REVIEWERS

PROFESSIONAL REVIEWER

Brian Horwitz
Director, Marketing and Operations
Management One
Cincinnati, OH

EDUCATIONAL REVIEWERS

Michael Aleci
Teacher, School of Business
Smithtown High School
Smithtown, NY

Sherrion D. Elmore
Lead Teacher, School of Business
Smithtown High School
Smithtown, NY

Scott Ferguson
Teacher, Marketing
East Paulding High School
Dallas, GA

Crystal Force
Teacher, Marketing Education
Wolfson High School
Jacksonville, FL

Irene A. Logan
Teacher, Occupational Education
Glen Cove High School
Glen Cove, NY

David Moutrie
Teacher, Marketing
Fraser High School
Fraser, MI

Nick Nicholas
GCE Instructor/Advisor
Rogers High School
Rogers, AR

Willotte Lowe Pittman
Coordinator, Marketing Education,
Muscogee County School District
Hardaway High School
Columbus, GA

Elizabeth S. Pitts
Coordinator, Marketing Education
Cass High School
Cartersville, GA

James P. Rademacher
Chair, Business/Vocational Department
Mainland High School
Daytona Beach, FL

Dr. Diane Ross Gary
Supervisor, Business Education
Bridgeport Public Schools
Bridgeport, CT

Gary D. Sealey
Teacher, Marketing Department
Menchville High School
Newport News, VA

William Turner
Teacher, Marketing Education
Washington High School
Washington, IN

Michael Vialpando
Business/Marketing Department
Westview High School
Phoenix, AZ

Paul A. Wardinski
Academy Administrator
Fairfax County Public Schools
Falls Church, VA

SPORTS AND ENTERTAINMENT MARKETING CONTENTS

TO THE STUDENT

Welcome to *Sports and Entertainment Marketing.* You have decided to embark on an exciting journey. Marketing is the tool that has allowed the United States economy to be one of the most successful in the world. Sports and entertainment are important parts of our modern economy. Fans and companies spend billions of dollars each year on sports. Entertainment is one of the largest exports from the United States to the rest of the world.

This book will take you on a step-by-step journey through the world of marketing. You will learn the basic functions of marketing and how those functions are applied to sports and entertainment. The basic functions of marketing are shown below. Marketing-Information Management, Financing, Pricing, Promotion, Product/Service Management, Distribution, and Selling are the foundations of marketing. Whenever a marketing function is presented in a lesson, it is marked with an icon indicating which marketing function is being used.

 MARKETING-INFORMATION MANAGEMENT FINANCING PRICING PROMOTION  PRODUCT/ SERVICE MANAGEMENT DISTRIBUTION SELLING

To help you on your journey through the world of Sports and Entertainment Marketing, this text has a number of special features to highlight interesting or unusual aspects of sports and entertainment.

Opening Act begins each lesson and encourages you to explore the material in the upcoming lesson. Opening Act also gives you opportunities to work with other students in your class.

Intermission provides you with an opportunity to assess your comprehension of material at key points in each lesson. Ongoing review and assessment of the lesson will help you better understand the material.

·SOUTH-WESTERN·

SPORTS AND ENTERTAINMENT MARKETING

Kaser and Oelkers

South-Western
EDUCATIONAL PUBLISHING
Thomson Learning™

Australia • Canada • Mexico • Singapore • Spain • United Kingdom • United States

Executive Editor	Eve Lewis
Project Manager	Enid Nagel
Production Manager	Patricia Matthews Boies
Editors	Darrell E. Frye, Nicole Christopher Toms
Editorial Assistant	Linda Adams
Art & Design Coordinator	Bill Spencer
Manufacturing Coordinator	Kathy Hampton
Marketing Manager	Nancy A. Long
Marketing Coordinator	Christian L. McNamee
Composition	New England Typographic Service

About the Authors

Ken Kaser has taught Business Education in Nebraska and Marketing Education in Texas for more than 20 years. He is the Marketing Coordinator at Clements High School in Sugar Land, Texas. Mr. Kaser has served as president of the Nebraska State Business Education Association (NSBEA) and the Mountain-Plains Business Education Association (M-PBEA). He has received the Outstanding Secondary Business Teacher of the Year Award from National Business Education Association, M-PBEA, NSBEA, and Texas Business Education Association.

Dotty Boen Oelkers is the Director of Career and Technology Education in the Fort Bend School District in Sugar Land, Texas. Recognized by the Texas Senate as the Career and Technology Regional Administrator of the Year for two different regions, Ms. Oelkers has sponsored the Texas DECA Chapter of the Year. She currently serves on the Texas Career and Technology Director's Advisory Council and the Executive Steering Committee for Tech Prep and School to Careers.

ISBN: 0-538-69477-7

Annotated Instructor's Edition ISBN: 0-538-69479-3

3 4 5 6 7 8 9 CK 07 06 05 04 03 02 01

Printed in the United States of America

Winning Strategies evaluates the strategies used by successful sports and entertainment marketing firms. The companies you will encounter include Wheaties, Tostitos, and Aware Records.

Cyber Marketing investigates Internet marketing and how the Internet is a major tool for today's marketers. Some of the examples of cyber marketing you will encounter include merchandising on pro team websites and celebrity fan clubs online.

Take a Bow acquaints you with people who have succeeded in sports, entertainment, and marketing careers. Some of the people you will meet are Pat Summitt, Sammy Sosa, and Gloria Estefan.

Marketing Myths explores some common myths that surround advertising and promotion in the sports and entertainment field. Among the topics you will explore are ambush marketing, misleading advertising, and non-traditional marketing strategies.

Judgment Call examines legal and ethical issues that exist in the sports and entertainment industries. Important issues you will examine include athletes with drug abuse problems, the welfare of sporting animals, and the television "V-chip."

Time Out introduces you to interesting facts and statistics about sports and entertainment marketing. For example, did you know that the Dallas Cowboys are the most popular football team in the United States?

Sports and Entertainment Marketing will provide you with an interesting journey through the world of marketing in sports and entertainment. Fasten your seatbelts and enjoy the ride.

CHAPTER 1

WHAT IS SPORTS AND ENTERTAINMENT MARKETING?

LESSONS

WINNING STRATEGIES

SPEEDY T'S

A screen printing and embroidering business in Lincoln, Nebraska, produces T-shirts and other apparel for University of Nebraska fans. Its agreement with the collegiate licensing company allows it to produce merchandise with the emblems of the University of Nebraska, but it must report sales of goods with the Nebraska emblems and pay royalties from those sales to the licensing company.

While the Nebraska football team was preparing to compete for the national championship on New Year's Day 1995, ART F/X began working on championship designs. It won exclusive rights to produce a "locker room" shirt for the winning team. Television coverage and newspaper photos made this T-shirt highly sought-after by fans. ART F/X purchased additional blank shirts and other clothing and put screens and equipment into a "go" state. Employees were alerted to start work as soon as the game was over. ART F/X brought in temporary help and ran the printing presses 24 hours a day the first week. Subcontractor printers were hired for additional printing as demand dictated. Sales for January 1995 showed an 895 percent increase over January 1994 due to the national championship.

Screen printing is a very competitive industry. There is always someone willing to do a job for less. ART F/X has maintained the quality that is necessary for exceptional results that keep satisfied customers.

THINK CRITICALLY
1. List as least three elements that made ART F/X's product/service planning a success.
2. How could ART F/X use its experience in producing the national football championship T-shirts to further market its services? Explain.

CHAPTER 1
LESSON 1.1

MARKETING BASICS

Describe the basic concepts of marketing.

Define the seven key marketing functions.

SCHEDULE
Block 45 minutes
Regular 1 class period

FOCUS
Ask students what goods and services consumers demand in the world of sports and entertainment. See if they can name any examples of marketing sports and entertainment.

OPENING ACT
Have students tell about commercials they like. Were any famous celebrities in those commercials? Why do companies spend large sums of money to have famous people endorse their product?

Answers for Opening Act Cooperative Learning
Michael Jordan, MCI; Mia Hamm, Nike; Alan Jackson (country singer), Ford; Tiger Woods, Titleist Golf Balls. Answers about buying decisions will vary.

OPENING ACT

Sports and entertainment play an important role in marketing. Athletes and entertainers play a prominent role by endorsing products and services. For example, American Express has had a long run of television commercials featuring comedian Jerry Seinfeld. In a recent survey by *USA Today's* Ad Track, the Seinfeld commercial came in third in consumer popularity. People like to be identified with celebrities and sports stars. Product endorsements by famous people are good marketing strategies.

Work with a group. Identify four advertising campaigns that feature other celebrities or athletes. Discuss with the group whether each strategy would affect your decision to purchase those products. Be sure to explain why or why not.

MARKETING CONCEPTS

Marketing is an important business function. You participate in the marketing process as a consumer of goods and services. About half of every dollar you spend pays for marketing costs. Marketing costs include product development, packaging, advertising, and sales expenses. Marketing includes a wide variety of business functions.

WHAT IS MARKETING?

According to the American Marketing Association, marketing is "planning and executing the conception, pricing, promotion, and distribution of ideas, goods, and services to create exchanges that satisfy individual and organizational objectives." This definition is complicated. However, it thoroughly describes the marketing process.

Another definition of **marketing** is the creation and maintenance of satisfying exchange relationships. This definition describes pieces of the entire marketing concept. *Creation* suggests marketing involves product development. *Maintenance* means marketing must continue as long as a business operates. *Satisfaction* implies that marketing must meet the needs of both businesses and customers when exchanging products or services. Finally, an *exchange relationship* occurs when people both give and receive something of value.

Marketing Mix To perform the tasks associated with marketing, marketers rely on a **marketing mix.** The marketing mix describes how a business blends the four marketing elements—product, distribution, price, and promotion. **Product** is what a business offers customers to satisfy needs. Products include goods like athletic shoes, and services like video rentals. **Distribution** involves the locations and methods used to make products available to customers. **Price** is the amount that customers pay for products. **Promotion** describes ways to encourage customers to purchase products and increase customer satisfaction. Promotion includes advertising, publicity, personal selling, and public relations.

Satisfying Customer Needs
The most important aspect of marketing is satisfying customer needs. Customers' needs should be the primary focus during the planning, production, distribution, and promotion of a product or service. This concept is not as easy as it might sound. To satisfy customers' needs, you need to perform three activities. First, you need to identify customer needs. Second, you need to develop products that customers consider better than other choices. And finally, you need to operate a business profitably. If you can do all of these items well, you will be able to market your products or services successfully.

In 1938, Congress passed the Wheeler-Lea Act. The act says, "unfair or deceptive acts or practices in or affecting commerce, are hereby declared unlawful." The law bans false advertising. It also requires businesses to tell consumers about negative features of their products. This law means that computer manufacturers cannot claim computers have more features than are available.

The law also means cigarette makers, who have sponsored a number of sporting events, must warn smokers about the medical risks of smoking. Currently, four different warnings appear on cigarette packs. The warnings change quarterly and range from a notice that quitting smoking can reduce the damage to your health to notice of dangers to unborn children. A movement is in process to strengthen the wording of the warnings.

THINK CRITICALLY
1. Do you think cigarette manufacturers should be required to warn people about the dangers of their products? Why or why not?
2. Do you think cigarette manufacturers should be held liable for the health problems of smokers? Discuss your opinion.

INTERMISSION

What is marketing? What are the elements of the marketing mix?

Marketing is planning and executing the conception, pricing, promotion, and distribution of ideas, goods, and services to create exchanges that satisfy individual and organizational objectives. The marketing mix is product, price, distribution, and promotion.

KEY MARKETING FUNCTIONS

There are seven key functions associated with marketing. They are product/service management, distribution, selling, marketing-information management, financing, pricing, and promotion. Every marketing activity will involve at least one key function.

USING THE KEY MARKETING FUNCTIONS

The key marketing functions are the basis of all marketing activities. You can find many examples of each marketing function in the business world. Every time you buy a product or service, all of the key marketing functions take place. Every time a business sells a product or service, all of the key marketing functions take place. Therefore, examples of all of the key marketing functions are numerous.

Product/Service Management is designing, developing, maintaining, improving, and acquiring products or services so they meet customer needs. Fisher Price tests new toy ideas with children and parents to make sure kids will play with the toys and parents will buy them for the children.

Distribution is determining the best way to get a company's products or services to customers. Television makers like Sony sell their products through electronics retailers like Circuit City. Sony knows that shoppers go to Circuit City because it sells electronic appliances.

Selling includes direct and personal communication with customers to assess and satisfy their needs. Selling involves not only satisfying customers, but also anticipating their future needs. Selling in today's world includes purchases made through the Internet with no personal communication whatsoever.

A famous example of selling in entertainment is singer Loretta Lynn. She and her husband spent months travelling around the country visiting radio stations to convince them to play her song "Honky Tonk Girl." The strategy worked. The song went to number 14 on the country charts and was Loretta Lynn's first hit.

Marketing-Information Management is gathering and using information about customers to improve business decision making. When Domino's first considered expanding operations into Japan, they used their marketing research to adapt the traditional Domino's pizza to Japanese tastes. They made pizzas smaller because the Japanese prefer pizza as a snack rather than a meal. Domino's also offered non-traditional toppings like corn and tuna because of local preferences.

With new technology, live cybercasts of music concerts can be heard and viewed around the world through the Internet. Huge companies are merging across communication lines and are using the Internet to bring all kinds of entertainment to consumers and to market items related to that entertainment.

THINK CRITICALLY
Visit the home pages of at least three movies that have related merchandise for sale. Determine what information is collected from customers. Work with a group. Discuss how the vendor could use this marketing information in the future to promote and sell other products.

Financing requires a company not only to budget for its own marketing activities, but also to provide customers with assistance in paying for the company's products or services. General Motors offers loans to customers through its GMAC division to help them buy cars from GM and to ensure steady revenue for GM.

Pricing is the process of establishing and communicating the value or cost of goods and services to customers. Prices may be set high if the seller knows people will buy at that price. Prices also may be set lower if the seller can count on selling a great volume of the good. Tickets for many professional sports events and concerts are often very expensive because demand is high.

Promotion is using advertising and other forms of communicating information about products, services, images, and ideas to achieve a desired outcome. For example, sports fans often find coupons on the back of ticket stubs after they go to a ball game. The coupons are used to promote products or services and to entice fans into trying them at a discounted price.

BASIS OF ALL MARKETING

The seven key functions are the basis of all marketing activities. You will need to refer to them often. Everything you learn about marketing will involve at least one of these functions. Make sure you understand these functions well. They are the responsibility of all marketers.

INTERMISSION

What are the key marketing functions? Name an example of each one.

Product/Service Planning, Distribution, Selling, Marketing-Information Management,

Financing, Pricing, and Promotion. Examples will vary.

Distribution means having your product at the right place at the right time. Imagine how successful ice cold Coke sales will be on a 90-degree football Saturday and how successful hot chocolate sales will be on a 40-degree football Saturday.

Selling involves personal communication with the customer. Fans in a stadium are a captive audience and food vendors have an opportunity to charge fairly high prices for hot dogs, soda, pizza, and popcorn. The next time you attend a game, watch how creative some of the sellers have become. They provide one more means of entertainment for the fans.

Marketing-information management is constantly seeking information about the desires of consumers. What new products will make a big hit?

Cyber Marketing
Successful movies are big business not only at the ticket office but also for retailers that sell merchandise directly associated with the movie. Think about a popular movie that ended up selling toys or fast food meals with memorabilia from the movie.

Think Critically
Answers will vary.

TEACH
It is easy for entrepreneurs to think their product is so great that consumers will pay big dollars for it. Realistically, competition may change this train of thought when determining pricing strategies.

Promotion can be as simple as word of mouth or as complex as a television commercial. Promotion is all about relaying an image to prospective customers.

It is important to understand the seven key functions of marketing. This entire book refers to these functions.

Ongoing Assessment
Use the Intermission as an opportunity to conduct ongoing assessment of student comprehension of the lesson material.

UNDERSTAND MARKETING CONCEPTS

Circle the best answer for each of the following questions.

1. Marketing, as a business function, is **c**
   a. encouraging customers to purchase products.
   b. another term for grocery shopping.
   c. creating and maintaining satisfying exchange relationships.
   d. none of the above

2. The elements of the marketing mix are **b**
   a. purchasing, distribution, financing, and price.
   b. product, distribution, price, and promotion.
   c. purchasing, planning, advertising, and distribution.
   d. planning, distribution, price, and advertising.

THINK CRITICALLY

Answer the following questions as completely as possible. If necessary, use a separate sheet of paper.

3. Think of three recent sports or entertainment purchases you have
   made. Identify how each purchase involved the seven key marketing functions.

   Answers will vary.

4. **Communication** You want to sell your almost-new stereo system.
   Create a flier to post on local bulletin boards to try to sell it. Use all
   of the marketing mix elements.

   Answers will vary. Possible answer:

   For sale: 1 stereo system—like new. CD player, dual cassette deck, turntable,

   AM/FM radio, equalizer and speakers included. Price—$500 obo. Call to

   schedule pick-up.

SPORTS MARKETING

CHAPTER
LESSON 1.2

OPENING ACT

Different sports compete for fan loyalty and revenue. College, professional, and amateur sports all want a piece of the spectator revenue. Spectators are actually consumers purchasing a service (the event). The ultimate goal for sporting events is selling the maximum number of tickets and other related items.

Marketing research is used to determine which sports are the most popular for different target markets. This research is not only important to event managers but also to sponsors interested in gaining the attention of potential customers. New sports make the entertainment scene even more competitive for spectators and sponsors.

Select your favorite sport. Who is the target market for this sport? Why? Who would be a good sponsor for this sport? Why?

Define sports marketing, and understand the importance of target markets.

Identify sports marketing strategies.

SCHEDULE
Block 45 minutes
Regular 1 class period

FOCUS
Ask students to name items sports fans purchase. List students' answers. Use this activity to point out the relationship of sports and related merchandise.

OPENING ACT
Marketing research is conducted to measure fans' desire. Special attention is given to a target market you look to for sales.

Answers for Opening Act Cooperative Learning
Answers will vary: College football target market; - 15-40 year-old males who like football; sponsor; Coca-Cola, a popular drink at sporting events.

TEACH
Spectators at sporting events also purchase other items such as food, apparel, programs, and souvenirs. Often product sales increase when the marketing strategies are related to sports or a winning tradition.

WHAT IS SPORTS MARKETING?

Spectators of sporting events are the potential consumers of a wide array of products ranging from apparel and athletic equipment to food items and automobiles. Sports spectators sometimes have more in common than just the sport. Finding out their interests and planning a product or service that the spectators will buy is a function of sports marketing. **Sports marketing** is using sports to market products.

DETERMINE THE TARGET MARKET

The first step in marketing a product to any audience is determining the target market. A **target market** is a specific group of people you want to reach. In order to promote and sell products and services, a company must know the needs and wants of the target market.

HOW TO FIND A TARGET MARKET

MARKETING-INFORMATION MANAGEMENT

A company with a product or service to sell must first identify the customer. The company must learn specific information, such as the age ranges in the group, marital status, gender, educational level, attitudes and beliefs, and income—especially **disposable income,** or income that can be freely spent. This information is known as **demographics.** Ideally, the company will find out why the consumers in the target group choose the specific items they buy. For example, past

experience, referral by a friend, and identification with an attitude are some of the reasons consumers buy an item.

SPENDING HABITS OF FANS

It is important to research the spending habits of fans in order to maximize profits on items they purchase at sporting events. The price fans are willing to pay for a ticket depends upon the interests of the target market, the national importance of the event, the popularity of the participating athletes, and the rivalry associated with the contest. Remember that fans are also willing to pay for team- or celebrity-identified clothing or equipment, and for the expenses of food and travel to and from a game.

INTERMISSION

What is a target market? Name some steps in identifying a target market. Why is it important to know the spending habits of fans? Target market is the specific group of people to whom you want to market. Steps include identifying demographics, matching products and services, and researching spending habits of the target market. Spending habits of fans will help you determine what products to produce and what prices to charge.

MARKETING STRATEGIES

PRODUCT/ SERVICE MANAGEMENT

In today's competitive market, product/service planners must be creative and two steps ahead of everyone else. Promotion is developed to attract the attention of the target group. Marketing strategies used by planners include sports logos on clothing, creation of new sports, gross impression, and perfect timing.

SPORTS LOGOS ON CLOTHING

Why do people wear clothing that has the logos of their favorite teams or that is endorsed by a sports figure? One reason is that team logos show fan loyalty. Another is that the value of the merchandise is increased in the eyes of the buyer. The same quality of T-shirt without the logo would cost less. A third reason is that some consumers feel more successful themselves if they own products endorsed by a successful person. Popular college and professional teams have earned large sums of money from such endorsements.

Major apparel companies, such as Nike and Reebok, realize the value of associating successful athletes and teams with their merchandise. Michael Jordan and the Chicago Bulls provided a huge boost for sales of Nike merchandise. Sometimes apparel companies will even name a line of merchandise after a successful athlete like Jordan. His "Air Jordan" shoes brought in over $100 million in new revenue.

NEW SPORTS, NEW OPPORTUNITIES

New sports markets offer new opportunities for endorsement and marketing. Arena football, founded in 1987, is one of the fastest-growing sports in the country, and for good reason. Tickets sell for an affordable price (around $12), players meet fans and sign autographs after every game, the action is continuous because the clock doesn't stop, and the scores are high—all elements that add excitement and build interest.

Recent seasons of arena football have had one million fans in attendance nationwide. The ABC network reported a television audience of two million for the Orlando Predators/Tampa Bay Storm game in 1998. This represents two million chances to promote a product.

GROSS IMPRESSION

Gross impression is the number of times per advertisement, game, or show that a product or service is associated with an athlete, team, or entertainer. Often, the message is a very subtle one. Brands shown in movies, television shows, and televised sporting events all represent gross impressions. Every time you see a product or company logo on the back of a pair of shoes, in a scene in a movie, or on the license-plate holder on a car, your brain records that image. Advertisers hope you will remember it when you are ready to buy such a product.

MARKETING MYTHS

Major companies pay millions of dollars to sponsor national sporting events. However, even though a company may purchase the exclusive rights to advertise during an event, competitors can advertise on local radio stations, competing networks, and billboards. Fans soon become confused about who the real sponsor is. This deliberate confusion is sometimes called *ambush marketing* or *stealth marketing*. It takes place when organizations participate in events to some degree rather than sponsor the events. For example, Coca-Cola might pay to be the official sponsor of a skating competition. However, Pepsi can pay to show an ad on the wall around the rink. Viewers can then see the ad as the skaters move across the ice.

THINK CRITICALLY

The company that uses ambush marketing obviously thinks it is beneficial. In the long run, is it? How might it eventually harm the company?

Many college and professional teams now have company or product logos on their uniforms. Marketers hope the spectators will see them, want to be associated with the elite team or athlete, and will buy the products.

Every time the media mentions a player, team, or product there is one more gross impression made on a potential customer. The more times a player, team, or product is mentioned, the better. College teams that receive a lot of media mention are more likely to end up in the national rankings, and athletes who receive extra mention are more likely to receive awards such as the Heisman Trophy.

TIMING

The popularity of teams and sports figures is based almost completely on continued winning. A team or celebrity on a losing streak can lose more than just points in a game. Timing is extremely important when marketing sporting goods. As you've learned, fans want products and services that identify them with a winner. Successful trends for athletes and teams must be monitored to determine when marketing strategies need to change. Similarly, the success of one major athletic company often sparks rivalry from a competitor. This, too, must be monitored so that a company's marketing can remain unique.

INTERMISSION

What is gross impression? Why is timing important for sports marketing? Gross impression is the number of times per advertisement, game, or show that a product or service is associated with an athlete, team, or entertainer. Timing is extremely important when marketing goods because fans want products and services that identify them with a winner.

UNDERSTAND MARKETING CONCEPTS
Circle the best answer for each of the following questions.

1. **Marketing Strategies**   Which statement is false about new sports entering the market? b
   a. New sports markets have opened more opportunities for endorsement marketing.
   b. Arena football has not gained much interest from fans.
   c. New sports fulfill the entertainment needs of people who cannot afford to attend professional games.
   d. Fans are willing to try new sporting events.

2. **Marketing-Information Management**   Specific information about people, such as income, age, and gender, is known as a
   a. demographics
   b. population variables
   c. poll results
   d. none of these

THINK CRITICALLY
Answer the following questions as completely as possible. If necessary, use a separate sheet of paper.

3. Design a new logo for a major sporting goods manufacturer. Explain what the logo represents and why it will be successful. This logo cannot resemble current logos.

   Answers will vary. Students should explain the relationship of the logo and the

   major sporting goods manufacturer.

4. **Research**   Watch a college or professional sporting event on television. Select a sports brand represented in this presentation and keep track of how many gross impressions were made during the telecast.

   Answers will vary. Students should record the sporting event, hours they viewed

   the event, brand, and the number of gross impressions.

ASSESS
Reteach
Make sure that students understand a target market. Give more examples of products and the target markets associated with those products. Then ask students to describe target markets for different products you write on the board.

Enrich
Give students a specific target market and information about a bowl game or a trip to the final four. It is their assignment to design a brochure for the target market in an attempt to sell the vacation package to the bowl game or the final four.

CLOSE
Wrap up the lesson by giving students examples of a target market, a marketing strategy for a target market, logos, and how royalties are calculated on items carrying the logo of a team or the likeness of an athlete.

CHAPTER 1
LESSON 1.3

ENTERTAINMENT MARKETING

GOALS

Understand why marketing must relate to the specific audience.

Relate advances in entertainment technology to changes in distribution.

Recognize the power of television as a marketing tool.

OPENING ACT

Television networks are desperate to attract male viewers ages 12 to 34. Professional wrestling and X-Games are two successful examples of television capturing the attention of this group. The large number of people spending their leisure time and money on pro wrestling demonstrates this success. ESPN presents the X-Games as sports, but the Games are considered by some to be a marketing gimmick.

Work with a group. Identify three additional TV shows aimed at these sought-after male viewers. Make a list of products that might be advertised on these shows. Discuss why the products' advertisers are interested in sponsoring these programs.

ENTERTAINMENT FOR SALE

Jammed between work, school, home, family, and other activities, people have a limited amount of leisure time and money. Influencing how they choose to use their time and money is the purpose of **entertainment marketing.** Entertainment marketing will be discussed in two ways. First, entertainment will be looked at as a product to be marketed. Second, marketing will be examined in light of how it uses entertainment to attract attention to other products. To market entertainment as the product is to pursue the free time of people who can also pay for the entertainment. An example of using entertainment to market a product or service is hiring celebrities to endorse related products.

WHAT EXACTLY IS ENTERTAINMENT?

Entertainment is whatever people are willing to spend their money and spare time viewing, rather than participating in. Entertainment can include sports or the arts, and can be viewed in person or in broadcast or recorded form. A distinction is often made between sports and entertainment. Sports are games of athletic skill. Entertainment can be movies, theater, the circus, or even traditional athletic contests.

Sometimes what qualifies as entertainment is a matter of opinion. For example, professional wrestling has little resemblance to the National Collegiate Athletic Association (NCAA) sanctioned sport of wrestling. Professional wrestling is an exaggeration of a real sport, but is it a sport? It attracts an audience any sport would be glad to have: 34 million cable-TV viewers a week in July of 1998.

A much-publicized pay-per-view pro wrestling match was held in July 1998. Basketball players Karl Malone and Dennis Rodman teamed up with pro wrestlers to present the "sweaty theatrics." In response to criticism for participating in the stunts that are portrayed as wrestling, the basketball stars claimed they are already in the entertainment business.

THINK CRITICALLY

Is there any difference between Rodman and Malone wrestling and Michael Jordan trying baseball or Deion Sanders playing both baseball and football? Explain.

IS A DISTINCTION REQUIRED FOR SUCCESSFUL MARKETING?

MARKETING-INFORMATION MANAGEMENT

Whether an event is a sport or entertainment, sponsors of the event want to gather as much marketing information as possible about the viewers. This marketing-information management enables sponsors to design product promotions specifically for that audience. The sponsoring companies must know their customers' needs and maintain accurate marketing information about them to succeed at marketing to them. Once the characteristics of the audience are understood, sponsors can plan their service or product, plan how to get the word out, and decide how to promote the product.

INTERMISSION

What are the two ways of looking at entertainment marketing? What is entertainment?

Entertainment marketing is either marketing of entertainment as a product, or entertainment to attract attention to other products. Entertainment is what people are willing to spend their spare time and money viewing.

MODERN ENTERTAINMENT MARKETING

At the beginning of the twentieth century, the performing arts represented a major form of entertainment. Performing arts include live theater, ballet, opera, and concerts. Marketing was limited to posters, newspapers, magazines, and word-of-mouth. In order to enjoy any professional entertainment, people had to travel to the theater, concert hall, or arena. Travel was slow and sometimes tedious.

THE BEGINNING OF CHANGE

Louis Le Prince made the first moving pictures in Britain in 1888. The Lumière brothers were the first to present a projected movie to a paying audience in a café in Paris in 1895. Promotion of films quickly followed with the construction of theaters for movies.

The first movie with sound, *The Jazz Singer,* opened in the United States in 1927 in the few movie theaters that were equipped at that time to handle sound. Mickey Mouse arrived in 1928 in Walt Disney's *Steamboat Willie.* Ten years later, *Snow White and the Seven Dwarfs* became the first full-length animated film. In a masterful marketing move, Disneyland opened in Anaheim, California, in July 1955. A totally new approach to the marketing mix of entertainment was born with the theme park. The live arts and recorded arts had been joined by an ever-evolving, technology-driven series of new media.

CHANGE ACCELERATED

PROMOTION

Once started, technologies of all sorts changed marketing advertising and distribution forever. Every new medium can be used for marketing and advertising. Besides television, radio, and the Internet, public buses are rolling billboards; subway cars carry ad panels; even sports stadiums are now named after advertisers. For example, the well-known Candlestick Park in San Francisco was renamed 3Com Park.

The marketing of entertainment is evolving faster and faster with daily changes in technology. Products that were innovative yesterday are out-of-date today. Information managers and promoters must be creative and forward thinking in order to anticipate the wants of the buying public.

INTERMISSION

Name three technological advances that have increased the possibilities for marketing.

Answers will vary. Possible answers: Internet, computers, television.

THE BIG EYE IN EVERY ROOM

When television began to arrive in great numbers of American homes, sports and entertainment marketers found a wide-open distribution channel into the billfolds of consumers. The market grew quickly and continues to advance throughout much of the world.

THE EARLY DAYS OF TELEVISION AND MARKETING

Nine television stations and fewer than 7,000 working TV sets existed in the United States at the end of World War II. In October 1945, more than 25,000 people came to Gimbel's Department Store in Philadelphia to watch the first demonstration of TV. That same year, the American Association of Advertising Agencies encouraged the start of television advertising. TV changed the marketing of entertainment in a profound way. Far more than newspapers and magazines had ever been able to, the audio-visual "life" of TV advertising hooked the imagination of the viewer-consumer.

In 1946, NBC and the Gillette Company staged the first television sports spectacular: a heavyweight boxing match. The program was a viewing success with an estimated audience of 150,000 watching on 5,000 TV sets. This was an average of 30 people watching the fight on each set.

TELEVISION'S INCREASING INFLUENCE

Even in its simplicity, early television took promotion and advertising to a new level. Major national corporations lined up to buy time and produce advertisements. The pricing of time for TV advertisements was quickly tied to the number of viewers the programming attracted. Television stations invited advertisers to use their expertise to create commercials. The nine TV stations of 1945 grew to 98 stations by 1949.

As you just learned, the United States had fewer than 7,000 TV sets in 1946. In 1996, just 50 years later, that number had grown to 223 million sets with many homes having at least two. Advertisers spent almost $42.5 billion on television advertising in 1996.

INTERMISSION

Name a few benefits of TV to marketers and advertisers. How have consumers' lives changed because of television?

Answers will vary. TV benefits include broadcast directly into homes, good return for

money invested, and multi-media advertisements. Consumers can now stay home

and get high-quality entertainment and find out about national-level new products.

UNDERSTAND MARKETING CONCEPTS

Circle the best answer for each of the following questions.

1. What is entertainment? c
   a. performing arts, such at theater, ballet, and symphony concerts
   b. professional sports, such as major league baseball
   c. whatever people are willing to spend their time and money watching
   d. a and b
   e. all of these

2. **Distribution** Name three technological advances that have helped marketing and advertising become a multibillion-dollar industry. a
   a. Internet, television, radio
   b. radio, newspapers, magazines
   c. Internet, billboards, bus advertising
   d. Internet, magazines, satellite dishes
   e. none of the above

THINK CRITICALLY

Answer the following questions as completely as possible. If necessary, use a separate sheet of paper.

3. **Communication** Name your three favorite television commercials. Explain why you like them. State whether you would find the same products so attractive if they were advertised in the newspaper.

   Answers will vary.

   _____

   _____

   _____

   _____

4. **Technology** Predict how the Internet will change entertainment marketing in the future.

   Answers will vary.

   _____

   _____

   _____

   _____

RECREATION MARKETING

CHAPTER 1
LESSON 1.4

OPENING ACT

" **T**oday's weather: Clear skies with seasonal snow showers." This is not a typical forecast for hot, humid areas close to the equator, but it is the daily forecast for Singapore's Snowland at Mega Leisure World in Megamal Pinang. Snow skiing and playing in the snow are attractive recreational activities. Promoted as the largest winter wonderland in Southeast Asia, Snowland is a great place to cool off and is one of many indoor winter wonderlands around the world.

Work with a partner. Discuss how the marketing mix can be used for recreational activities.

GOALS

Apply the marketing mix to recreation marketing.

Describe marketing for the travel and tourism consumer.

SCHEDULE
Block 45 minutes
Regular 1 class period

FOCUS
Ask students to make a list of entertainment and a different list of recreation events. Discuss the difference between entertainment and recreation.

OPENING ACT
Singapore is an island at the tip of Malaysia. Ask students to locate it on a map. What does having a snow skiing facility near the equator say about the economy of Singapore? Is this a luxury for people who have all their necessities met?

Answers for Opening Act Cooperative Learning
Answers will vary. Possible answer: product—mountain bikes; distribution—retail store or web site; price—varies; promotion—advertising, publicity, sales promotions, and direct mail.

RECREATIONAL SPORTS

Recreational sports marketers entice people away from home-based entertainment. Golf, tennis, bowling, hiking, snow skiing, snow boarding, and biking are a few of the more popular recreational sports. Travel and tourism are also recreational activities for an active, adventurous consumer. **Recreation** can be defined as renewing or rejuvenating your body or mind with play or amusing activity. **Recreational activities** are those involved in travel, tourism, and amateur sports that are not associated with educational institutions.

NOT FOR THE COUCH POTATO

Participation in recreational activities generally requires purchase of a combination of products and services. The participant must make a commitment of time and money for lessons, practice, equipment, and travel to a facility or location. Many opportunities exist for public and private facilities to combine their products and services into packages and to promote to specific groups of people. Marketing costs must be included in the financing of a recreational sports facility.

Planning the product or service is as critical as the blueprint drawings used in construction

Savvy planners schedule conventions at attractive locations with recreational facilities or natural attractions. Recreational activities are also planned into the convention time. A summer convention at a mountain resort will frequently include a lunch-time hike.

TIME OUT
Ask students to name locations that are great convention sites. Look for places large enough to handle many people, but attractive to a wide range of tastes.

TEACH
Use the list from Focus to discuss recreational activities. Are recreational activities important to people's health?

Ask what theme students would use in ads for recreational activities. Look for ideas about health and weight loss.

For adult groups, interests are more important than age in deciding on activities. Ask students to name recreational activities for a wide age range of adults.

Bowling is a popular recreation, but is not growing. Ask students to name other activities that might have stopped growing or are declining in popularity.

Ongoing Assessment
Use the Intermission as an opportunity to conduct ongoing assessment of student comprehension of the lesson material.

of a recreational sports facility. For adult participants, the marketing plan of a recreational sports facility should be geared more to the interests of the customer than to the age group. People are remaining active throughout their lives, and recreational activities can cross generations.

A BETTER IMAGE

Professional sports marketers work to increase interest in related recreational sports. They tap into the idea that people who like to participate in certain sports like to watch professionals play those same sports. For example, the Professional Bowlers Association is working to draw mainstream sponsors and a broader audience by promoting a new image of bowling. Ten million league members bowl at least once a week, and more than 55 million people in the United States bowled at least once during 1997. More people bowl than participate in any other recreational sport. People who frequently bowl also watch bowling on television and therefore make up a huge audience for advertising.

One of bowling's biggest problems, though, is lack of a famous, young icon. Bowling needs a marketable sports figure to catch the attention of the public. Exciting professional sports figures can increase interest in a recreational sport and can also increase the sale of related merchandise. U.S. golfer Tiger Woods was a worldwide celebrity before he played in the Million Dollar Golf Challenge in December 1998 in Sun City, South Africa. During and after the tournament, Woods played a key role in promoting the game with the black population in Africa who, prior to the end of apartheid and the elections of 1994, had been denied chances to play. A whole new audience and group of fans is being enticed to the sport of golf through promotional efforts.

INTERMISSION

What is recreation marketing? What is the relationship between professional sports and recreational sports?

Recreation marketing is attracting people to participate in recreational activities.

Professional sports encourage people to participate in the related recreation.

TRAVEL AND TOURISM

MARKETING-INFORMATION MANAGEMENT

The World Travel and Tourism Council estimates that, worldwide, the travel industry employs 130 million people and is the world's largest industry. **Tourism** is generally considered traveling for pleasure whether the travel is independent or tour-based. Tourism includes vacations, honeymoons, conventions, and family visits. Marketing travel for pleasure requires creating a desire to see and experience new places or return to old favorites. A major function of the travel industry is *data mining,* or collecting data about which people travel, where, and when. In the extremely competitive tourism business, the most successful firms make decisions based on marketing-information management. Understanding the customer is a key to marketing travel for pleasure.

RELAX AND SMELL THE ROSES

Summertime brings images of leisurely strolls through a tropical garden, with a cool ocean breeze blowing through the palm trees. If beaches are not for you, travel marketers can repaint the picture. A wealth of travel opportunities exist and can be tailored to the customer's vacation tastes and budget. People in the travel industry refer to recreational travel or tours planned around a special interest as **niche travel.** Niche travel can be designed for a group of music enthusiasts traveling through Europe listening to classical concerts or for people who prefer to spend their vacations performing works of public service, such as building houses for low-income buyers or helping with maintenance in the nation's parks. Throughout the country, farms and ranches also now offer vacation packages for those who want a taste of the country life or the cattle roundup.

British entrepreneur Thomas Cook began offering package tours to seaside resorts in the late nineteenth century. Improvements in trains, hotels, and ocean liners, and the invention of the automobile and airplane in the early twentieth century moved travel from toil to pleasure. Toward the end of the twentieth

Many Americans use round-trip, one-day air travel for business purposes. Prices for these and many other flights vary dramatically, depending on the city of departure. For example, if the departure city is a hub of a major airline, consumers can expect to pay more than they would from a nearby city. In August 1999, a day trip on Delta Airlines from Cincinnati (a Delta hub) to Washington, D.C. and back cost $824. A flight to Washington from Columbus, Ohio, two hours northeast of Cincinnati, cost $598. This is $226, or 38 percent less.

THINK CRITICALLY
Research the reasons for this cost difference. Can you cite three reasons for it? What is your opinion of the reasons? Is the price difference fair?

century, Disney theme parks began offering complete travel packages online, including hotel, airline, rental car, and park tickets.

The marketing mix in niche travel is critical to the success of the business. Planning the right tour, promoting and distributing it to the right customers, pricing it to attract them, and making a profit all require marketing information. Senior citizens would not likely enjoy the same travel that a high school student would. Although older adults are remaining more and more active, the same type of entertainment might be offered to them in a quieter setting.

INTERMISSION

Why is marketing information important to the travel and tourism business? Why is travel and tourism not a one-size-fits-all business?

It is important to understand customers' needs and wants and to focus the business

on a target customer. Travel for pleasure is based on individual interests.

TAKE A BOW

TOM PARSONS

Tom Parsons just may become a hero as big as any sports or entertainment star. He is one of the current forces changing the travel industry. He's a marketer, but he's selling discounts, not huge profits.

Parsons got his start in the mid-1980s when he discovered that a coworker had paid $100 less than he had for a ticket on a flight they were taking together. From that moment, he has spent his life digging up travel bargains that most other people can't find, and he's glad to tell everything he knows.

Parsons is the publisher of *Best Fares Discount Travel Magazine* and the author of

magazine articles as well as a new travel-tips book. He is also a frequent guest on many major radio and television talk and news shows. You can also check out his Web site, www.best-fares.com to learn more about travel deals and travel savvy.

THINK CRITICALLY
Look at Tom Parson's web site, and find costs for two different airline flights to the city of your choice. Then call the toll-free number of the same airline and ask for their best rate. Make a chart of your findings. What would you advise your friends and family to do before they travel? Are there any hidden costs?

UNDERSTAND MARKETING CONCEPTS

Circle the best answer for each of the following questions.

1. **Information Management**   Niche travel designs vacations for d
   a. snow skiers
   b. families with small children
   c. music enthusiasts
   d. all of these

2. **Promotion**   Recreational sports need a celebrity to endorse them in order to d
   a. attract more young people
   b. attract more of the population in general
   c. create more sales for equipment manufacturers
   d. all of these

THINK CRITICALLY

Answer the following questions as completely as possible. If necessary, use a separate sheet of paper.

3. **Geography**   Why do you think California attracts more visitors than any other state in the nation? Suggest how South Dakota and Oklahoma could attract more travelers.

   California is on the Pacific coast and has nice weather and natural attractions.

   Other states can advertise, offer bargains, create niche travel opportunities, or

   host conventions.

   _____

   _____

4. **Communication**   Work with a partner. Write a description of the marketing mix for a beach vacation facility.

   Answers will vary but should include all of the items in the marketing mix—

   product, distribution, price, and promotion.

   _____

   _____

   _____

   _____

CHAPTER 1 REVIEW

REVIEW MARKETING CONCEPTS

Write the letter of the term that matches each definition. Some terms will not be used.

_b_ **1.** the creation and maintenance of satisfying exchange relationships

_c_ **2.** a blend of the four marketing elements

_a_ **3.** whatever people are willing to spend time and money in viewing

_e_ **4.** renewing or rejuvenating your body or mind with play or amusing activity

_f_ **5.** can be used for marketing or advertising

a. entertainment
b. marketing
c. marketing mix
d. price
e. recreation
f. new media

Circle the best answer.

6. Assisting in the design and development of new products is
  a. financing
  b. marketing-information management
  _c_ **c.** product/service management
  d. none of these

7. Offering coupons to entice customers to try a product at a discounted price is an example of
  a. promotion
  b. product/service planning
  _a_ **c.** purchasing
  d. none of these

8. Gross impressions
  a. occur when you see a corporate emblem on the jersey of a favorite athlete
  _d_ **b.** is the number of media mentions of an athlete or a product
  c. can occur in any marketing, not just in sports marketing
  d. all of these

9. A target market is
  a. a specific group of people you want to reach
  b. people who have something in common
  _d_ **c.** people who might buy the same products if they knew about them
  d. all of these

THINK CRITICALLY

10. Spend five minutes discussing with another student how entertainment marketing changed after television became popular. Make a list of at least five changes since 1945. Share the list with the class.

Answers will vary.

11. You are the manufacturer of a new sports clothing line. Who is your target market? Choose a professional athlete to represent your company. Who did you choose? Why?

Answers will vary.

Example: soccer shorts

Target market: young people who play soccer and their parents who buy their clothes

Pro athlete: Mia Hamm

12. Using the Internet or sports magazines in your library, find and briefly describe three popular new recreational sports. They do not have to be team sports. To whom and how are these sports being marketed?

Answers will vary.

CHAPTER

REVIEW

MAKE CONNECTIONS

13. Mathematics You are a famous athlete whose image is on T-shirts produced by L&A Sport Products. You will receive 5 percent of the sales of any gear featuring your image. T-shirts sell for $18 at a major department store. Last quarter, 6,000 shirts were sold. How much will you earn from the sale of these shirts?

6,000 × 18 = 108,000

108,000 × 0.05 = $5,400

14. History You are a travel marketer in 1849 America. Your job is to promote migration to the west. Research such a trip and write a one-page sales feature describing how your clients will travel, what they will take with them, how long the trip will take, and the dangers they will face.

Answers will vary.

15. Communication You are now a travel marketer in the twenty-first century, and you want to praise modern travel. Using the information you learned in question 14, write a one-page paper comparing the pioneers' trip with a modern-day trip to the same destination. How will your clients travel now? What will they take with them? How long will the trip take by car? By plane? What dangers might they face?

Answers will vary.

16. Technology Now imagine you are a travel marketer in the year 2080. As part of your promotion, tell your client about the technological advances your ancestors had at the beginning of the twenty-first century that made travel safer and easier. List at least 10.

Answers will vary.

_____

_____

_____

_____

_____

PROJECT EXTRA INNINGS

Your travel marketing firm has been asked by a multimillionaire to create "the adventure trip of a lifetime" for her husband, who is turning 50 this year. She will go with him on the trip. Her husband has always wanted to go to an exotic location, but your client is unsure and wants to be sold on that destination. Your boss will give you a large bonus if you can successfully promote this trip.

Work with a group and complete the following activities.

1. Choose an exotic destination for your trip. With your town or city as a beginning point, discover the quickest route to your vacation site. Include the means of transportation necessary from point to point. For example, if you live in a small town, the first leg of the journey will probably be by car to a city with an airport.

2. Create a map of the world showing the travel route and time for each part of the trip. Use mapmaking software or a large piece of paper or poster board. Use different colors, and be sure to create a legend.

3. Write an exciting detailed report about your destination. Include descriptions of unique plants and animals, delicious foods, scenery, and languages spoken. Be sure to include a section on accommodations and activities available. Do advise your client of necessary vaccinations and other health issues. Include a section on local customs along with any precautions your client needs to take.

4. Provide a simple spreadsheet showing complete costs for the trip, including major transportation (car, plane, train, bus), hotel, tours, and meals. Include recommendations for tips.

5. Write an enthusiastic two-page cover letter telling your client why she'll be glad she and her husband made this trip.

Extra Innings
Have students use the Internet to map their trips. Have other maps available from your school library if the Internet is not available. Make sure students use spell check and grammar checker on their letters if possible. Letters should be persuasive with sales points including the features of the destination and references to gthe luxury and status of a visit to such an exotic site.

The *Sports and Entertainment Marketing* Teacher's Resource CD includes a spreadsheet template to help students complete this activity.

Look for the file p027 Extra Innings.xls in the Office Templates folder, or the file p027 XInS.txt in the Text Templates folder.

The *Sports and Entertainment Marketing* Teacher's Resource CD also includes a word processing template to help students complete this activity.

Look for the file p027 Extra Innings.doc in the Office Templates folder, or the file p027 XInW.txt in the Text Templates folder.

CHAPTER 2

COLLEGE AND AMATEUR SPORTS

LESSONS

WINNING STRATEGIES

CREATING A SUCCESSFUL BOWL GAME

What does it take to have a successful major college bowl game? A large stadium, favorable climate, adequate hotel accommodations, and tourist attractions. Even more important is the match-up of teams. A bowl will spark national interest if popular teams are participating and the results will have implications on the final college football ratings.

Major bowl games depend upon corporate sponsors. The Fiesta Bowl in Tempe, Arizona, has become a major bowl game not only because it has all of the necessary demographics to attract fans, but also because Tostitos is a significant financial sponsor. Sponsorship means both paying for expensive television time and coming up with creative promotional strategies during bowl game festivities. Tostitos also sponsors social events for bowl and university dignitaries as well as halftime activities.

Sponsoring a bowl game provides national exposure. A major goal of Tostitos is to have fans keep watching during commercials. Tostitos aired one commercial in which a comedian appears to be bungee jumping from an airplane with a Tostitos chip between his teeth in order to dip the chip in a jar of salsa on the football field.

The food vendors sell Tostitos products throughout the stadium. T-shirts and other bowl souvenirs all have the Tostitos trademark on them. Tostitos and the Fiesta Bowl are a winning combination—like chips and salsa.

THINK CRITICALLY

1. Why is Tostitos a good sponsor for a bowl game in the Southwest?
2. Create a new commercial for Tostitos for this year's Fiesta Bowl.
3. List three sponsors of other major bowl games.

MARKETING COLLEGE ATHLETICS

GOALS

Explain the importance of the NCAA and team rankings to college sports.

Define market segmentation.

Discuss the growing market surrounding women's college athletics.

SCHEDULE
Block 45 minutes
Regular 1 class period

FOCUS
Collegiate athletics are big business. Take time to break down what a typical game would cost a fan. Be sure to include the cost of a ticket, transportation, food, souvenirs, etc.

OPENING ACT
A sell-out crowd brings big revenue to the university. Major stadiums and arenas hold a lot of fans and generate huge revenue for a university. Ask students what they are willing to pay to see a game of their favorite university.

The *Sports and Entertainment Marketing* Teacher's Resource CD includes a spreadsheet template to help students complete this activity.

OPENING ACT

Successful college athletics provide huge revenues to the cities and states where the programs are located. Imagine how much revenue is generated on a football Saturday in Ann Arbor, Michigan, where the stadium holds over 100,000 fans. Successful programs such as the University of Michigan have national reputations.

Work with a partner. List five strong college football or basketball programs. Use the Internet to find out how many fans the stadium or arena holds for each of these schools and the ticket prices each school charges. How much revenue would be generated from ticket sales for a sold-out game?

EFFECTS OF COLLEGIATE SPORTS

A winning college team has economic implications not only for its school, but also for the community, region, and state. Universities offer products and services to fans, but fans also expect an adequate number of hotel rooms, restaurants, gas stations, and shopping malls. University cities must be alert to the needs of fans in order to reap the greatest financial benefits. A college community can benefit from the success of its primary team through media attention the team receives. Newspapers, magazines, and local sportscasts will focus on the team the entire year, and the home city will benefit.

PROMOTION

Strong Public Image Marketers strive to promote a strong public image of the team. Recall that promotion provides the means of communication to inform, persuade, or remind people about college athletics. A university might print schedule cards to distribute at different locations throughout the city. Frequently, posters are designed to build enthusiasm for approaching seasons. Colleges have sports information departments that produce promotional materials, and sports information guides are published annually for purchase by consumers. Additionally, colleges and universities now have web sites that allow fans to follow their favorite teams all year long.

RULES AND RANKINGS

The **National Collegiate Athletic Association (NCAA)** is the governing body of most college and university athletic programs. It creates and enforces guidelines and rules that schools must follow in order to remain in good standing. Guideline areas include recruitment, gender equity, scholarships, gambling prohibitions, and many ethical issues. The NCAA's overall goal is the promotion of college athletics, with a focus on the integrity of the athletes and their game. The NCAA strives to keep athletics an important, solid, and respectable part of college life and to help the athletes succeed with both their student and sports responsibilities. These qualities are what make collegiate sports so appealing to sponsors.

Any college or university may join the NCAA if it meets the following conditions:

- obtains accreditation by the recognized accrediting agency of its region

- offers at least four intercollegiate sports for men and four for women (one in each of the three traditional seasons)

- complies with all NCAA rules

- cooperates with the NCAA enforcement program and accepts penalties imposed by that program

FINANCING

In addition to supporting the student athlete and college sports programs, the NCAA serves as a magnet for important sponsors. The NCAA Corporate Partners support intercollegiate athletics financially and provide business and personnel expertise. Past Corporate Partners included: American Express, Continental Airlines, Hershey's, Ocean Spray, Rawlings, and Sears. These advertising dollars support the NCAA Championship, as well as allow expansion of NCAA programs for young people.

COLLEGE TEAM RANKINGS

Sports magazines and nationally recognized sports enthusiasts determine college team rankings based on past team performance, talent, team schedules, and personal preference. The first rankings for college football, basketball, and baseball occur before the seasons begin each year. Many different sports magazines are distributed nationally and regionally. Fans enjoy reading these publications and companies fill their pages with ads for a wide variety of products and services.

Why So Much Emphasis? Wise coaches and players try not to pay attention to preseason ratings and predictions, but early exposure does provide excellent promotion for a team going into a new season.

A highly ranked team builds excitement and strong attendance at games, creating fan loyalty and national respect. Preseason rankings influence major television networks to schedule games, and televised games mean more revenue for the team and its university. A high ranking at the beginning of the season is also important because it requires fewer steps to the lucrative number one spot.

Each team in the 1998-99 Rose, Sugar, Orange, and Fiesta Bowls earned an average of $12.5 million.

Other bowls paid from $700,000 to $3.6 million to each participating team.

TIME OUT

The University of Kentucky Wildcats men's basketball team brought $3.3 million in fan spending for business in downtown Lexington, Kentucky, in 1996-1997.

Post-season bowl games pay participating schools an enormous amount of money. Bowls want to invite teams that have a large fan base. The ultimate goal is to sell out the game and earn the greatest amount of fan dollars. In short, a national championship game leads to great financial gains for the bowl and many other businesses in the host city.

PROMOTION

#1 Has Lingering Effects Even after the celebration is over, a championship continues to bring favorable national recognition and increased potential for recruitment of top high school athletes. Retailers carrying the national champion's sportswear and other memorabilia will experience tremendous growth of sales. Also, being the official sportswear manufacturer for a consistent winner is good advertising. Fans see the manufacturer's ads in sports programs and magazines and throughout stadiums, arenas, and baseball fields, and their emblems on athletes' apparel.

INTERMISSION

What is the purpose of the NCAA? Why is a number one ranking lucrative?

The NCAA is the governing body of most college and university athletic programs. A

number 1 ranking attracts the attention of major television networks to schedule

games and produce revenue for the team and its university.

MARKET SEGMENTATION

MARKETING-INFORMATION MANAGEMENT

Sports publications for both college and professional teams use information management to determine rankings, feature articles, and cover stories. Using different players or teams on the cover of the same magazine in different parts of the country illustrates the concept of market segmentation. A **market segment** is a group of individuals within a larger market that share one or more characteristics. For example, millions of people in the United States enjoy college basketball, but a smaller group specifically enjoys University of Kentucky basketball. Sports magazine covers featuring the Wildcats will fly off the shelves in Kentucky, but the same publication featuring the Brigham Young University Cougars might not sell out in Kentucky.

FIVE ELEMENTS OF MARKET SEGMENTATION

Market segmentation is very much like target marketing. In order to make the most profit, you must focus on your customer's needs and wants.

Geographic segmentation is the dividing of markets into physical locations, such as eastern, northern, southern, and western regions of the United States or the urban and rural areas of a state. Geographic segmentation can even occur within a single city. Sports fans are likely to be loyal to their own region when purchasing products.

Demographic segmentation focuses on information that can be measured, such as income, profession, gender, and education. Marketers might use income information to advertise upscale hotels to corporate executives, or to advertise less expensive accommodations to those that want only to see the game and don't care for the extras.

Psychographics focus on characteristics that cannot be measured, such as attitudes and lifestyle choices. For example, if a major ballgame falls on a holy day of your faith, will you attend the game?

Product usage reflects what products you use, how often, and why. Marketers use this information to encourage you to use your preferred products more often or to try new, similar, or competing products.

Benefits derived are the value people believe they receive from the product or service. Examples in college sports are the enjoyment received from a good game, or from a sweatshirt with a team logo rather than an identical sweatshirt without the logo.

INTERMISSION

What is market segmentation? Give a college sports example relating to each element of market segmentation.

Market segmentation is finding a group of individuals within a larger market that share

one or more geographic, demographic, psychographic, product usage, or benefits

derived characteristics. Examples will vary.

WOMEN'S COLLEGE SPORTS

Women have participated in sports on both the professional and collegiate levels for decades, but it was not until 1980 that the NCAA focused attention on women's college sports. In 1981, the support was not only made formal, but 19 championship events were added to the women's programs. In 1987, the NCAA created the Women's Enhancement Program, which offers opportunities to college women in the form of postgraduate scholarships, internships at the NCAA national office, and career help for women who want to continue in intercollegiate athletics after their playing eligibility is over.

Increased Fan Support Fan support for women's athletic programs has increased dramatically in the last decade. Six national basketball championships at the University of Tennessee have inspired huge attendance figures at both home and away games. In 1987, ESPN televised 7 women's college games. Ten years later, the network ran 48. Attendance figures for the women's Final Four games averaged 17,500 between 1994 and 1998.

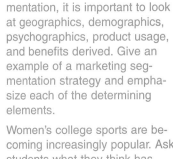

Average home-game attendance at the University of Tennessee women's basketball games increased from 2,725 in 1978-79 to 10,500 in 1996-97.

MARKETING OPPORTUNITIES IN WOMEN'S SPORTS

The creation of new sports opens up new marketing opportunities. While women's college athletics is not new, the attention coming to it is increasing as fast as or faster than with newer sports. Not long ago, marketers felt they could promote only clothing, beauty products, jewelry, and home appliances to women. With the astonishing increase of women in sports—and the increase in the number of fans—a powerful target market is opening up. Women now want soccer shoes, basketballs, golf clubs, state-of-the-art bats, and racing bikes. In short, the success of women in sports, and in college sports especially, has begun a tidal wave of marketing opportunities encompassing all the key marketing functions.

INTERMISSION

How have women's sports influenced product marketing?

Product marketing used to focus only on clothing, beauty, and home appliances for

women. Women now want soccer shoes, basketballs, golf clubs, and racing bikes.

TAKE A BOW

PAT SUMMITT

Pat Summitt, women's basketball coach for the University of Tennessee at Knoxville, is one of the most successful college basketball coaches. In her first 25 years as coach of the Lady Vols, Summitt has a win-loss record of 696-146. Her six NCAA championships are a record surpassed only by John Wooden, former men's coach at UCLA.

In 1966, Pat's parents moved their five children so she could attend a high school with a girls' basketball team. She later played for the University of Tennessee at Martin and for the United States women's national team. She helped lead the team to a World Championship in 1975. During this time, Pat was also teaching, working on her master's degree, and beginning her coaching career.

All of her hard work paid off. Many of her players at Tennessee went on to become stars in the WNBA. She coached the U.S. Women's national team to a gold medal in 1984. By 1996, Pat was the highest paid athletic coach at the University of Tennessee. Her friends and family attribute her amazing success to a single-minded determination to be the best. A large part of the success and marketability of womens' basketball can be attributed to Pat Summitt.

THINK CRITICALLY
Select the coach of one of the teams in the most recent NCAA women's basketball Top 25 poll. Prepare a display about the coach, including career highlights. Discuss the personal attributes that led to the coach's success.

UNDERSTAND MARKETING CONCEPTS

Circle the best answer for each of the following questions.

1. Market segmentation b
   a. involves looking at the entire marketplace as one
   b. involves dividing the marketplace into smaller interest groups
   c. usually decreases total sale
   d. is no longer used by successful marketing strategists

2. **Marketing-Information Management** Taking your little brother out for his birthday instead of going to a game with friends is an example of c
   a. demographic segmentation
   b. benefits derived segmentation
   c. psychographics segmentation
   d. product usage segmentation

THINK CRITICALLY

Answer the following as completely as possible. If necessary, use a separate sheet of paper.

3. **Technology** Use the Internet to find the latest rankings for a college sport. Choose one of the teams in the Top Five. Search again to find the history behind the success of that team. List the most recent steps to the team's success.

   Answers will vary.

4. **Research** Conduct research on schools that have been placed on NCAA athletic probation. List the reasons for the probation and the effects of the probation on the team's success.

   Answers will vary.

CHAPTER 2
LESSON 2.2

ECONOMIC IMPACT OF COLLEGE ATHLETICS

GOALS

Understand the benefits of college sports to the home community.

Identify benefits of sponsorship and licensing to a team.

Explain the reasons for realignment of college conferences.

SCHEDULE
Block 45 minutes
Regular 1 class period

FOCUS
Put a map of the U.S. on the board. Outline the states having teams in an athletic conference. Ask students why those teams might be a good combination for a conference.

OPENING ACT
A college sporting event provides a perfect setting for advertising all kinds of goods and services.

Answers for Opening Act
Cooperative Learning
Answers will vary. Sponsors have banners throughout the stadium, are announced during the game, or are listed in the game program.

OPENING ACT

Sponsorship plays an important role in college athletics. Sponsorship can be as inexpensive as advertising on the back of sporting event tickets or as expensive as buying television commercial time during the National Championship bowl game or the Final Four.

Have you ever noticed what types of sponsors have commercials during televised college sporting events? During one event you may see commercials for fast food, pizza, beer, soft drinks, automobiles, gasoline, airlines, and upcoming games to be televised. Sponsors want to be known for their loyalty to the local team and to be associated with winners.

Work with a partner. Watch a college game this weekend. Make note of which sponsors advertise during the contest. Why are these sponsors appropriate? If you attend a game in person, how can you recognize who the sponsors are by sitting in the stadium or arena?

BENEFITS TO THE COMMUNITY

The Cornhuskers of the University of Nebraska—Lincoln are year-round stars in a city of 200,000 people. Part of their popularity comes from Nebraska having no professional teams to compete for consumers' sports entertainment dollars.

GOOD FOR TOWN BUSINESS

On football Saturdays, the 76,000 seats in Nebraska's Memorial Stadium sell out. This means strong business for hotels, restaurants, shopping malls, concession stands, gas stations, and souvenir shops. Hotel rooms in Lincoln are booked on Friday and Saturday nights of a home football weekend. Restaurants and bars reap financial benefits as Husker fans patronize them. Tickets to sporting events are sometimes sponsored by local businesses as well as by major corporations. Restaurants might have special offers for fans if the home team scores a certain number of points or holds the opponent to a low score. Fans take their ticket stub to the restaurant to receive the special, which might be a free beverage, French fries, or

PROMOTION

sandwich. The restaurant can monitor how much business is stimulated by the special offer from the sporting event.

Retailers such as car dealers also promote themselves by having a popular coach or player present at the business site to sign autographs and visit with customers.

GOOD FOR STADIUM BUSINESS

Food items sold at athletic events grab the attention of additional consumers. Providers market their wares throughout sports complexes and sports publications. A major sporting event has a captive audience, so vendors can charge higher prices for food and beverages.

INTERMISSION

What can local businesses do to promote themselves to fans? Why can stadium vendors charge more for their goods?

Local businesses can put ads on the back of tickets, in the program, and on banners in the

stadium. Stadium vendors can change more because they have a captive target market.

A city with a popular college team can expect these revenues for one football game.

Ticket sales: $3 million

Hotel sales: $210,000 to $420,000

Stadium food sales: $380,000

Restaurants, shopping, transportation: $210,000 to $420,000

SPONSORSHIPS AND LICENSING

How much does it cost to have a corporate logo in the stadium of a major college football team? What is the value of corporate sponsorship to the university and the corporation?

SPONSORSHIPS

On one hand, sponsorship of college athletics is all about financing or generating revenue for the college programs. On the other hand, corporations are actually selling their products and services during major college sporting events. It is no accident that successful college teams are wearing Nike, Adidas, and Converse products. The name-brand apparel is very visible during the actual sporting event and televised post-game interviews. Corporations hope that fans who enjoy the success of a particular

Many college sports do not draw large crowds to the games or large numbers of people to a city. For example, college baseball traditionally has low attendance at games. In the 1999 season, the top 50 teams in home attendance had an average of 2100 fans per home game in the stands. A college football game can attract 100,000 fans or more.

THINK CRITICALLY
1. Find the average home attendance for baseball and football games for five different colleges or universities. How many times did more people attend the football games than the baseball games?
2. Are there any marketing advantages to having a smaller crowd? Explain.

Time Out
The success of a college athletic team determines the success of many retailers in the college community.

TEACH
Successful college teams bring big business to the community. Some major university cities receive over 50% of their annual sales during the three-month college football season.

Marketing Myths
Use the Internet to help research these questions.

Think Critically
1. Answers will vary.
2. Answers will vary. Possible answers: It is easier to determine the market segmentation for a smaller group of people

team will purchase the brand worn by that team. Television and radio payments from corporate sponsors add up to over $1 million each year for major universities.

Corporate sponsors often use creative promotional strategies to attract attention. A fan, for example, might shoot a half-court basket at halftime and win a new automobile. Such publicity stunts create goodwill among fans.

LICENSING

A **license** is the legal right to reproduce a team's logo in exchange for payment. For example, a bumper sticker manufacturer will pay an agreed-upon amount to a college for the right to make and sell stickers with the team's name and logo.

The mission of the athletic licensing and sales office at a university is to protect the use of the athletic department's name and symbols, and to ensure that the public can properly identify and associate logos on products bearing the institution's marks. It is common for a university to own and operate a store carrying the school's sportswear through its athletic department. Most universities put information on the Internet explaining the licensing process.

National retail sales of clothing items bearing a university's logo increase when one of the school's teams wins a national championship. An appealing logo makes a big difference in sales. Some universities have changed their logos to increase national retail sales. Many universities are updating their logos in order to increase sales of athletic apparel throughout the country. Each item containing a university logo provides income to the university. In 1997, colleges and universities had agreed to 2,000 licenses worth $2.5 billion. Just a few of the licensed items included clothing, posters, sunglasses, video games, software, rugs, and photographs.

INTERMISSION

Why are corporate sponsors important to college athletics? What is licensing?

Corporate sponsors generate signifcant revenue for college programs. Licensing is

the legal right to reproduce a team's logo in exchange for payment.

JUDGMENT CALL

College sports directors want an image of competitive young all-Americans studying among the ivy-covered columns of major universities. Unfortunately, some campuses across the United States have acquired reputations for parties and alcohol abuse. Many campuses have not legalized alcohol on campus or at sporting events. This regulation is especially important since many undergraduate students have not even reached legal drinking age. Often, college sporting events are sponsored by beer distributors who invest millions of dollars to advertise on television, signs, and banners.

THINK CRITICALLY

1. Is this sponsorship sending a mixed message to students that alcohol is acceptable since it is big money for sponsorship?

2. Why is it unusual to have beer corporations sponsor sporting events with athletes who are in top physical shape?

CONFERENCE REALIGNMENT

A **conference** is a group of college athletic teams within the same region. Conferences are created in order to have playing associations of manageable sizes and to be able to assign competing teams in an organized and fair manner. Examples are the Big 12 Conference (Kansas State, Nebraska, Missouri, Colorado, Kansas, Iowa State, Texas A&M, Texas, Texas Tech, Oklahoma, Oklahoma State, and Baylor) and the PAC 10 (UCLA, Arizona, Oregon, USC, Washington, Arizona State, California, Oregon State, Stanford, and Washington State).

The 1990s were a time of change for some of the college conferences. Changes within conferences are made, in part, to increase revenues. For example, the recent merger of selected teams from the Big 8 and Southwest Conferences increased revenue and publicity for the Big 12. Sometimes, too, conference changes create new rivalries, which, in turn, increase excitement, marketing opportunities, and revenues. Conference controllers continue to make changes in anticipation of greater revenue and television share.

INTERMISSION

Why are traditional athletic conferences breaking up and forming new alliances?

Athletic conferences are breaking up and forming new alliances to increase revenue

and exposure.

ENCORE!

UNDERSTAND MARKETING CONCEPTS

Circle the best answer for each of the following questions.

1. Sponsorships are d
   a. needed financing sources for universities
   b. recognition for major corporations and smaller businesses
   c. illegal in collegiate athletics
   d. a and b

2. Which of the following statements is false? b
   a. Sponsors receive exposure on television and on the playing field or arena.
   b. Sponsorships are relatively inexpensive for large corporations.
   c. Universities make a commitment to remain loyal to sponsors.
   d. Most sponsors prefer to associate their company with a winning tradition.

THINK CRITICALLY

Answer the following as completely as possible. If necessary, use a separate sheet of paper.

3. **Technology**   Use the Internet to research your favorite university or college athletic team. Discover who its corporate and local sponsors are and how much revenue is generated from the university logo.

   Answers will vary.
   _____
   _____
   _____
   _____

4. **Communication**   Your small city depends on the local college football team for a large percentage of its income. Help your Chamber of Commerce develop a brochure promoting the city's attractions that are not college or football related. List ten attractive features of the city, and write a short description of each.

   Answers will vary. The brochure could include information about local attractions
   _____
   and accomodations.
   _____
   _____
   _____
   _____

AMATEUR SPORTS

OPENING ACT

Busy adults use their leisure time participating in amateur sports. Families spend weeknights and weekends watching their children play sports. Participants enjoy the exercise, competition, and social interaction.

A physically active society is good for sports-related businesses, such as equipment and clothing retailers, sports-food manufacturers, and sports-injury clinics. A physically active society is also good for any local businesses that benefit from advertising in regional publications and from sponsorship of local teams.

Work with a group. Survey ten people to find out which amateur sport interests them most. Do they participate, or do they just enjoy spectating? How much do they spend on the sport?

GOALS

Discuss marketing and sponsoring of amateur sports.

Understand the economic benefits of amateur sports.

SCHEDULE
Block 45 minutes
Regular 1 class period

FOCUS
Before class, write a variety of amateur sports on the board or the overhead. Examples of amateur sports can include softball, skateboarding, skiing, golf, baseball, football, and many more. Ask students for additional amateur sports they would like added to the list and then take a vote to determine the students' favorite amateur sports.

OPENING ACT
Emphasize how amateur sports have become increasingly popular.

Answers for Opening Act Cooperative Learning
Busy adults are rejuvenated by participating in amateur sports. They enjoy the exercise, competition, and social interaction. Survey results will vary.

POPULARITY OF AMATEUR SPORTS

A professional athlete is someone who earns a living participating in a sport. An **amateur athlete** is someone who does not get paid but plays for enjoyment, challenge, or both. For most sports, professional athletes must be young, healthy, and strong. Amateur athletes can be of any age, and physical challenges are not prohibitions. The key to being an amateur athlete is wanting to be one. There aren't many professional athletes, but there are millions of amateurs.

Amateur sports have grown tremendously over the last few decades. Family social life often involves soccer, basketball, or baseball. Senior citizens participate in leagues and tournaments, as do youngsters who excel in the Special Olympics. Wheelchair basketball has been a passion for more than fifty years. Rodeo riding takes commitment and focus equal to or surpassing that needed in other sports.

MARKETING AND SPONSORING AMATEUR SPORTS

SELLING

Regardless of the sport, marketing and selling are essential. The amateur athlete, like the professional, must have top-quality equipment and the money necessary to compete. Companies are glad to make and sell the gear and to advertise and sponsor individual athletes or teams. Amateur sports provide significant income for manufacturers of athletic uniforms, shoes, equipment, lawn chairs, portable stadium seats, and coolers. Major corporations conduct marketing-information management studies to determine the latest trends and purchasing habits in amateur sports in order to

TIME OUT

The Special Olympics is a program of athletic training and competition for children and adults with mental retardation. One hundred fifty countries now compete in the programs started in 1968.

Top corporate sponsors give at least $1 million in cash plus other contributions that increase the Special Olympics' budget.

produce products and services demanded by broad and diverse groups of people. A recent wildly successful trend in marketing related to amateur sports is the minivan and the sport utility vehicle — vehicles big enough to carry team members and equipment.

LOCAL PROMOTION OF AMATEUR SPORTS

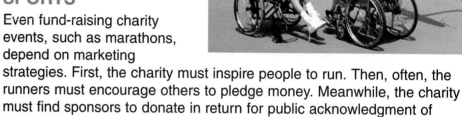

Even fund-raising charity events, such as marathons, depend on marketing strategies. First, the charity must inspire people to run. Then, often, the runners must encourage others to pledge money. Meanwhile, the charity must find sponsors to donate in return for public acknowledgment of the gifts.

Many communities rally around high school athletic teams. Businesses sponsor local teams and then print their names on uniforms. This form of promotion is good for the local team, and gives the business an image of being an active participant in the community. For smaller communities, high school sports are a big part of weekend life. Families travel many miles to attend athletic events and spend money in the process, frequently with businesses that advertise in the sport's program.

NATIONAL PROMOTION OF AMATEUR SPORTS

One of the strongest reasons for growth of certain amateur sports is the promotion that is used to elevate the attention of consumers. Television shows, movies, athletes, and media stars help to carry out successful promotional strategies for an amateur sport. For example, Mia Hamm, a member of the U.S. Women's Soccer Team, has sparked interest in women's sports. One television commercial pits Hamm against Michael Jordan in a one-on-one competition, with the song "Anything You Can Do, I Can Do Better" playing in the background. This commercial recognizes and encourages the growing interest in women's amateur athletics.

INTERMISSION

Why do communities rally around sporting events?

Local communities rally around the success of their local teams to be associated with a winner.

ECONOMIC BENEFITS

Communities, cities, and states can gain from amateur sports as well as from professional sports. Often the gain is financial, but sometimes it is just goodwill, enjoyment of a well-played game, and the mental and emotional support of the athletes.

MINNESOTA'S EXAMPLE

PRODUCT/ SERVICE MANAGEMENT

In 1987, the Minnesota State Legislature created the Minnesota Amateur Sports Commission. The Commission's tasks, which it has largely accomplished, were to bring out-of-state dollars into Minnesota through development of amateur sports events, and to create partnerships between athletes or athletic associations and public, private, or governmental organizations to support amateur sports. Its goals are:

1. To create economic development through amateur sports
2. To create the maximum opportunity for sport participation for all Minnesotans
3. To establish Minnesota as a national model for the Olympic and amateur sport movement

A few of the Commission's accomplishments in 1998 were to help increase sports opportunities for women, senior citizens, and people who have had few chances to play; to help construct 61 new ice rinks statewide; and to host three world championships.

ECONOMIC BENEFITS OF SPECIFIC SPORTS

Fans are limited to just watching professional sports, but almost anyone can participate in amateur sports. Some of the fastest-growing amateur sports today are soccer, ice skating, stock car racing, and baseball and softball.

The 26.2-mile Boston Marathon began in 1896, but it wasn't until 1966 that women were welcomed as participants. In 1972, wheelchair participants entered for the first time.

TEACH

Three ways that cities and states benefit from amateur sports include revenue, goodwill, and enjoyment of a well-played game.

Some states like Minnesota have made a dedicated effort to raise the importance of amateur sports. State governments realize the financial gain that amateur sports can provide.

Women, senior citizens, and people who have had few chances to play sports benefit from amateur sports.

Professional sports allow most people to be spectators while amateur sports allow people to be participants.

Ice skating is not limited to cold climates. Ice skating rinks in shopping malls allow skating enthusiasts year-round pleasure and mall retailers more revenue.

Soccer is the number one sport in the world and it is quickly gaining momentum in the U.S. The 1999 Women's World Cup Championship has helped spark increased awareness and enthusiasm for soccer.

Car racing has some of the most loyal fans. Car racing fans remain loyal to the brands advertised on their favorite driver's car.

Baseball games and tournaments help finance local economies.

These sports become weekend family affairs and now games are even scheduled between teams in different states.

Cyber Marketing
Think Critically
Answers will vary. Students must list equipment, items for sale through the Internet, fees to participate, and demographics of participants.

Ongoing Assessment
Use the Intermission as an opportunity to conduct ongoing assessment of student comprehension of the lesson material.

TEACHING STRATEGIES
Poor Self-Concept
Show students pictures of equipment used for different amateur sports. When they correctly identify the different sports, conduct a short discussion about what merchandise is sold for this sport and what products are sold to spectators watching the sporting event.

TEACHING STRATEGIES
Auditory Learners
Break the class into groups of two students. Make sure that each group has the appropriate diversity. Students select an amateur sport, conduct research, and report at least ten concepts about the sport to the class using a chart or software presentation.

Ice Skating   The popularity of ice skating has risen even in hot climates such as Houston, Texas. Shopping malls and gallerias now include ice rinks in their complexes. Not only does this provide a service, but the skaters must pass by stores on their way to and from the rink, providing exposure for more promotion and sales.

Soccer   Success of the U.S. Women's Soccer Team packed over 600,000 fans into stadiums for 32 matches during the 1999 Women's World Cup Soccer match. Marketers have found a new marketing niche—a sport represented by wholesome athletes and supported by suburban affluent families who are brand loyal.

Basketball   Amateur basketball is an extremely popular sport. "Pickup" games, which are unplanned matchups between players who happen to be on the same court at the same time, are a popular form of recreation for people of all ages and backgrounds. In 1996, author Chris Ballard and three friends traveled to 166 cities in 48 states to play pickup games. Their tour was sponsored by Nike, PowerBar, and Borden. Ballard recorded his experiences on a website diary and wrote the book *Hoops Nation: A Guide to America's Best Pickup Basketball.*

Baseball and Softball   Not only is money spent on the equipment needed for baseball and softball, but the economy has benefited from families traveling to games. Motels, restaurants, and gas stations all benefit from softball and baseball games and tournaments. Tournaments are important economic weekend events for the city hosting the games. Small communities in rural areas even fly softball teams to the West Coast to compete against teams in larger cities.

Use the Internet to research an amateur sport. Select a sport other than football, basketball, or baseball.

INTERNET EXTENSIONS
1. List the equipment you need to safely and adequately participate in the sport.
2. Find those items for sale through the Internet, and list the costs.
3. Research and list the fees you would need to pay in order to participate in a tournament or championship.
4. Do further research to find the demographics of those who are involved with this sport.

INTERMISSION

What kinds of products might be advertised during stock car racing and ice skating?

Answers will vary. Stock car racing—tires, gas, auto parts

Ice skating—winter clothes, ice skates, hot beverages

UNDERSTAND MARKET CONCEPTS

Circle the best answer for each of the following questions.

1. An amateur athlete d
   a. participates in a sport for money.
   b. participates in a sport for the enjoyment or challenge of it.
   c. can be any age or in almost any physical condition.
   d. b and c

2. Promotion   Marketers have many opportunities in amateur sports because d
   a. millions of potential consumers participate in amateur sports.
   b. amateur athletes want top-quality equipment.
   c. entire families become involved in amateur sports.
   d. all of these

THINK CRITICALLY

Answer the following as completely as possible. If necessary, use a separate sheet of paper.

3. List three amateur sports, the target markets for those sports, and marketing strategies for each sport.

Answers will vary.

_____

_____

_____

_____

4. Many families spend hours on weekends watching children play soccer. During the 1996 presidential election year, the phrase "soccer moms" became commonly used in political conversations. What do you think this phrase means? Why would someone running for a political office pay attention to soccer moms?

Soccer moms spend a considerable amount of time watching their children par-

ticpate in activities like soccer. Soccer moms have voting power and regulary

visit and talk with other soccer moms who vote.

_____

_____

ASSESS
Reteach
Give students a handout with pictures that represent four amateur sports or use a transparency to show the four sports. Students need to identify each of the sports, tell the reason for increased popularity of the sport, and identify a good corporate sponsor for each sport and why.

Enrich
Tell students to design a television commercial or a software presentation that advertises a special charity amateur sporting event. Students can also design a poster to increase interest in the charity event.

CLOSE
Design a magazine advertisement for apparel or equipment associated with an amateur sport.

CHAPTER 2 REVIEW

REVIEW MARKETING CONCEPTS

Write the letter of the term that matches each definition. Some terms will not be used.

__d__ **1.** the governing body of the athletics programs in colleges and universities

__c__ **2.** a group of individuals within a larger market that share one or more characteristics

__e__ **3.** the value people believe they receive from a product or service

__a__ **4.** the legal right to reproduce a team's logo in exchange for payment

__f__ **5.** someone who plays a sport just for fun

a. license
b. psychographics
c. market segment
d. NCAA
e. benefits derived
f. amateur athlete

Circle the best answer.

6. To maximize profits, cities with college sports teams must have
  a. adequate hotel rooms and restaurants.
  b. tourist attractions other than sports.
  c. shopping areas.
  d. all of these

d

7. Dollars from sponsors of NCAA sports support
  a. the NCAA Championship.
  b. expansion of NCAA programs for young people.
  c. a pool of dividends to be split among the sponsors.
  d. a and b

d

8. An example of product usage is
  a. your family's customs.
  b. your income.
  c. how often you eat corn chips.
  d. where you live.

c

9. Local businesses support amateur athletics because
  a. the promotion is good for the team.
  b. the business wants to be an active part of the community.
  c. sports fans will support the business.
  d. all of these

d

THINK CRITICALLY

10. List three major sporting goods manufacturers. Determine the methods of advertising each uses. Could each manufacturer on your list be more effective? Explain.

Answers will vary.

11. Think of the last college sporting event you or someone you know attended. What were the prices of some food and beverages? What would these or similar items cost outside the arena? Why are the prices different?

Answers will vary.

12. Some college or other amateur athletes must decide whether to become professionals. List five questions for such an athlete to consider when making this decision.

Answers will vary. Possible questions:

What is my long-term career goal?

How much job security will pro sports provide?

What career backup do I have if sports do not work?

CHAPTER 2 REVIEW

MAKE CONNECTIONS

13. Mathematics Your small-town restaurant supports the local high school athletic department by placing an ad in the town's weekly newspaper. The coupon offers free French fries to anyone who has a ticket stub and buys a burger and a soft drink after a game. French fries are $0.95. Burgers are $2.50. Drinks are $0.95. Your normal evening burger-fries-and-a-drink trade is 20 customers. On game nights, though, your customers increase to 60, but you give away the fries. Compare the revenue generated by sales of burgers, fries, and drink combos on a normal night with that on a night in which the promotion is in effect.

	Regular day	Game day
burger	$2.50	$2.50
fries	0.95	0.00
drink	0.95	0.95
	$4.40	$3.45
Customers	× 20	× 60
	$88.00	$207.00

Revenue increased dramatically with the promotion.

The *Sports and Entertainment Marketing* Teacher's Resource CD includes a spreadsheet template to help students complete this activity.

Look for the file p048 Make Connections-Mathematics.xls in the Office Templates folder, or the file p048 Conx.txt in the Text Templates folder.

14. Communication Your small city has just completed a beautiful new golf course that meets all standards for competition. Your city is not noted for tourism interests, but it is located 45 miles from a larger city that offers many attractions, including hotels, shopping, and restaurants. An interstate highway allows quick travel between the two cities. Write a one-page paper explaining why tourists should drive nearly an hour to come to your town and golf course.

Answers will vary. Possible answers: excellent golf course, small town hospitality, easy access to larger city.

15. History Use the Internet or magazines and books to research the history of women's basketball. When did basketball itself begin? When did women start playing in front of audiences? What did the first players wear? How has the game improved for women? How have women improved the game?

Basketball began in 1891. Women's basketball began in 1892. Other developments in-

clude intercollegiate play at Smith College in 1893 and the creation of the NCAA

Women's Basketball Championship in 1981.

PROJECT EXTRA INNINGS

Your family of four wants to attend the next basketball game at your favorite college that is in your state. You need to know how much money to set aside for the trip. Since it was your idea, the family has put you in charge of the budget.

Work with a group and complete the following activities.

1. Using the Internet, find ticket prices, parking prices, and prices for snacks and souvenirs within the arena. Could you take public transportation and save a parking fee? How much would the fares be?

2. Must your car be serviced before you go? If so, how much is a tune-up? If the car is in good shape, you'll still need gas. How many gallons will you need to get to the game and back? How much will that cost?

3. Find two hotels near the arena and two motels ten miles away from the arena. Assume your family will need one room for one night. How much will these rooms cost? Which will you choose?

4. Plan to leave home early Saturday morning and return Sunday. Your parents want to eat at one nice restaurant, but the rest of the meals can be at fast-food places or at less expensive dine-in chains. Estimate the costs for four people for two breakfasts, two lunches, and one nice dinner. Don't forget tips.

5. Use the cost spreadsheet provided on the template disk. Show itemized expenses and show what percent each kind of expense is of the total.

6. Produce a pie chart or bar graph from your spreadsheet information.

7. Just to show off to your parents, write a one-page report on why this money is being well spent.

Extra Innings

The Internet will be a valuable resource for this activity. Students can look up the web site for the various universities. They will also locate toll-free numbers for university athletic departments to obtain information and publications that will be good resources for this project.

The *Sports and Entertainment Marketing* Teacher's Resource CD includes a spreadsheet template to help students complete this activity.

Look for the file p049 Extra Innings.xls in the Office Templates folder, or the file p049 XInn.txt in the Text Templates folder.

CHAPTER 3

PROFESSIONAL SPORTS

LESSONS

WINNING STRATEGIES

THE ADVANTAGE OF ADVANTAGE

Advantage International is a sports management firm based in McLean, Virginia. Advantage is the management agent for Women's National Basketball Association player Sheryl Swoopes. In 1997, Swoopes informed her Advantage agent, Tom George, that her first child would be born during the first month of the first season for the WNBA. Swoopes was one of the new league's most popular players and she would be out for at least part of the season.

Advantage made the perfect moves for Swoopes and played up the impending birth. The cover of the first issue of Sports Illustrated for Women featured Swoopes during her pregnancy. Advantage continues to market Swoopes as a mother and sports star. Being a supermom has opened additional opportunities for Swoopes to endorse products. Advantage markets Swoopes to her advantage.

THINK CRITICALLY

1. How did Advantage International turn Swoopes' missing the new league's opening games into a positive promotion?
2. What would be the characteristics of consumers who would associate with Sheryl Swoopes? What products might they use?

CHAPTER OVERVIEW
Chapter 3 addresses the economic value of professional sports, the ethics of acquiring a team, how pro teams as a product are distributed to specific marketing areas, the role of agents and managers, and the relationship of ethics to sports.

Lesson 3.1
Big League Sports
This lesson discusses the financial benefits of a professional team and the perks associated with professional sports.

Lesson 3.2
Attracting a Professional Team
In this lesson, students will describe acquiring and financing a pro team.

Lesson 3.3
Agents, Managers, and Ethics
In this lesson, students learn about sports agents and the impact of ethical behavior on an athlete's promotional value.

TEACHING RESOURCES
❑ CNN Video, Chapter 3
❑ CD-ROM Resources, Chapter 3

Winning Strategies
Talk with students about the role of an agent in promoting an image for a pro athlete. Ask students if they think it is important for a famous athlete to be portrayed as having a normal family life off the playing field.

Think Critically
1. Instead of trying to cover up or deny, Advantage keyed on Swoopes as a Super Mom. This marketing plan gives women the confidence that they can have a profession and be a good mother.
2. Characteristics of consumers —female, interested in sports, young wives and mothers. Products: sports equipment, children/baby products, cosmetics.

CHAPTER 3
LESSON 3.1

BIG LEAGUE SPORTS

GOALS

Discuss the financial impact of professional sports.

Identify the perks associated with big league sports.

OPENING ACT

The values of a culture are reflected in the products or services people demand and the amounts they are willing to spend to fulfill those demands. This concept explains the money side of professional sports. Professional players, some just graduating from high school, sign multimillion-dollar contracts. Many Americans love professional sports and are willing to pay high prices to see the action.

How much are you willing to pay for a ticket to the Super Bowl? Survey 10 other people to find out what they are willing to pay for this event. Ask each person why, and record the answers.

FINANCIAL IMPACT

The Dallas Cowboys franchise was valued at $320 million in 1997. Paul Allen, owner of the NBA Portland Trail Blazers and the NFL Seattle Seahawks, is worth at least $17 billion. Nike and Reebok have spent almost $400 million in worldwide advertising. Hockey player Joe Sakic earned $7 million annually from 1996 to 1999. In today's market, professional sports provide a handsome profit for owners, players, and sponsors (advertisers).

Professional sports, like college sports, are big business. They depend on a large financial commitment and a large financial return. A city gains a special identity with a professional team, and a winning tradition fuels the financial fire.

BIG LEAGUE PRICING AND PLANNING

PRICING

The "big" in "big league sports" refers to revenue potential or commercial value (money) as much as to the skill level of the actual physical competition. Marketers consider the product or game they have available to distribute in order to determine what prices to charge for the event and what advertising strategies to use. For example, a team fresh off of a national championship will probably have sold-out games the next season because fans will expect continued success.

As professional team owners plan for financial success, they must determine the cost of obtaining the top professional athletes. Multimillion-dollar contracts for professional athletes require huge ticket sales. In order to keep ticket sales strong and charge high prices, owners must provide a winning product or team. Corporations pay extra fees to obtain their group of tickets for professional contests. These tickets come in handy when entertaining business clients.

FINANCIAL PLANNING FOR A SPORTS TEAM

FINANCING

Team owners and managers must prove financial viability of a team before the team can find a home city. This is especially important in light of the huge costs to the city. Owners and managers must convince the city that the costs of a team or new stadium will be repaid through increased spending by fans—most importantly by fans coming to the events from outside the area—and by increased tax revenues. An NFL team can be a financial asset to a city if:

1. Everyone and everything involved with the team (staff, headquarters, practice areas, and pre-season training facilities) stays within the home city area.

2. The stadium/arena is used for events other than those for which it was built.

3. The team attracts other business development like hotels, restaurants, and retail shops.

BRINGING ALL THE RESOURCES TOGETHER

PRODUCT/ SERVICE MANAGEMENT

Once the financial viability of a sports team is proven, then media support, marketing arms, charitable concerns, and other organizations come together to back it. For example, the Dallas Cowboys have turned $60 million in profits in the last three years from their off-the-field products such as media rights, luxury suites, and team sponsorships. Also, even though Coca-Cola is the official beverage of the NFL, Pepsi is paying $40 million over the next ten years to be the official beverage of Texas Stadium, home of the Dallas Cowboys.

The Cleveland Browns were without a football team or stadium for almost 5 years. Their merchandise still sold in the top 10 percent of all NFL gear during their absence.

MARKETING MYTHS

Sports movies are often criticized for poor acting and little plot. The top five income-producing sports movies may change that mind-set.

1. Jerry Maguire (1996): $153,620,822

2. Rocky 4 (1985): $127,873,716

3. Rocky 3 (1982): $122,823,192

4. Rocky (1976): $117,235,147

5. A League of Their Own (1992): $107,439,000

THINK CRITICALLY

What can you conclude from the popularity of sports movies?

TEACH
Conduct a short discussion on possible reasons why a city and sports fans are willing to spend large sums of money on professional teams. Ask students to give examples of financial benefits for a community that hosts a professional team and write the list on the board.

Ask students if they would be willing to pay higher sales tax in order to snag a professional team for their city.

Marketing Myths
Sports enthusiasts are not only loyal fans attending games, but they also enjoy sports movies.

Ongoing Assessment
Use the Intermission as an opportunity to conduct ongoing assessment of student comprehension of the lesson material.

INTERMISSION

What can cause higher prices for tickets to sports events? How can a team be good for a city? A high demand for tickets, rivalry, or championship game can cause higher prices. A team brings additional revenue into a city.

A team can give a city something to rally around and can revitalize a downtown area.

One New York Mets game at Shea Stadium generates $2 million in economic activity, $62,000 in taxes, and 850 jobs.

PRESTIGE, POWER, PROFITABILITY

The value of sports franchises has skyrocketed due to prestige, power, and profitability. Football's Philadelphia Eagles sold for $65 million in 1985 and for $185 million in 1994. A group of investors bought the New England Patriots for $106 million in 1992 and $160 million two years later. A deal in late 1999 valued the Cincinnati Reds at more than $180 million.

PERKS AND PAYOFFS

In addition to the usual benefits such as salary, people often receive perks (an abbreviation of *perquisite*). A perk is a payoff or profit received in addition to a regular wage or payment. Employees of companies may receive tickets to a sports event as a perk.

The position of team owner has many perks, including money and media exposure. Jerry Jones, owner of the Dallas Cowboys, has appeared on national television numerous times. However, there is more to ownership than publicity. The Cowboys are one of sports' most popular teams. Jerry Jones paid $140 million for them in 1989 ($65 million for the franchise and $75 million for the stadium). The value of both has more than doubled, and this doesn't include the off-the-field dollars mentioned earlier.

POLITICAL CLOUT

Franchise owners who bring millions of dollars in business activity to cities often find themselves with political clout, especially in a city that either wants a new franchise or wants to keep an existing one. Mayor Philip Bredesen of Nashville, Tennessee, supported Nashville's successful bid to become the new home of the Titans football team. Some of his reasons were new local jobs and businesses, a new image for the city, and a motivation for young people to stay in Nashville. The fact that a city might lose a team because many other cities will offer a new stadium with all the modern amenities, rent-free gives owners more clout than most ordinary citizens have.

Americans seem eager to contribute to multimillion-dollar contracts for professional athletes. Some tickets for Super Bowl XXXIII sold for well over $5,000. Even championship college bowl games attract customers willing to spend more than $1,000 per ticket.

THINK CRITICALLY

With so many people living in poverty today, is it right for athletes to earn so much money or for attendees to pay so much for a few hours of pleasure? What does this imply about the value system in the United States?

PROFESSIONAL TEAMS AND THE COMMUNITY

Professional teams bring enthusiasm and heightened emotion and morale to a city. People perceive teams as bringing many new jobs to a city. Teams offer construction jobs for the new stadiums, jobs for the

TEACH

Professional teams bring a lot of good to a community. Ask students to give examples of what a professional team brings to the community. Emphasize the new jobs created by bringing a professional team to a community.

Ask students if they are emotionally tied to a professional or college team. In other words, are they die-hard fans? Describe how fans become very attached to a team and how they feel empty if the team leaves the community.

Emphasize how the success of a professional team calculates into financial success for a community. Make sure students understand that communities make a large financial commitment for a professional team in expectation of a large financial return.

The goal of business is profit. Emphasize the major reason for a professional team is to make a profit. Money attracts the best players and teams.

citizens once the team is operating, tourist dollars both in and out of the stadium, a boost for surrounding businesses, dollars spent by regional residents who come to the events, and even increased newspaper sales (for the sports page). Even professionals like lawyers in private firms can benefit from a team in town. The law firm of Snell & Wilmer in Phoenix has created a new department that handles contracts, tax issues, and financial planning for sports and entertainment personalities.

SOCIOLOGICAL TIES TO A PROFESSIONAL TEAM

Sports have a sociological impact on cities and their citizens. Advocates of professional sports teams talk about the "image enhancement" teams bring to a city and about the pride residents feel from having a team. Many people identify with their teams. With a professional sports franchise in town, fans have something to talk about at work and at home. They have a place to go for wholesome family entertainment, and a certain amount of pride in their hometown. Such identification with a team can be so strong that the loss of the team can bring on bitterness and depression. Art Modell, the owner who moved the Cleveland Browns to Baltimore at the end of the 1995 season, received bomb threats, hate letters, and death threats for his action.

THE BOTTOM LINE

FINANCING

Winning is everything in sports. Players are lured to other teams with special incentives for winning. Rickey Jackson signed with the San Francisco 49ers for the league minimum of $162,000 in 1994 after a 13-year career with the New Orleans Saints. Jackson thought the 49ers could make it to the Super Bowl with his help, so he had a bonus clause in his contract giving him $838,000 if the 49ers made it to Super Bowl XXIX. The 49ers won the Super Bowl and gladly paid Jackson his bonus money.

Power, prestige, and money also apply to college sports. Merging conferences and alliances is done for fiscal, not geographic or academic, reasons. Penn State University joined the Big Ten for three reasons: more television coverage, better exposure, and more money.

INTERMISSION

List three perks for a franchise owner. List three benefits a professional team brings to a community.

Perks include media exposure, money, and political clout. Benefits include enthusiasm, heightened morale, jobs, and an economic boost.

TAKE A BOW

ANTHONY MUÑOZ

Anthony Muñoz of the Cincinnati Bengals was inducted into the Pro Football Hall of Fame the first time he was nominated. He played in 11 Pro Bowls, was a member of the NFL's 75th Anniversary All-Time Team in 1994, was in two Super Bowls, and has received numerous other honors.

But Muñoz also has a heartfelt appreciation for his mother who worked several jobs to provide for him and his four brothers and sisters. His family had the basics but nothing more.

"It was tough ... but what an example of ... having to work for everything," Muñoz has said. "... (T)hat's where I learned that hard-work ethic and what it was all about." This lesson carried him through three operations in his four years at the University of Southern California and on to his sterling career in football.

Anthony Muñoz did not let stardom destroy his life. Sam Wyche, former Bengals coach, said of Muñoz, "He's a better person than a football player, and he's a Hall-of-Fame football player. Anthony is one of the rare ones in this league."

THINK CRITICALLY
1. Name three other professional sports figures that have the reputation of decency that Anthony Muñoz has. Name three that have the opposite reputation.
2. Research the salaries of both groups you named. How do they compare? Does being a "nice person" pay better?
3. Assuming the pay were the same, whom would you choose for a role model? Why?

UNDERSTAND MARKETING CONCEPTS
Circle the best answer for each of the following questions.

1. Sports franchise ownership carries ___?___ power with it. **e.**
   a. financial
   b. social
   c. political
   d. (a) and (c)
   e. all of the above

2. The amount of money spent on big league sports in the United States indicates **d.**
   a. intense demand for professional sporting events
   b. that consumers are not willing to spend huge sums of money on sporting events
   c. that cities compete to land teams
   d. (a) and (c)
   e. all of the above

THINK CRITICALLY
Answer the following as completely as possible. If necessary, use a separate sheet of paper.

3. **Technology** Use the Internet to find the ticket prices at three major league stadiums or sports arenas in the United States. How many seats are available in each facility? What is the total revenue for a sell-out performance?

   Answers will vary. Students should research three major stadiums and list ticket

   prices, seating capacity, and revenue for a sell-out performance.

4. **Mathematics** A businesswoman has agreed to purchase a 35% share of a professional football team. She is paying $68.6 million for her share. Based on this deal, what is the total value for the team?

   $35\% = 0.35$

   $\dfrac{\$68.6 \text{ million}}{0.35} = \$196 \text{ million}$

   The total value of the team is $196 million.

CHAPTER 3
LESSON 3.2

ATTRACTING A PROFESSIONAL TEAM

GOALS

Describe the distribution process for a professional sports team.

Explain the process for financing a professional sports team.

OPENING ACT

Economists believe the economic value of a professional sports team does not measure up to the social and psychological significance of the team. Most team owners and sports fans would disagree. For an existing team to move to a city or for expansion teams to be approved, there must be financial benefits to the league member owners, to related businesses, and to the cities in which the team will locate. Success cannot occur if one makes a profit and the others lose money.

Work with a group. Brainstorm benefits other than financial that might come to a community acquiring a professional sports team. Post the list of these benefits in the classroom.

GETTING IN THE BALLGAME

Since there are more cities that want professional sports teams than there are teams available, the league controls the location of the teams based on the business benefits to the league and owners. The leagues are in business to make a profit. Additionally, the groups of owners make up an exclusive club that holds the key to membership. Similarly, cities hope to increase their own income by hosting professional sports teams.

DISTRIBUTING THE GAME

DISTRIBUTION

Individual teams within a league are separately operated businesses, but they are not in competition with each other as they would be in a free open market. Instead, each team is a member of a cartel. A **cartel** is a combination of independent businesses formed to regulate production, pricing, and marketing of a product. In the case of professional sports, the cartel is a number of independent sports teams grouped together and governed by a league agreement to control the market mix and set up the distribution of the products. Since teams must have other teams to play, they must stay in the league or start a new league. The league controls the distribution of the teams, including the locations of the teams and the number of teams allowed to operate within the league. In most cases, cartels are prohibited by federal antitrust law. However, professional sports leagues are allowed to form a cartel because of special legislation exempting the leagues from antitrust laws.

HOW DISTRIBUTION IS DECIDED

Regions with a large potential customer base are considered favorable for the location of a team. In many cases, owners want public funds to subsidize the new team. For tax-paid subsidies to be available, local governmental agencies must have the support of voters. Many people consider these subsidies to be a form of corporate welfare.

In 1998, the National Football League awarded Cleveland, Ohio, a franchise to operate the thirty-first NFL team rather than moving an existing team there. Work began immediately on a thirty-second team to join the league. Twenty-four of the thirty-one current NFL owners must agree to the selection of a new city to receive a team. The owners set the price of the new team and split an "expansion fee" among them. Players do not share in the expansion fee.

Bringing a team to a city takes more than just a new owner's desire for a team. The potential owner has to have the financing to pay the NFL as much as $450 million to $600 million for an expansion team. Additionally, the new team has to have a place to play.

INTERMISSION

How does the operation of a professional sports team differ from the operation of most other businesses in the U.S.?

The league controls production, pricing, and marketing. The competition between teams

is regulated by the league. Most of the practices would be prohibited in private business.

The new Paul Brown Stadium will open for the Cincinnati Bengals in the year 2000. Some of its off-the-field, tax-financed price tags are:
• Scoreboard: $5.4 million
• New offices, without furniture: $2.67 million
• 679 wooden-backed chairs etched with the team logo: $135,000
• Window treatments for the administration building: $48,106
• One custom-made desk: $4,854

ATTRACTING A SPORTS TEAM

FINANCING

There are fewer NFL teams than the market can support. The lack of teams forces cities to compete whenever a team becomes available through expansion or moving. Offering the best facilities at the best price is one of the enticements used to attract teams. Until about 1960, teams generally owned their own playing facilities. Since that time, some state and local governments have been eager to share in subsidizing major sports by financing stadiums. Some franchises are selling the naming rights of stadiums to subsidize the cost of building these facilities. But in the late 1990s, taxpaying voters began showing some resistance to helping build facilities. When taxpayers pick up facility costs, owners use the money coming in from attendance, broadcasting, and concessions to pay the salaries of professional players. These salaries continue to increase dramatically.

IT TAKES MONEY

The economics of pro sports involves huge amounts of money and risk on the part of the owners. Few are willing to jeopardize their fortunes without the opportunity to profit from the venture. New stadiums offer luxury suites and upscale restaurants that increase the chances of

profits, but these are not a guarantee of attracting a team. In 1989, voters in San Antonio, Texas, passed a referendum for construction of the Alamodome, a $156 million publicly financed stadium. Voters were convinced that it would help attract a professional football team. In 1999, San Antonio still did not have a NFL team, but it did have the NBA-champion Spurs to fill the Alamodome. However, the Spurs now want a new arena.

Pricing of tickets, concessions, luxury seating, and merchandise related to a professional team all contribute to the financial picture. The biggest profit center is television revenue. This revenue is generated through the sale of advertising time on TV channels that offer the game. Networks sell the ad time and buy the right to air the games. The cost per minute of TV advertising is based on the number of viewers. In determining what city will win a pro team, TV ratings are a major concern. When 3 of the 14 biggest TV market areas (Cleveland, Houston, and Los Angeles) lost their NFL teams, ratings for NFL viewing dropped considerably.

AND MORE MONEY

The award of the thirty-first expansion team to Cleveland left Los Angeles and Houston to battle for number thirty-two. Houston, the nation's fourth largest city, is located in an area that has no American Football Conference team. There are roughly 50 million TV viewers throughout the Houston region. Los Angeles is estimated to have about three times the number of TV sets as Houston. When the NFL announced plans for an expansion team, Los Angeles had two possible owners, and Houston had one excellent organization ready for a team. Having multiple sites competing for the expansion team allowed the NFL owners the option of increasing the team price.

When the two Los Angeles groups competing for the team had neither the financing nor taxpayer support by spring 1999, NFL Commissioner Paul Tagliabue announced that the league itself would consider financing the construction of a new stadium in Los Angeles. Los Angeles taxpayers did not appear eager to help finance the stadium. The estimated cost of $400 million would have to be repaid by the new team owners who would be selected later. A Houston franchise would not have such a heavy debt because taxpayers had already agreed to pay more than 60% of the $310 million proposed retractable-roof stadium. Houston philanthropists and billionaire Robert C.

McNair had put together a seamless package to entice the current team owners. But the lure of big TV revenue from Los Angeles appeared to hold more long-term attraction for the NFL owners.

ANOTHER OPTION

FINANCING

An alternative to the sky-high public financing of professional sports teams is community ownership. This is where the local government or the fans own the team. For example, the Green Bay Packers sell publicly traded stock in their team, and they have been very successful in nearly 80 years of belonging to the people. They have won three Super Bowls, and they have managed to keep their facilities up-to-date without adding more burdens to the taxpayers.

In spite of the apparent benefits to cities and citizens, the major leagues currently forbid public ownership in most cases. Perhaps as private ownership costs continue to soar, this will change. Several political action groups are already organized to help. Congressional Representative Earl Blumenauer from Oregon has sponsored the "Give Fans a Chance Act" toward this end. In Minnesota, a group named "Yer Out!" is working against state legislators who vote to subsidize professional teams with taxpayer money.

INTERMISSION

What part do the stadiums or arenas play in financing a professional team? What part do TV ads play in financing sports?

New stadiums have attractive income-producing features like luxury suites and

restaurants. TV ads pay the cost of broadcasting the game and are used to pay the

team for broadcast rights.

TEACH
Ask students who benefits from the decision on where a pro team is located. Ask students which city ended up with the thirty-second expansion team.

Public ownership means individuals own stock. Lead students in a discussion about why the league owners object to public ownership of sports facilities as a way to finance the facility. Discuss the difference between public ownership as individuals choosing to own stock in the facility and taxpayer subsidized facilities as not being the individuals' decision.

TEACHING STRATEGIES
Gifted Students
To challenge gifted students, ask them to propose strategies to present a tax-paid stadium to three different groups: voters in low, middle, and high income levels.

TEACHING STRATEGIES
Visual Learners
Teach students to web an idea. On the board, draw a circle and write "pro team" in the center. Draw lines radiating out from the circle. Ask students to name the major groups of people who must come together to acquire a pro team. Write those groups on the lines, forming the web.

Ongoing Assessment
Use the Intermission as an opportunity to conduct ongoing assessment of student comprehension of the lesson material.

UNDERSTAND MARKETING CONCEPTS

Circle the best answer for each of the following questions.

1. Which three cities recently lost their NFL teams? a.
  a. Cleveland, Houston, Los Angeles
  b. Los Angeles, Dallas, Cleveland
  c. Baltimore, Houston, Tampa
  d. Denver, Los Angeles, St. Louis
  e. Nashville, Houston, Cleveland

2. Financing Which of the following will have to work together to bring a team to a city? e.
  a. the league
  b. other team owners
  c. local government
  d. the new team owner
  e. all of the above

THINK CRITICALLY

Answer the following question as completely as possible. If necessary, use a separate sheet of paper.

3. Research Choose a local pro or semipro team, or choose one of your school's athletic teams. Use the library or the Internet or talk with city, county, or school officials about how the team affects the budget of that governmental body. What effect does the sports team have on employment in the area? How many people are employed in related jobs? What are the jobs? What other information is available? What conclusions can be reached? Are sports and entertainment events profitable for a community? Under what circumstances are they profitable?

Answers will vary. Positive effects include jobs like coaches, retail salespersons,

referees, concession workers, groundskeepers, journalists, and advertising

workers. Events are profitable if marketed so as to attract fans and sponsors.

AGENTS, MANAGERS, AND ETHICS

OPENING ACT

Sports and entertainment celebrities can earn millions of dollars from endorsing products *if* companies value them as spokespersons. But it is not just fame that contributes to a celebrity's endorsement value—it is also that person's personality, reputation, and character. When determining which celebrity to finance, sponsors look for someone whom people might want to have living next door. They do not want an angry, impulsive person who has no self-control or respect for others. Young athletes who suddenly find themselves millionaires frequently make bad decisions about finances and behavior. Sponsors drop celebrities who break the law or otherwise disgrace their own character.

Work with a group. Brainstorm about sports, entertainment, and ethics. Make a list of what you think about ethics in sports and entertainment marketing. Post your list for the class to see.

Understand the role of sports agents.

Explain ways professional sports organizations and their sponsors develop an athlete's character.

Assess the importance of ethical behavior on an athlete's promotional value.

SHOW ME THE MONEY

An **agent** is the legal representative of a celebrity. The celebrity pays the agent to manage the celebrity's career, including negotiating contracts with a team, filmmaker, or concert producer as well as negotiating endorsements. Most agents for big name celebrities are either attorneys or accountants. The complexity of contracts requires knowledge of laws as well as negotiation skills. The agent is paid a percentage of earnings to protect the client's financial resources. Agents can take the credit for the high salaries of top celebrities and athletes.

Sports agent Frank Scott was the first agent to show that his clients could sell products as well as play ball. His clients included Yogi Berra, Roger Maris, and Mickey Mantle.

Since professional sports players won the right to become free agents, allowing them to play for the highest bidder, promotion of the players' interests have been handled by firms who serve as the players' agents. Sports agents have responsibilities similar to those of agents for entertainers. Agents represent the players to management, and also promote the stars to companies that might have endorsement opportunities.

INTERMISSION

What are the responsibilities of a sports agent?

Agents' responsibilities include managing a celebrity's career, soliciting work, negotiating contracts and salaries, promoting players, and representing the player to management.

POLISHING THE MARKETING VALUE

Celebrities can pay to have people look out for them both professionally and personally, but ultimately they must be responsible for their own behavior. Character development takes time and effort, but it can make the difference between a superstar and a wanna-be.

PRODUCT/ SERVICE MANAGEMENT

The National Basketball Association provides an annual training program for rookie players. The program provides information on dealing with finances and the news media and on avoiding drugs and alcohol. Some players arrive in professional sports mature enough to handle their own business and behavior, but some do not. The number of crimes committed by pro sports players disturbs the general public. Pro players are establishing a history of arrests that is hurting the ability to attract sponsors for teams and individuals. Offenses include illegal drug use, gambling, and, more and more frequently, physical harm to other people.

Aggression that may be acceptable on the field of play is not

In April 1999, Darryl Strawberry, outfielder for the New York Yankees, was arrested for cocaine possession. In 1990, while with the New York Mets, Strawberry entered the Smithers Center for alcohol rehabilitation. In April 1994, while with the LA Dodgers, Strawberry entered the Betty Ford Center for treatment of substance abuse. Major League Baseball suspended him for 60 days in 1995 after he tested positive for cocaine. In August 1999, Strawberry's suspension for his latest drug incident was lifted, allowing him to return to the Yankees.

THINK CRITICALLY
Do you think Darryl Strawberry should have been re-employed by Major League Baseball? Why or why not?

acceptable off the field. Some players fail to understand this principle. While professional sports teams, leagues, and commissioners tend to overlook or forgive transgressions by highly skilled athletes, sponsors may not. Fans worldwide support teams and athletes with unique and inspirational stories, and corporations like to be connected with what fans like.

HANDLERS

Many sponsors are now paying **handlers** to work closely with athletes who are unable or unwilling to police themselves. For athletes to remain valuable to the firm, they must behave. Henry Gaskins serves Philadelphia 76er Allen Iverson as almost a foster parent. Gaskins, who has a master's degree in business administration with a focus in marketing, was employed to act as a full-time mentor, companion, and off-court coach to Iverson. Iverson's agent, David Falk, knows that preventing problems is in the best financial interest of both Iverson and Reebok, whose products Iverson endorses. Neither the company nor the athlete can afford negative publicity. Pricing of the sponsor's product is affected by the costs of hiring someone to watch over the sponsor's investment.

ADVISORS

Some advisors are financial and business counselors rather than behavior monitors. Under the guidance of Nike's Howard White, Michael Jordan became the nation's richest athlete and spokesperson. White is credited with keeping Jordan at Nike since 1984. Advisors who act in this capacity keep the athlete and sponsor together for the benefit of both. Part of the job is to make athletes feel the company cares about them as human beings, not just as income-producing faces.

INTERMISSION

Why would the NBA care about players' behavior outside of working hours? How is a handler's job different from that of an advisor? Answers will vary. Possibilities include negatively affecting fans

and ticket sales, hurting the team image, and reducing advertising revenue. Handlers

are like foster parents; advisors deal with financial matters.

Young people are looking to non-traditional sports for heroes. Andy MacDonald, a champion skateboarder, was signed on to do an ad for the Partnership for a Drug-Free America, while some football, basketball, and baseball players continue to be arrested for drug use.

Time Out
This is an opportunity to discuss the ethics of pro athletes. Which pro athletes are asked to endorse products that appeal to people the age of the students? Do these celebs have arrest records?

TEACH
Ask students if they think athletes admire other athletes who are ethical. Ask them if they know of examples.

Hold a class discussion regarding principle-based behavior. Help students understand that principle-based behavior is how you act when no one is watching.

Discuss if pretending to be ethical can fool people into thinking you are ethical over a long period of time.

Ongoing Assessment
Use the Intermission as an opportunity to conduct ongoing assessment of student comprehension of the lesson material.

DO ETHICS COUNT?

A perception exists among the general public that sports and entertainment celebrities no longer value ethics. **Ethics** are a system of deciding what is right or wrong in a reasoned and impartial manner. A look at what takes place when it matters most will provide another point of view. The bitter NBA lockout during the 1998-99 season was finally settled on the verge of a totally lost season. The credit for saving the season should go to a single player. Hakeem Olajuwon of Houston Rockets, known as a quiet and very religious man of principles, met with Billy Hunter, the NBA Player's Association negotiator. Olajuwon, with Shaquille O'Neal, Jayson Williams, and their agents, persuaded Hunter to set up the last-minute meeting that led to the settlement. O'Neal is a marketing giant, but he needed the thoughtful man of substance Olajuwon to bring the battle to an end. The players wanted the man of ethics to represent them when it mattered the most.

ETHICS AND CHARACTER MATTER

Ethical behavior is based on solid moral principles or high standards in both business and personal life. Almost all societies can agree on some moral principles such as "don't kill" or "don't steal." Moral development can be divided into stages in which people advance from childish behavior to mature and responsible behavior.

In early stages of moral development, a child learns that exhibiting bad behavior will result in punishment, while exhibiting good behavior will result in rewards. As a child matures, the influence of others' expectations of him or her grows. Eventually, the child may reach a stage of maturity in which he or she acts on the basis of a set of principles.

PROMOTION

Students today may have difficulty developing the later stages of ethical behavior due to lack of mature adult role models. Exposure to frequent news accounts of unethical behavior by politicians, sports and entertainment figures, and even religious leaders may cause a cynical view of the value of ethics. Are these stories new or are they just being reported more now than in previous decades? Either way, there is no way to rationalize unethical behavior. Just because "everybody is doing it" doesn't make it the principle by which to live, nor does it improve the marketability of a product. Lack of ethics can result in publicity that can undo the best marketing plans.

INTERMISSION

How are a person's ethics developed? How can unethical behavior impact the promotion of a product?

Ethics are developed as a person matures and are based on a set of principles the

individual adopts as his or her standard for behavior.

UNDERSTAND MARKETING CONCEPTS

Circle the best answer for each of the following questions.

1. **Promotion** A handler fills which need(s) for a professional athlete? **e.**
   a. mentor
   b. business counselor
   c. companion
   d. promoter for endorsement opportunities
   e. a and c

2. Ethical behavior includes **e.**
   a. honesty
   b. respect for oneself and others
   c. aggression
   d. anger
   e. a and b

THINK CRITICALLY

Answer the following questions as completely as possible. If necessary, use a separate sheet of paper.

3. **Ethics** In what ways does unethical behavior by sports stars affect the sport?

   Unethical behavior can turn off fans, limit advertisers who want to be associated,

   reduce TV contracts, and leave a negative image of the whole sport.

4. **Communication** Begin with the list of ideas about ethics created in the Opening Act. Review the list and add to it everything else you know or think about ethics in sports and entertainment marketing. Describe how these elements relate to your own life. Do you admire these qualities? Why or why not?

   Answers will vary.

CHAPTER 3 REVIEW

REVIEW MARKETING CONCEPTS

Write the letter of the term that matches each definition. Some terms will not be used.

_f_ **1.** the legal representative of a sports or entertainment celebrity

_d_ **2.** people hired by an advertising sponsor to act as a companion to a sports figure

_e_ **3.** a system of deciding what is right or wrong in a reasoned and impartial manner

_c_ **4.** a group of independent sports teams governed by a league agreement

_b_ **5.** the bottom line in sports

a. image enhancement
b. winning
c. cartel
d. handlers
e. ethics
f. agent

Circle the best answer.

6. The "big" in "big league sports" refers to the

c
a. size of new stadiums
b. number of people who attend games
c. revenue potential or commercial value
d. none of these

7. An NFL team can benefit a city if

d
a. those involved with the team stay in the home city
b. the stadium can be used for events other than home-team sports
c. the team attracts other business development
d. all of these

8. The biggest profit center for professional sports is

c
a. TV revenue
b. sale of luxury suites
c. larger stadiums that provide more ticket sales
d. none of these

9. Ethical behavior generally improves as people

a
a. mature
b. earn higher salaries
c. become famous
d. none of these

THINK CRITICALLY

10. Name the last sporting or entertainment event you attended. Then name all the costs to you, including transportation (bus, subway, gas for your car), your ticket, snacks, souvenirs, and your time.

Answers will vary. Students should list all expenses and dollar amounts. Examples of

expenses include tickets, food, gas, snacks, and souvenirs.

11. Refer to your answers in exercise 10. Write a paragraph explaining whether you were satisfied with how you spent your money and your time. What influenced you to attend and spend the money? What functions of marketing were involved?

Answers will vary.

12. Taxpayers and cities spend millions of dollars to attract and keep professional sports teams. Should the players and owners be required to "give something back" to the cities? Explain.

Answers will vary.

CHAPTER 3 REVIEW

MAKE CONNECTIONS

13. Mathematics   The Philadelphia Eagles sold for $65 million in 1985 and for $185 million in 1994. What percent increase is this in nine years? What does this say about the marketing of professional sports?

$185 million — $65 million = $120 million

This represents a 185% increase.

Answers will vary. Possible answer: professional sports are a good investment.

14. Communications   Are you a fan of professional sports or not a fan at all? Write a one-page paper explaining your position and why the other point of view is a good one.

Answers will vary.

15. History   Look into the history of a professional sports club that is still in the city where it started out—for example, the Chicago Cubs. Write a short paper comparing the club in the 1950s and the 1990s. Mention the playing facilities, attendance records, and any interesting cost comparisons you can find.

Answers will vary.

16. Technology   Use the Internet to research the beginning of instant replay in professional football. Discuss how it has changed games from the days when the officials had only their eyes to trust when making calls. Express your opinion on whether or not this technology has improved professional football. What is the possible financial impact of the instant replay?

Answers will vary. Instant replay will lengthen games because more time is required to

look at the replay. People might be more or less willing to watch or attend games that are

decided by instant replay.

PROJECT EXTRA INNINGS

Extra Innings
Good resources for this project include the Internet and the Austin Chamber of Commerce. Students can gather valuable information by researching cities that are currently building new stadiums.

You are a planning consultant hired by a medium-sized city that does not currently have a professional sports team. Your job is to design a comprehensive proposal that will bring a professional football or basketball team.

Work with a group and complete the following activities.

1. Your proposal should include a report detailing the top 5–10 reasons for the team to move. Include city and regional demographics and information about the city (climate, hotels, restaurants, potential fan base, community support).

2. Also include in your report a section outlining the special incentives (for example, a new stadium) you will offer and how you will finance these incentives.

3. Include a spreadsheet detailing cost and revenue projections for both the team and the city.

4. Create graphics (maps, blueprints) showing the location and design of the stadium or arena. Search the Internet for pictures or schematic drawings of stadiums and choose the best design for your stadium.

5. Present your proposal to the class.

CHAPTER 4

MARKETING PRODUCTS AND SERVICES THROUGH SPORTS

LESSONS

WINNING STRATEGIES

CEREAL STARS

One of the classic winning strategies of all time is the story of Wheaties® cereal. Wheaties came into existence by accident in 1921 when a man fixing his breakfast dropped an oatmeal-like wheat bran mix on a hot stove and the splat cooked into a crispy flake. The man ate it, loved it, and recommended it to the Washburn Crosby Company. Washburn Crosby marketed the discovery as Gold Medal Wheat Flakes. Later, the name was changed to Wheaties, and General Mills took over Washburn Crosby.

Wheaties' first-featured star was a fictitious character from radio, Jack Armstrong, All-American Boy. In 1936, athletes became a permanent fixture on Wheaties boxes with the appearance of Lou Gehrig. Stars from baseball, aviation, tennis, skating, auto racing, basketball, swimming, track, gymnastics, hockey, and golf have appeared.

Having your face on a Wheaties box has become such a boon to a career that some athletes have it as a goal and consider being asked a great honor. But beyond just the promotional aspect of the athletes, Wheaties in 1999 launched a five-box series of packages honoring women in sports. The featured athletes were members of the U.S. Women's Soccer Team. Wheaties Marketing Manager Jim Murphy said, "A new era of heroes (was) born. We wanted to do something special to permanently honor these women and their achievements."

THINK CRITICALLY
1. Explain the benefit to Wheaties of having a star athlete on its box. Explain the benefit to the athlete.
2. Name some risks to Wheaties of having real people on its boxes.
3. Discuss the elements of sponsorship, promotion, and endorsement in relation to Wheaties.

CHAPTER 4
LESSON 4.1

USING SPORTS TO MARKET PRODUCTS

GOALS

Understand the enormous market for sports.

Explain emotional ties to sports and earning power of women in sports.

Discuss the marketing cycle.

OPENING ACT

The beginning of the twenty-first century is a wonderful time to be a marketer. The modern marketer has an audience almost too big to be counted. The audience is made up of all races, socio-economic groups, and ages. This audience is enjoying good financial times and is enthusiastic about sports.

Today's marketers also have means of promotion unheard of in years past—from the Internet to state-of-the-art television sets with access to hundreds of channels. These tools, combined with sports fans' seemingly limitless desire to watch and participate, make an ideal world for the professional marketer.

Work with a group. Think about America fifty years ago. How was society different then? How would you have marketed men's sports shoes? Who would your audience have been? How would you market those shoes now? Who would your audience be?

MARKET AUDIENCE SIZE

A wide range of demographic groups enjoy sports. The young market flocks to the X Games. Baby boomers with hearty disposable income and a focus on their personal fitness are participating in all types of sports. Sports medicine and training centers are in every major city. Web sites for participants and fans are innumerable.

THE AUDIENCE

PROMOTION

Many businesses want to align themselves with a sports team or athlete. Sports events attract more viewers and participants than any other entertainment today. For example, 1970 records show 11.2 million golfers; 1997 records show 24.7 million. Estimated spending by sports advertisers in 1997 was $152 billion. U.S. television featured 800 hours of sports in 1971, but 1,800 in 1992—and that was before the expansion of cable channels. Play time in games has been changed in order to wedge in more commercials.

Sports sponsors fully understand the size of the sports audience today. An audience full of avid fans is captive. If they want to see the team, the game, or the athlete, they have to see the advertisements.

INTERMISSION

Explain how sports popularity has grown over the last two decades. What does this say about the potential for product sales?

The popularity of sports has more than doubled over the last two decades. The

potential for product sales has greatly increased as well.

Television networks ABC, CBS, ESPN, and Fox signed eight-year contracts with the NFL worth $17.6 billion in the late 1990s. The Turner networks and NBC agreed to pay $2.64 billion for four years of NBA games.

THE POWER OF SPORTS

More time and money are spent on sports than on any other recreational pursuit in the country. Sports fans also spend a lot of mental energy on their favorite teams and athletes. Sports promoters and investors spend a lot of time creating new possibilities for revenue.

POWER OF EMOTIONAL TIES

The power of athletics as a marketing aid can be explained partly by the emotional ties people feel toward sports. It is safe to say that millions of people feel intense love, hate, joy, or disappointment over sports. Some enjoy the intrigue of the skill and psychology of the players. Some are proud that their city has a professional team and believe a team brings the city a better image. Others are emotionally involved with their own performance or that of their children or local amateur teams. Still others find their own self-worth or personal contentment influenced by the success or failure of a team. At the last game of the original Cleveland Browns in 1995, men wept openly at losing their team. The Browns' owner, Art Modell, received hate mail and bomb threats because of his decision to move the team to Baltimore.

The elation some fans feel at a team victory is also powerful as evidenced by rioting after championship games. Chicago police were out in full force after the Chicago Bulls win in 1998 in an attempt to control rowdy fans. Downtown Lexington, Kentucky, suffered damage from happy fans after the University of Kentucky's win over Utah in the NCAA Men's Basketball Championship, also in 1998.

Many fans overlook an athlete's tasteless or criminal behavior as long as he or she still scores and entertains. The pay-per-view audience for the January 1999 fight between Mike Tyson and Francois Botha was almost one million. Each fan paid $45.95 to see the fight on TV. Fans contributed to Tyson's $100 million earnings in 1995, shortly after he was released from prison. People who feel strongly about their teams or favorite athletes will likely make loyal customers of products they learn about through event advertising or endorsements.

TIME OUT

In 1971, 1 in 27 girls played high school sports. In 1998, 1 in 3 played.

POWER OF A NEW MARKET

The rising popularity of women's athletics is causing companies to take a closer look at their marketing campaigns, especially in light of WNBA attendance of 13,000 per game and 2 million television viewers for a New York Liberty game.

WNBA and Women's World Cup Soccer players are members of the first generation of girls who grew up with sports as a real option and a regular activity. Thanks are due in part to Title IX, the prohibition against gender discrimination in school programs that receive federal funds.

SELLING

Women make 80 percent of all purchasing decisions. Women also spend more than $5 billion a year on sportswear. Companies have started to rethink their campaigns to attract more of this money.

Men still have a much larger portion of promotion and endorsement dollars, but women are coming along. Professional tennis players Steffi Graf and Gabriela Sabatini earned $6.5 million and $4 million respectively from endorsements in 1994, and Nike named a shoe after Sheryl Swoopes.

INTERMISSION

Explain how the rise of women's sports is changing marketing.

Successful women's sports teams and female athletes have caused companies to rethink campaigns to attract more sales to women.

MARKETING THEORY

Marketing products through sports is an interconnected process. First, a company buys the rights to advertise during a game or to use a logo on products it makes. Next, television and radio stations and networks sell broadcast time to teams and their sponsors. Cities buy the rights to host teams, but they often must sell this idea to the taxpayers. Finally, the consumer buys the products advertised during the game.

HOW COMPANIES DECIDE

Many companies that want to advertise their products through sports hire outside consulting firms to help them do it. Other companies have started their own special sports marketing groups within their marketing departments.

**MARKETING-
INFORMATION
MANAGEMENT**

One of the largest marketing firms is the ESPN CHILTON Sports Poll. This group, begun in 1994, offers its clients "the most efficient and effective ways to reach (their) target market." ESPN CHILTON offers demographic data, as well as information about the mood of the sports consumer at any point in time, and advice on how a company can best attract a particular market.

As you will learn in the rest of this chapter, marketing products through sports involves sponsorship by companies, promotion of those products, and endorsement of the products by athletes.

INTERMISSION

How are companies, the media, cities, and consumers all involved in buying and selling products through sports?

Companies buy the rights to advertise through sports. TV and radio sell broadcast

time to teams and sponsors. Cities buy rights to host teams and sell the idea to

taxpayers. Consumers buy products advertised during games.

TAKE A BOW

ARTHUR ASHE

Increasing sales through the popularity of sports is the focus of sports marketing, but dispersing goodwill through sports is also important. Arthur Ashe was a sterling example of dignity, honor, and good sportsmanship. He grew up in Richmond, Virginia, during the last decades of segregation. He began playing tennis because a nearby black-only playground had four courts.

Ashe was an African-American athlete before sports were fully open to blacks. He was also in a sport that had historically been limited to upper-class whites. He was insulted in public and on the court, but he mastered blocking out the ridicule to concentrate on his game and his goals.

Ashe had many accomplishments besides tennis. He co-founded the National Junior Tennis League with the goal of attracting more minority people to tennis. He encouraged colleges to raise, rather than lower, academic standards for student athletes. He publicly denounced apartheid in South Africa. He created the Arthur Ashe Foundation for the Defeat of AIDS.

THINK CRITICALLY

1. Write about five ways that marketing has changed since Arthur Ashe's day.
2. Can a company making a profit help make society a better place? Research and write, highlighting three examples.

UNDERSTAND MARKETING CONCEPTS

Circle the best answer for each of the following questions.

1. **Marketing-Information Management** Sports spectators are seen as good potential customers partly due to their **b**
   a. amount of free time available for watching sports.
   b. emotional ties to sports.
   c. ability to travel long distances to see games.
   d. none of these

2. **Marketing-Information Management** One reason for the rise in popularity of women's sports is **a**
   a. the current generation having grown up with sports under Title IX.
   b. a falling interest in men's sports.
   c. a higher calibre of sponsors for women's sports.
   d. none of these

THINK CRITICALLY

Answer the following questions as completely as possible. If necessary, use a separate sheet of paper.

3. **Communication** Discuss the status of women's athletics in your school. How does the funding compare to men's athletics? How does attendance at women's events compare? How can marketing help women's sports at your school?

   Answers will vary.

   _____

   _____

   _____

   _____

4. **Communication** Write about two people you know who have emotional ties to sports. Explain what it is that your friends love about their favorite sports or athletes. What will your friends give up in order to watch the sports?

   Answers will vary.

   _____

   _____

   _____

SPONSORSHIP

CHAPTER

LESSON 4.2

OPENING ACT

Athletics at the amateur, college, and professional levels have experienced success partly due to money generated by sponsorship. Businesses of all sizes consider the possibility of profiting from sponsoring a team or an athletic event. Supermarkets sponsor little league teams by buying uniforms for the players. Corporations sponsor tournaments like the NCAA Final Four. Businesses sponsor teams and athletic events for favorable publicity.

Work with a partner. Discuss who in your community would be a good sponsor for high school athletics. Why? Who would be a good sponsor for the World Cup Soccer Tournament? Why?

GOALS

Understand sponsors and their investments.

Discuss prohibited sponsorship.

SCHEDULE
Block 45 minutes
Regular 1 class period

FOCUS
Make sure students clearly understand sponsorship. Before class begins, write the numbers 1 – 7 on the board and open the class by listing seven reasons why a business would want to sponsor a sporting event.

OPENING ACT
Athletic sponsors come in all sizes, including small grocery stores and corporate bowl game sponsors. Athletic sponsors realize the benefits of associating with athletics.

Answers for Opening Act Cooperative Learning
Answers will vary. A restaurant, grocery store, newspaper, or sporting goods store might be good choices as sponsors, because all of these businesses provide necessary goods.

Umbro would be a good sponsor for World Cup Soccer since they make soccer apparel.

SPONSORS AND INVESTMENTS

A **sponsor** is a person, organization, or business that gives money or donates products and services to another person, organization, or event in exchange for public recognition. A local veterinary clinic, for example, might sponsor a neighborhood girls' softball team. The clinic's name might be on the players' uniforms, or the recreation association might publicly thank the clinic and other sponsors through the local newspaper, a direct mail flyer, or posters hung in local shops.

REASONS FOR SPONSORSHIP

Businesses become sponsors for many reasons.

- to increase sales

- to introduce a new product or service to a large audience

- to compete where many potential customers are in one place

- to be identified with an event in which the target market is interested

- to earn the goodwill of the audience

- to show their commitment to the community

- to enter new markets

- to entertain clients, employees, or potential customers

- to enhance the companies' image

NEED FOR PROFIT

A business becomes a sponsor to receive a guaranteed amount of exposure, recognition, or acknowledgement. This exposure is used to increase sales and profits. If the business no longer makes a profit from the sponsorship, it either cancels the relationship or creates a new ad campaign. To make sure its investments are working well, a business turns to market research to measure the results of its sponsorships.

Sponsors monitor the value of their investments, and want a good return on them. A **return** is the profit the sponsor earns from its support of an athlete or team. For example, a veterinary clinic would like to see an increase in new patients because of its sponsorship of the girls' softball team. Also, businesses carefully watch the returns on sponsorships since the costs can be high. A 30-second commercial for a recent Super Bowl cost $1.6 million.

SPONSORSHIP IN NICHE MARKETS

Niche marketing involves researching a target market to determine the specific items or services a small group of people will buy. Businesses must thoroughly understand both the larger target market and the smaller niche market for each event they sponsor. Common niche markets include women and men in different age groups (for example, 12–24, 25–34, 35–44, 45–54, 55 and up) and different ethnic groups. Sponsors try to appeal to a diversified market while at the same time introducing their products to new target markets.

EXAMPLES OF NICHE MARKETS

Auto racing is the number one sport for fan loyalty, and racing fans are also the most loyal to the sponsors of their favorite drivers or teams. Sponsors get the recognition they want with their logos on the driver's uniform, helmet, and car, and they receive extra publicity when their team or driver wins. Value is added to the sponsor's return when the business name is mentioned during the race broadcast.

One of the most sought-after target markets today is young men ages 12 to 34. Television networks and sponsors are clamoring to attract this group through variations of extreme sports presentations. ESPN started the X Games in 1995 and has been extremely pleased with their popularity—more than 250,000 teens attended the 1998 Games in San Francisco. In 1999, NBC set out to capitalize on this market by creating and televising a variation of the X Games called Gravity Games. NBC was eager to draw an even larger young male market by adding more prize money and live bands. Networks are aiming at a mostly male, mostly young market that doesn't enjoy sports

like baseball and football. Soft-drink makers, technology businesses, and clothing businesses among others are the main sponsors of extreme sports. NBC also signed X Game celebrity Michael "Biker" Sherlock to help with the logistics of the Gravity Games. Advantage International, the marketing firm you learned about in Chapter 3, is the operations manager for the Gravity Games.

INTERMISSION

What does a sponsor expect in return for its investment? What is niche marketing?

A sponsor expects exposure, recognition, and increased sales and profit. Niche

marketing involves researching to determine the specific items or services a small

group of people will buy.

CAN ANYONE SPONSOR ANYTHING?

Sponsors come in all sizes and all ranges of budgets. Few businesses can afford to sponsor major league sports, but newer sports offer attractive opportunities for smaller businesses.

FINANCING

One option for smaller businesses that want to become sports sponsors is minor league baseball, which has grown in popularity since the major league players' strike in 1994. Many fans were disappointed and angered by the strike, the increasing cost of tickets, the building of new stadiums with taxpayer dollars, and what was perceived as arrogance of players and owners. In protest, they transferred their loyalty to the minor league teams. Sponsors can advertise with the minor league and still reach the same baseball-loving market.

Another option for smaller sponsors is what is sometimes called **affinity sports.** These are niche markets whose participants are just as passionate about their sports as are enthusiasts in the more traditional sports. Bass fishing and rope

Sports sponsorship works two ways. Sponsors can look for an individual, team, or sport to sponsor or individuals, teams, or sports seek sponsors. A business that wants to sponsor a sport can research on the Internet. Once a match is found, the business must confirm the financial soundness of its decision to sponsor.

THINK CRITICALLY

1. Visit the web site for SSI Pro Tour of Sky-surfing. Read about their sponsorship opportunities.

2. Explain how SSI makes sponsorship attractive to sponsors.

As of 1999, there were 181 minor league baseball teams. Some of the more popular teams are located in Columbus, OH; Buffalo, NY; and Durham, NC.

jumping are examples of affinity sports that have thousands of participants and significant tournaments nationwide. Such niche markets are prime opportunities for a business to achieve its sponsorship goals.

LOSS OF SPONSORS

The end of the twentieth century saw a backlash against sports sponsorship by tobacco and alcohol businesses. This backlash not only ended tobacco ads on television but also cancelled or cut back many sponsorships.

Two results of the Multistate Tobacco Settlement of 1998 on tobacco sponsorship were:

- tobacco sponsorship is prohibited for concerts, events in which the participants are under 18, or for football, baseball, soccer, or hockey

- tobacco sponsorship is limited to one event and one brand per year per business

Tobacco businesses have sponsored auto racing for the last 25 years, contributing fees of $15 million per year to NASCAR, $50 million per year to the Indianapolis 500, and $10 million per year to the National Hot Rod Association. Concern among auto racers and fans is that replacement sponsors of that magnitude will be hard to find.

In 1998, United States Health and Human Services Secretary Donna Shalala called for a ban on alcohol advertising in college sports. Even before her challenge, some colleges, such as the University of North Carolina, Baylor, and Brigham Young, had already prohibited alcohol advertising. Further limitations are sure to be discussed in the next few years.

Many fans of NASCAR racing are angry about the potential damage to their sport due to the Multistate Tobacco Settlement limitations on tobacco sponsorship. Opinions such as "Companies have a right to advertise and make a profit" and "These limitations are an infringement on free speech" are circulating among the auto racing crowd.

THINK CRITICALLY
Express your own opinion on the two statements. What is your opinion about government regulation of advertising of products that have been proven harmful?

INTERMISSION

Name two controversial sponsors for athletic events. Why are these sponsors controversial?

Answers will vary. Controversial sponsors include alcohol and tobacco companies be-

cause they sell products that are harmful to consumers' health.

UNDERSTAND MARKETING CONCEPTS

Circle the best answer for each of the following questions.

1. Sponsorship involves d
   a. donating products
   b. donating services
   c. financing an event
   d. all of these

2. **Financing** Sponsors pay careful attention to budgets because
   a. their image is on the line b
   b. sponsorship has become very costly
   c. there are so many sponsorship options from which to choose
   d. all of these

THINK CRITICALLY

Answer the following questions as completely as possible. If necessary, use a separate sheet of paper.

3. **Communication** You run a business in a small community where funds are limited for athletic equipment and uniforms for the high school women's track team. Devise three different sponsorship packages to help the team.

   Answers will vary. The company could sponsor the scoreboard, the athletic uni-

   forms, or the transportation cost to and from events.

4. **Communication** The greatest percentage of auto racing fans is in the 25–34 age group. You would like to reach this niche market with appropriate accommodations at an auto racing event. List five products and/or services you propose to offer the 25-to-34-year-old market at the auto racing event. Give rationale for each of your ideas.

   Answers will vary.

CHAPTER 4
LESSON 4.3

PROMOTION

GOALS

Discuss promotion and its objectives.

Understand the tools used in promotion.

OPENING ACT

Promotion is getting the word out to consumers. The ultimate purpose of promotion is to inform or remind people about the products or services of a business or event. Promotion is also used to generate a favorable public image. Sporting events use unique strategies to increase attendance. Promotional strategies can range from giving away free items to having a fireworks display following the event.

Work with a group. Discuss three sporting events and the promotional strategies that were used to increase attendance. Were these strategies effective? Why or why not?

PROMOTION

SELLING

Strictly speaking, selling is the exchange of a product or service for another item of equal or greater value. Different kinds of things can be sold. A physical or tangible item or product, such as a soccer ball, can be sold. So can the right to have a service performed, such as valet parking at a stadium. Teams can also sell the right to attend an event, in the form of a ticket to a game.

Selling with respect to marketing includes a number of other activities. Selling can involve determining the needs of customers and responding to those needs. Usually the response includes planned, personal communication to help influence a customer's decision to purchase. Selling is also concerned with enhancing future business opportunities.

PROMOTION

Promotion is publicizing or advertising a product, service, or event with the goal of selling it. Promotion is *information* about the product, service, or event that is given to the consumer. The purpose of the information is to make the consumer want the product. People must know about something in order to want to buy it. Promotion leads to selling. Promotion can include developing a communication process with customers, writing promotional materials, or using publicity to draw attention to a product or service.

PROMOTION EXAMPLE

Good promotion serves both the buyer and the seller of the promotion. For example, Faye's Auto Repair sponsors the Marion County High School Musketeers basketball team. The high school promotes, or advertises, the season's games and acknowledges Faye as a sponsor. Faye's business is promoted every time anyone sees the school's ads. Faye publishes her own advertising for her garage and includes a game schedule and the notice that her business is a proud sponsor of the Musketeers. The team and Faye both benefit from the promotion of the other. People who follow the Musketeers will see Faye's ads, and people who don't follow them but bring their cars in for repair will learn about them.

PROMOTION TARGETS

Attracting new markets and keeping old ones are equally important. The primary goal of promotion is to increase sales or attendance, either by finding new customers or persuading regular consumers to buy more.

Promotion is a critical stage in winning new customers. In the early 1990s, professional tennis began to lose audience share, especially among the youth market. Part of the loss was due to lack of charismatic stars, such as Jimmy Connors or Chris Evert, and lack of exciting player match-ups. Managers with the U.S. Tennis Association wanted to keep its strong audience of affluent 21-to-35-year-olds, but develop a love of tennis in the upcoming younger generation. As part of its promotion strategy, the Association created Arthur Ashe Kids' Day. The annual family-oriented day includes appearances by such celebrities as Rosie O'Donnell, Britney Spears, Pete Sampras, and Venus and Serena Williams, plus tennis clinics, shows, games, and giveaways.

Maintaining customer satisfaction, loyalty, and repeat business is also a crucial goal of promotion. A related goal is increasing customers' usage. Sports event promoters often offer special prices for different groups, such as a half-price ticket for the first 500 people who show up wearing a team cap. Also, for long-time supporters, promoters might offer an upgrade in season tickets or discounted parking.

PROMOTION OBJECTIVES

Before a company spends a cent on a promotion campaign, the company must know exactly what it wants to accomplish. First, the target market must be decided. The company should name the market, then research the five elements of market segmentation (demographic, psychographic, geographic, product usage, and benefits derived) of that target market to make sure the product and the market will suit each other.

Next, the company must decide on the message it wants to send with its campaign. Does the company want to persuade the customers to try a new product, inform the customers about new or special features of an existing product, create a new attitude about an existing product, or just broaden awareness of a product?

During its first three years, Arthur Ashe Kids' Day raised over $1 million for the Arthur Ashe Foundation and other charities.

Promotions encourage consumers to visit the store, buy a new product, or buy more of a product they already like. Stores can offering special prices at a Grand Opening, give better prices with a ticket stub or coupon in a sports program, or give free samples of a new product.

Sometimes other entertainment outlets such as movies can provide the perfect promotional strategy for sporting events. Movies have also successfully used sports as a central theme.

Ongoing Assessment
Use the Intermission as an opportunity to conduct ongoing assessment of student comprehension of the lesson material.

Many professional athletes refuse to sign autographs. One of the more famous is Barry Bonds, outfielder for the San Francisco Giants, who makes roughly $9 million a year.

Finally, the company must determine what it wants consumers to do, whether that involves trying a new product, coming to a certain store or event, or buying more of something they already buy. Once these decisions are made, the company can go forward with its promotional plan.

A 1998 advertising campaign by Fox Sports Online illustrates the determination of promotion objectives. Fox wanted to capture a niche market of the larger target market of males 18 to 49 years old that had been a fond audience for the movie *There's Something About Mary.* Fox ran a series of television commercials showing young men so focused on Fox Sports Online that they ignored everything else going on around them. The commercials ran during NFL games as well as at other times. Fox had to decide its target market, males between 18 and 49 with a particular sense of humor, and then learn enough about them to know how to get their attention. Next, Fox had to decide what message it wanted to send and what it wanted the viewing audience to do. The message, that the site is interesting and fun, achieved the desired outcome of new site users.

INTERMISSION

What is promotion? What are two ways to increase sales?

Promotion is publicizing or advertising a product, service, or event with the goal of

selling it. Two ways to increase sales are finding new customers and persuading

regular customers to buy more.

PROMOTIONAL TOOLS

A **promotion plan** (sometimes called a **promotion mix**) has four elements: personal selling, advertising, publicity, and sales promotion.

PERSONAL SELLING

An in-person, face-to-face communication between a seller and a customer is **personal selling.** It can be between a vendor and a business buyer, such as the representative of a sportswear manufacturer and the manager of a college bookstore, or between a retail store clerk and a customer. Personal selling is also illustrated by telemarketers—salespeople who promote their products by telephone rather than in person. Personal selling has, as an advantage, the opportunity for the seller to overcome any hesitation on the part of the consumer, but the seller must be familiar with the product and must want to sell it. The seller can offer more information, comparison with a similar product, or stories about personal experiences with the product. Often, human interaction will make the sale. Even if a current sale is lost, customers are likely to return to the business if they are treated courteously and professionally.

ADVERTISING

Paid communication between the product maker or seller and the audience or customer is **advertising.** Effective advertising should clearly explain the benefits of a good product. However, even the best advertising won't bring customers back to a bad product. Advertising can occur almost anywhere, and can reach millions of people quickly in both diversified and target markets.

PUBLICITY

Any free notice about a product, service, or event is **publicity.** Articles in newspapers or magazines or "sound bites" on television or radio are examples of publicity. Newspapers' front-page stories about 1999 Tour de France racer Lance Armstrong's victory over cancer promoted interest in the race that no amount of paid advertising could have brought. The news features brought free promotion not only to Armstrong but also to the entire race, to other racers, and to bicycle-related business owners who were quoted in the article.

Publicity also means just keeping your name, event, or organization in public view through press releases, speeches, volunteer work, donations other than sponsorship, and letters to the editor.

SALES PROMOTION

Sales promotion includes any action or communication that will encourage a consumer to buy a product. Usually, sales promotions are short-term "specials." Examples include limited-time memberships to health clubs, giveaways, coupons, items with the company's name printed on them, and free samples of a product. Sales promotions are aimed at consumers, as with the giveaway or sample product, or at vendors, as with a free display rack with the agreement to sell a certain sports magazine.

MARKETING MYTHS

Wilson Sporting Goods introduced its new line of golf balls in 1996. Its promotional strategy included handing out a free sample and an information sheet at 1,500 golf courses across the country. After using them, 85% of golfers said they would buy the new brand. This promotion, plus television, newspaper, and magazine advertising, brought Wilson a 7.4% share of the $600 million golf ball market in 1998.

THINK CRITICALLY
Explain how advertising alone is not always as effective as a promotion such as a product giveaway.

INTERMISSION

What are the elements of a promotion plan?

Personal selling, advertising, publicity, and sales promotion.

UNDERSTAND MARKETING CONCEPTS

Circle the best answer for each of the following questions.

1. Promotion is a
   a. information about a product, service, or event
   b. the exchange of a product or service for another item of value
   c. another word for target marketing
   d. none of these

2. **Promotion**   An example of publicity is d
   a. buying advertising space on a city bus
   b. helping customers find an item in a shoe store
   c. offering a taste of new crackers in a grocery store
   d. being featured on the evening news

THINK CRITICALLY

Answer the following questions as completely as possible. If necessary, use a separate sheet of paper.

3. Look at a program for a sports event from this year. Are sponsoring businesses listed? Who are the sponsors targeting?

   Answers will vary.
   _____
   _____
   _____
   _____
   _____
   _____

4. **Communication**   Think of the last time that you experienced personal selling and sales promotion. Write a paragraph about the experience. Include details about how you were treated, whether you were given any solid information, and whether you bought or intend to buy the product. Suggest how your experience could have been better.

   Answers will vary.
   _____
   _____
   _____
   _____
   _____

ENDORSEMENTS

CHAPTER 4

LESSON 4.4

Sammy Sosa's and Mark McGwire's home run records made these athletes much sought after by businesses with products to endorse. Popular coaches on the college and professional levels are also chosen to endorse products. When a team wins a national or world championship, its most charismatic athletes are invited to endorse a wide array of items. Endorsement success depends on matching the personality of famous athletes with the products they endorse.

Work with a partner. List three athletes or coaches who would be good endorsers of products. Why did you choose these individuals? What characteristics of these individuals can you compare to characteristics of a product or service?

GOALS

Define endorsements and their restrictions.

Describe qualifications for endorsers.

WHAT IS AN ENDORSEMENT?

The Federal Trade Commission (FTC) defines an *endorsement* as "any advertising message [that] consumers are likely to believe reflects the opinions, beliefs, findings, or experience of a party other than the sponsoring advertiser." In other words, an **endorsement** is a person's public expression of approval or support for a product or service. Endorsements are a promotional tool rather than a form of sponsorship.

PROMOTION

The FTC also offers clarifying examples of what is and is not an endorsement. For example, a film critic's comments, if used by the filmmaker in an advertisement, are legally endorsements. The critic is a known and real person and that review is an opinion independent of any comments by the filmmaker.

A commercial featuring two unidentified teenagers talking about a product or store is not an endorsement because the teens are not "real" and are acting as spokespersons for the company. However, a commercial starring a well-known racecar driver for a brand of tires is an endorsement. The second example is an endorsement because the public

- knows the person is a real professional driver

- assumes the comments are personal opinion whether that fact is made plain or not

- assumes the driver would not make the comment if he or she did not believe it

Similarly, the FTC points out an ad for golf balls in which a famous golfer is shown hitting the balls. Even though the golfer doesn't speak, the ad is an endorsement because the golfer's likeness is used.

In today's marketing environment, the most influential endorsements are made by entertainment or sports celebrities, even though other people, including politicians, professionals, and ordinary citizens, also endorse products.

LEGAL RESTRICTIONS ON ENDORSEMENTS

The Federal Trade Commission has several guidelines that must be met by the endorser and the sponsoring company. A few of these guidelines follow.

1. Endorsements must always reflect the honest opinions, findings, and beliefs or experiences of the endorser.

2. The endorser must have real experience with the product.

3. The endorsements may not contain any deceptive or misleading statements. The statements must be able to be substantiated by the advertiser.

4. Endorsements may not be presented out of context or reworded so as to distort in any way the endorser's opinion.

5. The endorser must use and continue to use and believe in the product for as long as the endorser is used in the advertisements.

6. If the product changes in any way, the company must notify the endorser, and the endorser must continue to use and believe in the new or revised product.

INTERMISSION

Name some examples of endorsements.

Examples will vary.

ATHLETE ENDORSEMENTS

In 1998, American businesses paid more than $1 billion to athletes for endorsements. There were more than 2000 athletes who made endorsements. Endorsements have advantages and disadvantages as well as surrounding controversy.

ADVANTAGES AND DISADVANTAGES

Advertising endorsements are advantageous to businesses in at least three ways. First, studies have proven that consumers will buy products endorsed by celebrities more often than products that are not so endorsed. Fans and businesses like to be identified with a winning team or athlete.

Young people, in particular, often copy their role models, the endorsers. Second, viewers, listeners, and fans are less likely to turn off a commercial featuring a celebrity than a commercial featuring a fictitious character. Third, consumers tend to believe celebrities, especially those who are chosen for their good public image.

Endorsement as a means of promotion has a few disadvantages, too. One disadvantage is that endorsements are very expensive to the sponsoring company. Another is that the endorser may not agree to endorse only one product. For example, Michael Jordan has endorsed Gatorade, Nike, McDonald's, Rayovac, MCI, and Sara Lee products. This creates the possibility of consumers' doubting the sincerity of the endorser. A third disadvantage is the risk of negative publicity if the endorser commits a crime or a serious social blunder.

HOW CONTROVERSIAL CAN AN ENDORSER BE?

One of the common-sense decisions to be made when choosing an endorser is whether the endorser is a positive representative for the product or service. Most businesses and advisors turn away from any sort of negative publicity. But there is a difference between harmful endorsement and questionable endorsement.

For example, Dennis Rodman is a flamboyant personality with a strong will of his own. Even though his behavior offends many people, some businesses consider him an acceptable endorsement candidate. Consumers who consider themselves outside the mainstream, especially teens and young adults, find Rodman attractive, as do businesses that are willing to take a risk with an unpredictable personality. Rodman has endorsed Comfort Inns & Suites, his own Converse athletic shoe, and a new camera for Eastman Kodak. He did, however, lose a contract with Carl's Jr., a California restaurant chain, for attacking a photographer.

SHOULD ENDORSERS SPEAK OUT ON ANYTHING BESIDES THE PRODUCT?

A current debate is whether celebrity endorsers have a moral obligation to speak out on human rights or other controversial topics. As is almost always the case, some people say yes, and others say no.

Tiger Woods, for example, receives tens of millions of dollars from Nike for his endorsements. Nike has been harshly criticized for what some call exploitation of workers in its factories in Vietnam. Some believe Woods should take a stand against this abuse. Lee Fentress, a writer for ESPN SportsZone, makes two arguments against athletes and entertainers being expected to stand up for a cause. First, he says, athletes are experts in their own field, not in the field of politics, labor, human rights, or global issues. Second, he asks why athletes and other celebrities should be expected to support a cause most of the rest of the citizens of the country are not expected to support. If athletes are expected to fight for causes, then, he

The top five paid endorsers among athletes in 1998–1999 were:
Michael Jordan— $42 million
Tiger Woods— $40 million
Shaquille O'Neal— $28 million
Arnold Palmer— $23 million
Jack Nicklaus— $19 million

fallen celebrity) on the board. Ask students if they can give examples for each disadvantage.

Controversy sometimes sells merchandise. Ask students why they think controversy attracts the attention of consumers.

Dennis Rodman is controversial, but he has endorsed hotels, athletic shoes, and a new camera. Companies must carefully consider the possible backlash from having a controversial figure endorse their product or service.

Endorsers make large sums of money promoting products. Some people believe that endorsers have a moral obligation to speak out on ethical issues such as sweat shops producing athletic apparel. Ask students if they think endorsers have an obligation to speak about ethical issues involving the product they endorse.

Athletes are experts in their field and they should not be asked to tackle political or human rights issues that ordinary citizens overlook. Ultimately, the ethical issues come back to corporations producing merchandise.

Athletes have clout while they are active players. If they intend to make a difference, they must speak out while they are still actively participating in sports and not wait until they retire.

"What might have been" is hard to determine. Corporations probably cannot accurately project the increased dollar amount of sales that an endorsement will reap. It's best not to count chickens before the eggs are hatched.

Companies actually "buy a personality" when selecting an endorser for their product. Ask students what this means.

List the characteristics that businesses look for when selecting an endorser. Put the list on the board or overhead and ask students to give an example of athletes for each characteristic.

Companies can work on speaking ability, personal appearance, and educational background of an endorser. Ask students what kinds of specialists can be hired to improve these areas for an endorser.

Ongoing Assessment
Use the Intermission as an opportunity to conduct ongoing assessment of student comprehension of the lesson material.

says, television stations should turn down advertising by Nike, and consumers should refuse to buy its products.

On the other hand, Tom Farrey, also writing for ESPN SportsZone, maintains that athletes have a responsibility to know what's going on with the businesses they endorse and to speak up if bad conditions become known. He further states that athletes must speak out while they are still active players. They cannot wait until they retire because once they're out of the game, they lose their clout.

WHAT ABOUT "WHAT MIGHT HAVE BEEN"?

An interesting turn in the endorsements issue is the "what might have been" question. In 1993, Celtics star Reggie Lewis died suddenly of heart failure. In 1999, his widow, Donna Harris-Lewis, sued Lewis's doctors for failing to correctly diagnose and treat the heart condition that resulted in his death. Ms. Harris-Lewis sought the income her husband might have earned had he lived. A sports agent testified that Lewis could have earned nearly $115 million if he had been able to finish his playing career and had become a popular endorser. The jury could not agree on a verdict, and the judge declared a mistrial.

WHAT BUSINESSES LOOK FOR IN AN ENDORSER

PROMOTION

Brad Vom Bauer, the director of account planning at Harris and Love, a Salt Lake City advertising firm, once said, "If you want to create a personality for your product, the easiest way to do it is to buy a personality."

When searching for a celebrity endorser, businesses look for:

- someone with a positive, charismatic, trustworthy image; someone respected by consumers

- a celebrity most consumers know

- a celebrity whose career is in process (rather than someone who has retired)

- someone who presents few risks

- someone who has a believable relationship with the product

Speaking ability, personal appearance, and educational background are not among the top requirements. Businesses believe these deficiencies can be remedied with voice coaches and wardrobe assistants.

INTERMISSION

List advantages and disadvantages of having a product endorsed by a celebrity.

Answers will vary. Consumers will buy products endorsed by celebrities more often

than products that are not endorsed. Endorsements are expensive.

UNDERSTAND MARKETING CONCEPTS

Circle the best answer for each of the following questions.

1. Promotion An endorsement is **d**
   a. a promotional tool.
   b. a person's approval of a product or service.
   c. often most successful when made by a celebrity.
   d. all of these

2. Promotion Which of these television ads would be an endorsement? **c**
   a. a shoe ad showing Mia Hamm in the background
   b. a group of teens talking about the next televised X Games
   c. Lisa Leslie of the WNBA telling you to drink your milk
   d. none of these

THINK CRITICALLY

Answer the following questions as completely as possible. If necessary, use a separate sheet of paper.

3. Which male athlete would you ask to endorse your new sportswear shop? Which female athlete would you ask? Explain the advantages and disadvantages of both your choices.

Answers will vary.

_____

_____

_____

_____

_____

4. As you continue to promote your sportswear shop, how will you make sure your athlete endorser stays within the legal guidelines for endorsements?

Keep the endorser happy with complimentary products to ensure that he or she

keeps using the products. You might have to increase the pay for your endorser.

_____

_____

_____

_____

TEACHING STRATEGY
At-Risk Students
Use posters and bulletin boards to reinforce concepts associated with endorsement. This will allow students to recall the major topics by looking around the room.

TEACHING STRATEGY
Visual Learners
Show students television commercials and magazine advertisements endorsed by famous athletes. Ask students if the endorsement will increase sales and why.

ASSESS
Reteach
Review the necessary elements for an endorsement and remind students of the legal restrictions for an endorsement.

Enrich
Students select a famous athlete to endorse a product. They must give rationale for their selection, relate the player to the product, and state why consumers will purchase more due to the endorsement.

CLOSE
Students will research an endorsement by a famous athlete. They must describe the endorsement and tell the class the results from the endorsement. Did the endorsement accomplish the goals set by the business?

REVIEW

REVIEW MARKETING CONCEPTS

Write the letter of the term that matches each definition. Some terms will not be used.

__f__ **1.** the powerful and influential feelings people have for sports

__d__ **2.** the publicizing or advertising of a product, service, or event with the goal of selling it

__a__ **3.** a person's public expression of approval for a product or service

__e__ **4.** what a business must be sure of before it advertises a product

__b__ **5.** the profit a sponsor earns

a. endorsement
b. return
c. bartering
d. promotion
e. promotion objectives
f. emotional ties

Circle the best answer.

6. Endorsers must

    a. have a real experience with a product

d   **b.** not make any deceptive or misleading statements

    c. actually use the product or service

    d. all of these

7. A person or business who donates money or products and services to another person or event in exchange for public recognition is a(n)

    a. endorser

c   **b.** promoter

    c. sponsor

    d. none of these

8. An important new sports market in terms of dollars spent is the

    a. women's market

a   **b.** 50-and-older market

    c. Generation X market

    d. none of these

9. Any face-to-face communication between a seller and a customer is

    a. publicity

c   **b.** sales promotion

    c. personal selling

    d. none of these

THINK CRITICALLY

10. Write a paragraph discussing the merits versus the risks of a company using a controversial athlete to endorse its products. How could the company's promotion plan succeed? How could it fail?

Answers will vary. Consumers outside the mainstream might be attracted to controversy.

The strategy might backfire due to public disgust with a controversial athlete.

_____

_____

_____

_____

11. Name three sports that appeal to adults over 50. Next, name three that appeal to the 12-to-34 market. Third, name three sports that appeal to all ages. Then, name three products that could be promoted successfully through each of those sports.

Answers will vary.

_____

_____

_____

_____

_____

12. Write a one-paragraph publicity feature about a popular brand of sports equipment. Remember that publicity is free. Then, change that feature into an advertisement that you will pay a magazine to publish. Explain how the two promotions differ.

Answers will vary.

_____

_____

_____

_____

_____

REVIEW

MAKE CONNECTIONS

13. Mathematics Your bagel shop has just given $500 to help build a neighborhood skateboarding park. In return for your donation, your shop's sign will hang in the park for one month. The skateboarders' association expects a thousand people to see your sign. The average profit on a purchase at your shop is $0.96. How many new customers will you need to make a profit of $500 to cover the donation?

500 ÷ 0.96 = 520.83

You will need 521 new customers to cover the donation.

14. Communications Write letters to two local businesses asking the owners to sponsor one of the less prominent sports at a local high school. Describe the sport, and explain what it needs in the way of equipment, promotion, and professional advice. Propose an outline of objectives for the sponsorship. Be sure to tell the business owners what they will receive in return.

Answers will vary.

15. History Research and write about the early days (late 1800s) of women's basketball. Include comments about societal standards in those days. Speculate on how the sport would have been promoted to the public and what kinds of businesses might have been sponsors. Mention any special rules, and point out any special players.

Answers will vary. Women's basketball was started in 1892 by Senda Berenon at Smith

College. In 1938 it was a two-court six-player game. Female basketball players did not

dribble like male players did. It was a halfcourt game. In 1971 it became a five-player

game with a 30-second clock. Standards for women's sports have changed from passive

interest to competitive sport complete with rules and star athletes. The pace of women's

athletics has picked up a lot of steam. Previous sponsors probably emphasized cosmet-

ics, perfumes, etc. Today the sponsors sell female apparel and the endorsers are popular

female athletes.

PROJECT ●●●●●●● EXTRA INNINGS

Your advertising company has been asked to design an attention-getting and income-producing promotional campaign for the National Wheelchair Basketball Association.

Work with a group and complete the following activities.

1. Using the Internet, research the history of wheelchair basketball. Learn how and when it started and how it has expanded over the years. Be sure to learn how it has included women and college students. Make notes about its tournaments and championships, and don't leave out information about its star athletes. Find out the audience market size of wheelchair citizens.

2. Write an outline of points you think the public would be interested to know.

3. Help the NWBA determine its promotion objectives.

4. Determine how, through promotion, the NWBA might move from a niche market to a mainstream market.

5. Write a one-page publicity piece about the NWBA. Plan to send it to major newspapers across the country.

6. Work with the NWBA to determine influential endorsers.

7. Prepare a proposal for three major corporations, asking for their sponsorship of the next NWBA championships.

EXTRA INNINGS
The Internet will probably be the best resource for this activity. Students can learn a wealth of information about the National Wheelchair Basketball Association. This exercise is good because is shows how physical challenges do not necessarily keep individuals from participating in sports. Students should relate the benefits of a corporation sponsoring games played by individuals with disabilities.

The *Sports and Entertainment Marketing* Teacher's Resource CD includes a spreadsheet template to help students complete this activity.

Look for the file p097 Extra Innings.xls in the Office Templates folder, or the file p097 XInn.txt in the Text Templates folder.

CHAPTER 5

PUBLIC IMAGES

LESSONS

WINNING STRATEGIES

LISTENING TO HORSES

Equestrians worldwide have heard of Monty Roberts' gentle horse training techniques. Roberts' book *The Man Who Listens to Horses* became the surprising number four best seller on the London Times list within two weeks of its release in 1996.

While controversy has surrounded some of Monty Roberts' stories, spectators who watch him conduct a seminar are hard pressed to deny his remarkable talents as a horseman and trainer. Jack Canfield, co-author of the *Chicken Soup for the Soul* books, stated, "Observing Monty's philosophy and method of working with horses and people is one of the most profoundly deep, awe-inspiring, and heart-opening experiences I've ever witnessed. I highly recommend this book to everyone."

Roberts' follow-up book, *Shy Boy: The Horse that Came in from the Wild*, also became a number one best seller. He has also released audio and video versions of these books and his horse training techniques, which he calls "join up" and "follow up." In his quest to "make the world a better place for horses…and humans," he travels the world providing workshops and demonstrations. At his own farm in Santa Barbara, CA, he offers classes to riders and trainers. England's Queen Elizabeth II has put his methods into place for training cavalry horses. Roberts is working to create an International Learning Center, but he accepts only donations, not sponsorships.

THINK CRITICALLY

1. Visit Monty Roberts' web site to learn more about this trainer, his methods, and his goals. Do you think he is using public relations strategies to the best of his ability?
2. Why do you think that Roberts does not accept sponsorships to further his goals? Do you think that this contributes to or detracts from his public image? Explain.

CHAPTER 5
LESSON 5.1

PUBLIC RELATIONS

Discuss the importance of positive public relations for sports.

Explain how public relations firms assist in creating favorable images.

Evaluate how athletes can affect public perceptions.

OPENING ACT

Marketing firms, athletes, and fans all contribute to positive public relations. For sports teams and individuals to be successful, they not only have to play their sport well, but also must provide a positive image to their audience. These tasks are achieved by creating promotions, adding social value by donating proceeds to worthy causes, being positive role models, and convincing their fans to display good sportsmanship. Some sports figures must overcome negative publicity created by either their behavior or that of fans.

Work with a partner. Think of sports teams or individuals with a positive public image and those with a negative image. List the reasons that your examples have gained their reputations. How have their images affected them in terms of media publicity, fans, salaries, and the opportunity to advance their careers?

IMAGE IS EVERYTHING

Think about sports that interest you. You may be involved with a sport that has a smaller audience, such as cycling or rowing, because you enjoy participating. If you follow any major sports, chances are that you choose your favorite teams and athletes based on their ability and their image. Many people who don't watch weekly football tune into the Super Bowl. The publicity surrounding the event attracts a larger audience.

Part of the reason that baseball, football, basketball, and ice hockey are major sports is due to extensive marketing campaigns that draw attention to them. **Public relations** is the arm of marketing that concerns itself with creating a favorable public opinion for an individual or organization. Public relations professionals work hard in the sports world to create positive images of the game and the players.

AN ACTION PLAN

PROMOTION

Before contracting with a public relations firm, a sports manager should acquire a letter of intent that details exactly the firm's services and responsibilities in promoting a player, a team, or a particular sports event. A plan of action is an important part of the public relations process. The plan should answer the following questions:

- *Which forms of media are most appropriate for promoting the event or tournament?* Depending on the budget, the person or event to be promoted, and the location, sometimes only one medium is used. For key promotions, a firm may choose all major forms of advertising: TV, radio, newspapers, magazines, and the Internet. A good public relations firm will determine the contacts to make and the contracts to sign.

- *What will be used to create a favorable image for the player, team, or event?* Associating a major event with a public cause, such as disabled or homeless children, can create a wider audience for the event. For example, some spectators may not care much for the game, but they may be drawn to attend because a portion of their ticket money will be contributed to their favorite charity.

- *How will the public relations firm promote the event and the cause?* Successful ad campaigns will increase awareness and sales.

It doesn't help to be a superior athlete or have a great event scheduled if no one knows about it. The job of public relations is to publicize these things and to enhance them by promoting their connections to special causes and public service.

THE BIGGER PICTURE

MARKETING-INFORMATION MANAGEMENT

The importance of a positive image extends beyond the athletes and events. The location of a sporting event also needs an attractive presentation. Outside fans are more likely to attend a sporting event if they believe they will enjoy the location. Businesses need to maintain a reputation for excellent service, cleanliness, and safety. Fans are also more likely to support their team on the road in cities whose fans are known to be good sports. Marketing-information management tracks public perceptions of events and locations. To be successful, athletes, events, and locations must maintain positive relationships with the community and with fans.

CONSUMER DEMAND

With all of the choices consumers have for entertainment, sports must compete for their participation. This involves ensuring that all components—athletes, fans, hotels, restaurants, and city attractions—put their best foot forward.

INTERMISSION

What are public relations? What role do athletes, fans, businesses, and cities play in public relations?

Public relations is the arm of marketing that concerns itself with creating a favorable

public image or opinion. This public image depends on the performance and actions

of athletes, fans, businesses, and cities. Each of these entities either makes a

positive or negative impression.

TEACH
Public relations aim to satisfy the customer. This process may involve listening to consumer complaints and concerns in order to make adjustments that will keep them coming back to sporting events.

Even in a technological world, time must be spent to develop consumer trust by building personal relationships.

Judgment Call
Heat is a major factor affecting summer sporting events in Atlanta. The Summer Olympics presented a challenge for equestrian events involving horses not used to the heat. Atlanta built special accommodations to make sure that the horses received appropriate care in the excessive heat.

Think Critically
1. Custer did not ignore the issue and she took positive steps to protect the health of the horses. This action demonstrated concern and humane treatment for animals.

2. Public relations were very important in this case not only for animal activists, but also other concerned individuals. If a horse would have died during the Olympics due to nonaction on the part of Custer, the negative publicity would have been hard to overcome. Banning the event was an option that would have taken away from the Olympics. Ignoring the problem had potential for negative publicity.

SPECIAL EVENTS

Businesses can be involved with sports in many ways. They can sponsor a team or event, take part in promotional parades, advertise in the event program, and accommodate fans' needs. By doing so, they not only promote goodwill, but also increase their business by creating a good reputation. **Goodwill** is a general willingness to work with or assist a person or organization based on a positive reputation or relationship.

KEEPING THE CUSTOMER HAPPY

MARKETING-INFORMATION MANAGEMENT

Cities must consider many factors when they choose to host a sporting event, whether a college bowl game or the Olympic Games. Each time, problems must be solved to create an enjoyable experience for visiting fans so that they will want to return. These issues include transportation and traffic, sufficient accommodations, adequate police protection, quality attractions, and other features that people look for when visiting a new place. Major problems, like traffic, can keep people from wanting to visit a city.

Atlantans had very positive comments about their experiences in Minnesota for the NFC Championship game prior to the 1999 Super Bowl. They found locals to be accommodating and friendly, in spite of the rivalry for a place in the Super Bowl. Cities hope that by knowing their visitors and meeting their needs, they will be seen as welcoming and tourist friendly. For example, cities with traffic problems can still be successful hosts by providing public transportation shuttles.

JUDGMENT CALL

Residents of Atlanta affectionately refer to their city as "Hot'lanta" in the summer. Temperatures routinely peak in the 90s. Additionally, the city has significant pollution problems.

These concerns plagued the city as it prepared to host the 1996 Olympics. Many people were concerned with the well being of horses from around the world for the equestrian events. The U.S. Humane Society tried to have the three-day competition banned, as many horses were unaccustomed to high heat and humidity. To solve the problem, special cooling stations were constructed throughout the horse park.

Rather than confront or ignore the concerns of animal rights activists, Cheryl Fisher Custer, district attorney for the Rockdale Judicial Circuit, listened to concerns, watched tapes, and consulted equine veterinarians to correct the potential problem.

THINK CRITICALLY

1. How did Custer help avert a negative perception during the Olympics?

2. How important do you think public relations were in this case? What other actions might have been taken, and what could have resulted?

MAKING PUBLIC RELATIONS WORK

The goal of public relations is to create a satisfying experience for customers. Attentive listening to customers' complaints and problems, problem solving, and understanding their needs are elements of good public relations work. Successful public relations marketers put customers first, use networking successfully to package and promote a good product, and evaluate the experience to determine its strengths and weaknesses.

In this technological, fast-paced world, the role of personal service and the time it takes to establish personal relationships often get left behind. Successful marketing firms remember the importance of these qualities and use them to build trust, loyalty, and networks of association.

INTERMISSION

Why would businesses be concerned with having popular sporting events in their communities?

Popular sporting events bring large revenues to communities. The event produces

revenue for restaurants, retailers, hotels, etc.

ATHLETES AND PUBLIC GOODWILL

Think of sports figures that come to mind as public role models as well as expert athletes. What about those athletes contributes to their favorable image? How do they affect your perception of their sport? Now think of athletes who have received negative publicity. What details have contributed to their poor image? Have they been able to overcome it? How does negative sports coverage affect your response to the player and/or the sport in which they are involved?

In October 1998, the National Basketball Association announced the cancellation of all games through November and a postponement of the entire 1998-99 season due to stalled contract negotiations with the players. The financial loss was dramatic, as season ticket holders were promised refunds plus six percent interest on all cancelled games, and individual tickets could be refunded or used as "rain checks" for future games. Additionally, when the Collective Bargaining Agreement was finally supported by players and the league in early January 1999, many fans were disgruntled and uninterested in the season. This has also happened when baseball players have gone on strike. While players may have legitimate concerns to express to the league, fans want the games to proceed, and they may perceive the players as poor sports.

African American baseball player Jackie Robinson broke image barriers built on racial prejudice when he entered Major League Baseball in 1947. One of the greatest baseball players of the century, Robinson is also a role model and hero because of the reputation he created fighting racial injustice.

SPORTS HEROES

Some of the best athletes receive negative publicity when fans read about their latest multimillion-dollar contracts. They can be perceived as greedy, thoughtless individuals. Athletes can overcome this image by supporting or creating their own foundations and charities. Many become spokespersons for special causes, such as Big Brothers/Big Sisters, Special Olympics, and The March of Dimes. Many athletes support the Children's Miracle Network, a non-profit association that raises money for affiliated children's hospitals around the world.

FANS AND IMAGE

When fans have a bad reputation, public relations firms have to work harder to ensure that visitors have an enjoyable experience. Cities known for locals that display bad sportsmanship can make visiting fans reluctant to attend games in their location. Sometimes marketing campaigns can divert fans by promoting venues with the best reputations. Extra police protection at the event itself can help control unruly fans.

On the other hand, fans known for good sportsmanship are a bonus to public relations. Agencies can confidently promote the pleasant experiences visitors are likely to encounter both at the sports venue and in surrounding areas. Friendly locals create many benefits for their communities in terms of business opportunities and reputation.

INTERMISSION

How can athletes create positive images for themselves? What are the end results of a positive public relations image?

Answers will vary. Athletes can demonstrate good sportsmanship on the field and

positive involvement in the community. In the long run, positive public relations will

net the athlete more income.

UNDERSTAND MARKETING CONCEPTS

Circle the best answer for each of the following questions.

1. What is/are the goal(s) of public relations? **d**
   a. to promote a positive image of athletics
   b. to market the strong features of a community
   c. to problem solve when consumers complain
   d. all of these

2. Promotion Which of the following examples would a public relations firm want to downplay? **c**
   a. having a Special Olympian throw out the first ball at a baseball game
   b. media coverage explaining that an athlete was unjustly accused of taking drugs
   c. paying the star of a professional team a record salary
   d. offering a percentage of event proceeds to a children's hospital

THINK CRITICALLY

Answer the following questions as completely as possible. If necessary, use a separate sheet of paper.

3. Research Fans can make or break the image of their team and community. Look through the newspaper, sport magazines, or online to find two examples of fans displaying good sportsmanship and two in which they created a negative image. Explain what demonstrated good and bad sportsmanship in the four scenarios.

Answers will vary. Students should demonstrate a clear understanding of good

and bad sportsmanship.

_____

_____

_____

4. Research List three of your favorite athletes. Do they have a good public image? Why or why not? Read about them to discover public service in which they are involved that enhances their reputation.

Answers will vary.

_____

_____

_____

_____

ASSESS
Reteach
Ask students to define "public relations" and to give examples of what fans, athletes, and communities can do to demonstrate positive public relations.

Enrich
Ask students to design an award for the most hospitable college football or basketball fans in the United States. What are the criteria to decide this award? What should be the award for the fans or the university?

CLOSE
Image is extremely important for successful sporting events. This image is the joint responsibility of marketing firms, athletes, fans, and the cities where the sporting events take place.

CHAPTER 5
LESSON 5.2

FANS

GOALS

List the advantages of fan clubs to both fans and athletes.

Discuss the importance of marketing research before undertaking a licensing agreement.

Describe successful sports licensees and sponsors.

OPENING ACT

Fans' commitments to their favorite athletes often spill over into fan club activities. When they join a fan club, fans have access to athletic statistics, personal facts, schedules, and other information about the sports figure. The World Wide Web has increased access to fan clubs and information about favorite players.

Work with a partner. Choose a sports figure who has a fan club on the Internet. What features does the club offer to its members? Do you think it is worth joining? Why or why not? Discuss your findings with the class.

FAN CLUBS

PROMOTION

Fans are as important to star athletes as the athlete heroes are to their fans. What attracts fans to a particular athlete? Perhaps it is their sports specialty, their personality, their community service, or a combination of these qualities. Fans give athletes loyalty, positive media attention, and a following that results in ticket sales and sales of promotional materials, such as T-shirts, trading cards, jackets, hats, and other items.

A fan club offers a perfect opportunity for an athlete to build a positive image. Through it, he or she can communicate directly with fans. On Tiger Woods' Internet Club site, for example, he personally answers five emails each week, which encourages fans to remain connected to the site in hopes that their question will receive his attention.

BENEFITS OF FAN CLUBS

SELLING

Fans are generally admitted to a fan club for a small fee, but some clubs are free. While membership fees generate little revenue, products and special events offered to members can result in high sales profits. Fan club members often receive a small discount on merchandise, such as official clothing, posters, calendars, etc. The discount motivates fans to buy. Some athletes offer special outings or seminars to fan club members, again resulting in profits to the sport and unique opportunities for the fans. Frequently the profits, or a percentage of them, are donated to the athlete's favorite foundation or charity. Such a gesture improves the athlete's image and promotes goodwill.

INTERMISSION

In what ways are fan clubs beneficial to both players and fans? How has the Internet increased the popularity of fan clubs? Fan clubs are beneficial to players for visibility, public relations, and income. Fans get discounted merchandise, information on celebrity appearances, and a feeling of closer contact with the athlete. The Internet has made it easier to join fan clubs and update player information.

LICENSING AND MERCHANDISING

The sports merchandise craved by so many fans has created a multibillion-dollar industry in licensing sports merchandise to third-party companies that produce, distribute, and sell the merchandise. Some products can be purchased through fan clubs. They are also sold in licensed department stores, through magazines, and at sports events.

Team Licensing Business, or TLB, is the industry magazine that reports on trends, statistics, and predictions for the 20,000 retailers involved in the business. For instance, they reported that the National Basketball Association had 109 licensees in 1997, resulting in $3 billion of gross retail sales worldwide. The Chicago Bulls ranked first in sales, and the top licensee was Champion. Collectibles and electronic games were the fastest growing product lines for the league. For the National Football League, the Green Bay Packers topped the 1997 list for sales, and Fruit of the Loom sold the most licensed items for the league.

The World Wide Web has made it easier than ever to become a fan club member. The most popular celebrities, athletes, and teams have web sites that offer membership in a club.

THINK CRITICALLY
1. Find a celebrity fan club web site.
2. What information did you find? Is the site an "official" fan club site or is it an unofficial site put up by a fan?
3. Read the directions on becoming a member. Is there a fee? Do you want to join? Why or why not?

MARKETING MYTHS

Not all sports licensing stories have happy endings. A classic example is the attempt by NBC and Cablevision to make a profit from the 1992 Summer Olympics. The companies offered coverage of every event, using pay-per-view. Fans found the $100 fee to be too high. Cablevision lost $50 million and NBC lost over $60 million on the venture.

THINK CRITICALLY
1. Why do you think the venture failed? Can you think of a way the companies could have made this plan a winner?
2. Do you ever watch pay-per-view events? Why or why not?

"EVERGREENS"

Product manufacturers love to create "evergreen products" that remain valuable from year to year. Sports trading cards are one example of this phenomenon.

Baseball cards were first added to cigarette packs in the 1880s to promote sales. In 1930 baseball cards were added to bubble gum packages to increase sales. Cards remained popular until their production stopped during World War II. In 1951 the Topps Company reintroduced baseball cards with its bubble gum. As they became more popular, other sports cards were added to gum packages.

These days the companies with the biggest sales are playing card companies rather than gum manufacturers. Old cards with great players from the past are quite valuable to collectors. There are hundreds of web sites offering cards for sale. To keep interest in current cards, some companies are adding gimmicks. Upper Deck has added CD-ROMs to selected packs, with additional information on the athletes on the cards.

SUCCESS AND NEW FEATURES EQUAL SALES

MARKETING-INFORMATION MANAGEMENT

New trends, new athletes, changing positions of teams, and consumer demand are all variables that affect merchandise sales. Fans can be fickle, supporting one player or team when they are on top, but dropping them the next season if they don't maintain their peak performance. The retirement of a highly regarded player may allow another

one to take his or her place as the new hero. Merchandising companies watch these trends carefully to make predictions about what to market and what quantities to produce. They also use trends to set prices.

INTERMISSION

Why is sports merchandise licensing such a lucrative business? How do sports card companies maintain consumer interest in the cards?

Fans crave the merchandise and spend large sums of money on it. Sports cards are

collectible and some now include information about the athlete on CD-ROM.

PREDICTING THE MARKET

Licenses are expensive to obtain, so manufacturers must analyze the market to determine the risks involved with becoming licensed to reproduce particular sports images. In addition to the license price to reproduce the symbol, emblem, or likeness of an athlete, team, or sports league, they will also invest in designing, manufacturing, shipping and distributing, marketing and promoting merchandise, and keeping track of inventory.

The market can be unpredictable. For instance, the Oakland Raiders—and their licensees—took a chance when they became the first team to add black to their color scheme to promote a cutting-edge image. Would it sell? As it turned out, they were not only successful in sales, but they also provoked a new trend in uniform styles and designs. While their ticket sales to games were low, the Raiders made money on their design gamble.

SUCCESSES IN THE MARKET

Some companies have been more successful at reading the market than others. Starter, Rawlings, and Champion have a consistent record in successful licensed merchandise. Upper Deck has done well in trading cards sales for many years. Other companies have boosted their sales by becoming official sponsors of events or leagues. For example, Kodak boosted sales by becoming an Olympics sponsor.

INTERMISSION

How do companies determine whether or not to purchase a license? How can licensing benefit the licensor?

Companies analyze the market to determine risks and potential for profit. The licensor

earns royalities from the sale of merchandise.

UNDERSTAND MARKETING CONCEPTS

Circle the best answer for each of the following questions.

1. Fan clubs can benefit fans because c
   a. they are free
   b. they guarantee discounted merchandise
   c. they offer fans an opportunity to communicate with other fans and learn more about the athlete in ways not available to non-members
   d. they plan seasonal parties

2. **Marketing-Information Management** How can third-party companies predict future successful sports merchandise? b
   a. disregard past trends
   b. keep abreast of news in trade magazines
   c. ignore licensing agreements in order to create less expensive products
   d. none of these

THINK CRITICALLY

Answer the following questions as completely as possible.
If necessary, use a separate sheet of paper.

3. **Promotion** Design a trading card for your favorite athlete. What kinds of details would you put on the back, and why?

   Answers will vary. Evaluate projects for creativity and choice of information to

   include on the back of the card.

   _____

   _____

   _____

4. Identify five licensees or official sponsors of a major sporting league or event. Why would a company spend additional money to become a licensee or an official sponsor?

   Examples will vary. Official sponsors receive great publicity and visibility.

   _____

   _____

   _____

   _____

PUBLISHING AND SPEAKING ENGAGEMENTS

OPENING ACT

Have you ever heard a good motivational speaker? What kinds of information did he or she include in the presentation? For how long did it affect you? Athletes and coaches with strong reputations and winning personalities can make a great deal of money on the lecture circuit. Fans will often buy tickets to hear them repeatedly, as the emotional impact of hearing the first presentation is likely to fade.

Inspirational books work much the same. Athletes often write about how they reached their level of success, and readers hope that by reading the information, they too might increase their sports abilities.

Find a book in the library or a bookstore that is written by a sports figure. Would you want to read it? Why or why not?

GOALS

Explain how a sports figure can be successful in the lecture circuit.

Describe the steps in the creation of popular sports books.

MOTIVATIONAL SPEAKING

Many people enjoy listening to speeches by well-known individuals, making public speaking a natural job extension for professional athletes and coaches. Particularly in tough physical sports, such as football and ice hockey, athletes can't plan on a lifelong career in their sport. However, many extend their association with sports through speaking engagements.

Speaking engagements can range from giving motivational talks to large auditoriums full of people to small leadership training seminars. Speakers' success and the price they can charge will depend on more than their sports prowess. Public speakers need a different set of tools to do well: excellent speaking and communication skills; well-written speeches; the ability to handle unexpected questions and comments in an authoritative, confident manner; and a message that the audience is interested in hearing. A sense of humor, sincerity, and refined people skills will also enhance their popularity on the speaking circuit.

SCHEDULE
Block 90 minutes
Regular 2 class periods

FOCUS
Most athletes realize that their careers are limited due to the physical nature of sports. Other possible sources of revenue include publishing and speaking engagements. Ask students which athletes or celebrities they think would be good to speak at a convention. Would they purchase a book written by their favorite athlete or coach? Why?

OPENING ACT
What would entice you to listen to a speaker again? Why is the publishing business a good financial outlet for some athletes?

Answers for Opening Act Cooperative Learning
Answers will vary. Some of the books focus attention on game strategies while other books have a deeper philosophical value.

AIDS TO SUCCESS

Speakers can't do all the work by themselves. They rely on strong marketing and promotional campaigns and an agent to book speaking engagements. These specialists are paid a percentage of the fees charged for the speech. One agency, Promotional Sports Stars, Inc, formed a sports speakers bureau that grooms its sports speakers and since 1985 has arranged thousands of speaking engagements. The company's top speakers include Rick Pitino, Tommy Lasorda, Bonnie Blair, Picabo Street, Mia Hamm, and Joe Greene.

Because this peripheral job in the sports industry is big business, the training for it can be as rigorous as training for a big game. Potential speakers may hire speech writers, coaches, and specialists to help them create a positive public image. They may also have to create sample videos, as organizations may request a sample before hiring the speaker.

THE PRICE OF MOTIVATION

The best of sports speakers collect a high price for their motivational talks. For example, winning basketball coach Rick Pitino receives $20,000 and a round-trip, first-class plane ticket for his presentations on managing and motivating. Business companies hire him to talk to upper management about team building and coaching. When he speaks to salespeople, he addresses them as sports recruits. He also makes the word "TEAM" into an acronym to organize his presentations.

Superstars of sports can earn between $7,500 to $25,000 for a single speaking engagement. "Average" sports speakers earn from $3,500 to $7,500 for an hour of speaking. These jobs can also lead to other related careers, such as sports broadcasting.

ONGOING SUCCESS

If you've ever been to a motivational speech or weekend seminar, you may be familiar with this pattern: The speech can excite and motivate you. When you try to pass on your fervor to others, however, they tend to respond with a "guess you had to be there" attitude. After a while, the effects wear off on you, too. Yet it is likely that you would want to hear that speaker or a similar presentation again.

Sports speakers can expect high demand when their talks are good, because followers will want to hear them again. An annual visit to the same city is not unusual. They present to a large percentage of the U.S. meeting and convention industry, representing an estimated $75 billion annually.

INTERMISSION

Why are athletes popular for speaking engagements?

Athletes who give speeches are often able to motivate listeners and excite them with

the possibility of a bonus like an autograph.

WRITING THEIR STORIES

DISTRIBUTION

There are other ways to extend a sports career profitably. People love a good story about someone's personal experiences, failures, triumphs, and lessons learned. A well-written biography of a sports hero is likely to sell well. These books can also set off a national publicity tour. For an athlete also gifted in speaking, the two career options can go hand in hand.

BROADENING THE AUDIENCE

The target market for books written by sports celebrities is people who are also involved in their particular sport, but some will draw a larger audience because of universal themes and concerns. One example is *I am Third,* a book written more than thirty years ago by football great Gale Sayers. More than a book about football, this autobiography is an inspirational narrative about friendship, faith, and love. It inspired the highly acclaimed 1971 television drama, *Brian's Song.* The story is of Sayers and his friendship with fellow Chicago Bears player Brian Piccolo, whose life was ended early by cancer. A more recent example is *My Sergei: A Love Story,* published in 1996, in which young Russian Olympic pairs skater Ekaterina Gordeeva narrates the story of her skating career, romance, and marriage with her partner Sergei Grinkov, who died on the rink of a heart attack at the age of 28.

THE PUBLISHING PROCESS

Many sports "authors" do not actually write their own books. Instead, they tell their stories to a ghostwriter, often a sportswriter or sports reporter, who then commits it to paper for a fee.

Book prices are determined on public demand and the extent of the distribution. If the book is intended for national distribution, it generally will command a higher price than one planned for regional or local distribution. The publisher typesets the manuscript, provides a cover design, and arranges for the printing and distribution of the book. The author usually receives a royalty, which may be 10 percent or more of the price for every copy sold. While this percentage seems small, an author can make several million dollars on a best seller.

Top-selling sports books:

Dave Pelz's Short Game Bible (golf)

The Glory of Their Times (baseball)

The Winner Within (basketball)

Everyone's a Coach (football)

TEACH

Many athletes and coaches have interesting stories to tell by writing books. If the athlete is also a good speaker, they can sell their books at their speaking engagements. Personal triumphs, failures, and unusual experiences tend to sell books.

Sometimes books not totally devoted to the sport or the athlete have a greater rate of return. *I am Third* is an example of autobiography that goes beyond the sport and pulls the emotional strings of consumers.

An athlete may hire a ghost writer to actually write their story. Public demand determines the price of books. The author can receive a royalty of up to 10 percent of sales, which might amount to several million dollars for a best-selling book.

Promotions may involve ad campaigns. Appearances by the athlete on television and radio, and at bookstores for signings also help to sell copies. Sports authors often hire a literary agent who, for a percentage of the sales, will plan the marketing campaign and book appearances.

PROMOTION

INTERMISSION

What are some reasons that athletes and coaches choose to write books? How can an athlete promote a book?

Reasons include income, visibility, and pleasure. The book can be promoted with

book signings, TV and radio appearances, and public speaking engagements.

TAKE A BOW

MICHELLE KWAN

Born in 1980 in Torrence, CA to Hong Kong immigrants, Michelle Kwan took to the ice at the age of 5. She watched her brother Ron play hockey. At the age of 12, she qualified for senior skating status, but her youth kept her in the shadows of Nancy Kerrigan and Tonya Harding.

In 1996 Kwan won both the U.S. National and World Championships. She was the favorite for the 1998 Olympic Games, but a painful toe fracture limited her training schedule. In spite of the hardship, she skated one of her best programs at the 1998 U.S. Nationals. She got 15 perfect scores, the most ever awarded to a skater. At the Olympics, Tara Lipinski defeated Kwan, but she graciously accepted the silver medal.

Kwan is well loved by skating fans and non-skaters alike, due to her grace on and off the ice. She is a role model for girls because of her athletic ability, her love for her family, and her concern for others. She is a national spokeswoman for the Children's Miracle Network. She has contracted with Hyperion Books to write a series of books on skating success and motivation. Kwan signed with Electronic Arts in 1999 to create an interactive figure skating game with Michelle as the main character. There are numerous web pages devoted to Kwan, created by admiring fans.

An A-student and avid reader, Kwan accepted the role of national campaign chair to the American Library Association's Teen Read Week in October 1999. She is currently a freshman at UCLA.

THINK CRITICALLY
1. A recent ad's caption reads, "Michelle Kwan showed America how to turn silver into gold." What do you think that means?
2. In class, discuss your favorite sports heroes. Are any of them role models for U.S. teens? Why or why not?

UNDERSTAND MARKETING CONCEPTS
Circle the best answer for each of the following questions.

1. Speakers may need the services of d
  a. a speech writer
  b. a speaking coach
  c. a promotional agency
  d. all of these

2. Which of the following statements is false? d
  a. Book tours increase the sales of an athlete's book.
  b. Sports books that extend beyond the topic of the sport may generate interest for a wider readership.
  c. Athletes' autobiographies are often ghost written.
  d. An athlete usually does not count on much income from writing a book.

THINK CRITICALLY
Answer the following questions as completely as possible.
If necessary, use a separate sheet of paper.

3. **Communication**   Rick Pitino uses "TEAM" as his speech acronym. Come up with your own acronym for developing a speech. Explain what each letter of your acronym represents and how it could help you to organize your speech.

Answers will vary.

_____

_____

_____

_____

4. Which sports figure would you want to have write a book, and why? What do you think the contents should include to make it a best seller?

Answers will vary.

_____

_____

_____

_____

CHAPTER 5 REVIEW

REVIEW MARKETING CONCEPTS

Write the letter of the term that matches each definition. Some terms will not be used.

__d__ **1.** the arm of sports marketing that concentrates on creating a positive image for athletes, teams, and events

__b__ **2.** professionals that help athletes market their books

__e__ **3.** what a company needs before it can market products with the likeness of sports figures, team emblems, or other official sports insignias

__a__ **4.** the term applied to the amount that an author receives in book sales

__c__ **5.** organizations that help athletes and coaches succeed in the lecture circuit

a. royalties
b. agents
c. speakers' bureau
d. public relations
e. license
f. promotion
g. goodwill

Circle the best answer.

6. The element that can make or break a sports figure's relationship with fans is
    a. salary
c **b.** book sales
    c. image
    d. autographs

7. Public relations firms work to
    a. improve city streets
d **b.** help athletes find jobs after their sports careers are over
    c. teach fans etiquette skills
    d. none of these

8. Which answer is not true? Fan clubs benefit athletes and sports organizations by
    a. providing large revenues through membership fees
a **b.** promoting positive public relations
    c. increasing fan loyalty
    d. offering opportunities to organize special events and raise money for athletes' favorite charities

THINK CRITICALLY

9. A major new sports store has hired you to promote its grand opening. What special promotional items do you want on hand? Which athlete(s) will you want present to sign autographs, and why? What kinds of media advertising will you use, and why?

Answers will vary. You would want the right mix of male/female professional athletes and

coaches available to sign autographs in order to attract more customers into your store.

You would choose popular winners based upon regional appeal. Special promotional

items could include free food, soft drinks, and caps. A radio station could broadcast from

your store and drawings could be held to give away free merchandise. The newspaper

and radio would provide cost-effective advertising. Television advertising could be used

for a more extensive market.

10. Choose a favorite product that you regularly purchase and develop a marketing campaign associating that product to your favorite sports league. Include at least three promotional strategies relating the product to the sport.

Answers will vary.

11. List five current athletes or coaches as possible guests for an autograph session. What is the value of each person for this session?

Answers will vary.

CHAPTER 5 REVIEW

MAKE CONNECTIONS

12. Mathematics How many speeches per year would Rick Pitino need to make to earn an annual salary of at least $200,000?

Rick Pitino earns $20,000 per speech.

$200,000 \div 20,000 = 10$

He would have to give 10 speeches per year.

13. Communication Design a promotional poster for a popular sports book.

Answers will vary.

14. History Use the Web to research some popular sports figures from the early part of the twentieth century. How were they promoted to the public? If possible, find out what salaries they made.

Answers will vary. Possible sites include sports almanacs. Popular sports figures from the early part of the 20th century did not have all of the promotional avenues available for publicity today. Their publicity depended on athletic performance and not nearly as much money was pumped into the promotional process.

15. Communication Write a newspaper press release for an upcoming sports event at your school. Consider all aspects of the event that you can use to attract a large audience. Using that copy, rewrite it into a more concise, catchy radio ad.

Answers will vary. The news release should include the time, date, location, price, and

competitiors for the event. Special features such as the halftime show or homecoming

activities should also be included in the news release. The radio ad would emphasize

time, date, location, and competitors for the event. The radio ad should grab the attention

of prospective customers.

PROJECT EXTRA INNINGS

Imagine that you live in a city of 50,000 people that has just been chosen to host a major event and you have been chosen to handle the public relations for the event. The citizens are very excited. A major event has never occurred in the city before, and everyone is anxious for the event to be successful. Businesses are hoping to make extra profits from the many visitors who are expected to attend.

While the town is generally positive about the event, there are factions that could create a bad image for the location. A local bar in the city is known for its rough clientele, and there has been a rash of drunk driving accidents in the area of that establishment. Additionally, some people would prefer to keep the town quiet, and they do not want the media attention and crowds that the event will draw.

Work with a group and complete the following activities.

1. What will it take to create a positive experience for the town and visiting fans? Create a special "Welcome to _____!" promotional kit to hand to fans as they attend the event. What items would you include, and why?

2. Who are several celebrities that are taking part in the event that you can use to create a positive image for the event?

3. What special opportunities at the event and in the town can you promote that will draw attention to positive aspects of both while distracting visitors from negative aspects?

4. Organize a meeting in which you invite area business people to discuss ways they can promote their businesses. Also address specific concerns such as traffic and sufficient accommodations and ways to solve the problems.

5. Create promotional materials to advertise the event: press releases, posters, newspaper ads, and mailers, etc.

Extra Innings
Divide the class into groups. Assign each group a sports or other entertainment event. Suggestions for the event include a film festival, a comedy festival, the Summer Olympics, the Winter Olympics, the Super Bowl, a college football bowl game, a World Cup finals game, a tennis tournament, or a golf tournament. Ask each group to design a strategy to attract this event to your city or town.

CHAPTER 6

ADVANCING THE CAUSE

LESSONS

WINNING STRATEGIES

TEEING OFF FOR FAMILIES

Tiger Woods is something of a legend. One of the youngest players on the PGA Tour, Woods is also the most successful African American to play professional golf. Tiger was a golf prodigy, putting with Bob Hope on the Mike Douglas Show at the age of 2 and shooting a 48 for nine holes of golf at the Navy Golf Club in Cypress, California while only 3. At 15, he was the youngest to win the U.S. Junior Amateur Championship, and at 16, the only one to win it twice. Woods won it a third time the following year. Tiger was Sports Illustrated's Sportsman of the Year when he was only 20. At 23, Woods had won over $5 million with nine victories and 30 top-10 finishes in 51 golf events worldwide.

Woods has concerns beyond golf. He has created the Tiger Woods Foundation to help children and families. Woods says about the Foundation, "It is celebrating the spirit of inclusion in all aspects of human existence.... I was always taught that being a role model means more than having individuals look up to you. A role model is someone who embraces the responsibility of influencing others positively."

The foundation supports groups that make golf accessible to inner-city children. Alan Wallack, Director of Bridgeport, CT, Board of Education, said, "When I tell people I've worked with the Tiger Woods Foundation, it lends instant credibility."

THINK CRITICALLY

1. How does the Tiger Woods Foundation advance Tiger Woods' image?
2. How important do you think it is for a winning athlete to be involved in philanthropy? Explain.

CHAPTER 6
LESSON 6.1

COMMUNITY SERVICE

GOALS

Describe the importance of charities and tournaments to the successful images of athletes and teams.

Explain why athletes become involved with or create their own foundations.

SCHEDULE
Block 90–135 minutes
Regular 2–3 class periods

FOCUS
What is community service?
How does community service benefit the person performing it?

OPENING ACT
How can an athlete strengthen their public image off the field?
Have students search the Internet to find athlete's charitable activities.

Answers for Opening Act
Cooperative Learning
Answers will vary.

Mia Hamm: Bone Marrow Research

Cynthia Cooper: Kim's House for Less Fortunate Children

Tiger Woods: inner-city kids

You would associate with a public service that visibly helps a worthy cause.

OPENING ACT

Top-ranked sports personalities are in the spotlight as much as politicians and movie stars. The public examines their every move, both in and out of the sports world. To be popular with fans, these athletes must always consider their public image. One way of maintaining a favorable image is by participating in activities that have the public's approval. Perhaps that's what Denver Bronco running back Terrell Davis had in mind when he appeared with Elmo and friends in a 1999 episode of *Sesame Street* to recite the alphabet. Voted Most Valuable Player in 1998, Davis shows kids what's most important—reading and education—when he's off the field.

Work with a partner. Think of other famous athletes and ways in which they have supported admirable public causes. If you were in their place, with which kind of public service would you associate yourself, and why?

COMMUNITY SERVICE

Athletes don't have to look for negative publicity. The media always manages to find that. Contract disputes, multi-million dollar contracts, athletes involved in drugs or gambling, and other instances of poor conduct always find their way to the front pages of the sports section and sports magazines.

Many athletes, however, use their extra time and money to support charitable organizations and special events to help others, and not just because they know it will give them a good image. Cathy Rigby, a former U.S. Olympic gymnast, has created a video explaining bulimia and the process of recovery. She once suffered from this eating disorder and now campaigns to help others overcome it. Soccer star Mia Hamm created a foundation to raise money to further research on bone marrow disease. Her brother died from this illness.

RAISING AWARENESS AND VISIBILITY

PROMOTION

Sports figures increase the public's awareness of important causes in many ways. They organize special events, become spokespersons for charities, take part in promotional campaigns, and contribute financial support to charitable organizations. Media information services do not necessarily publish this information on their own, so athletes must work with public relations firms to create press releases about the events and charities that will benefit. Marketing firms also help to distribute information to those who may wish to participate in such events.

TOURNAMENTS FOR CHARITIES

Tournaments, popular with sports such as golf and tennis, are frequent avenues that athletes choose to organize and host for charities. Since 1997, tennis Hall of Fame member Roy Emerson has hosted the Annual Vic Braden/CHOC Tennis Tournament for the Children's Hospital of Orange County, California. Between 1997 and 1998, the tournament raised over $100,000. This money, along with other contributions, allows the hospital to treat over 90,000 children per year, regardless of their families' albility to pay.

PRODUCT/
SERVICE
MANAGEMENT

Golf is a sport that capitalizes on creating tournaments for charity. There are web sites devoted to listing the many golf tournaments that raise funds for children's hospitals, the American Lung Association, Special Olympics, cancer centers, scholarships, and more. There are even marketing firms, including Golf Tournaments Inc., that specialize in organizing golf tournaments for athletes and organizations. This corporation helps with all the details of event planning: choosing the time of year, deciding on a course, budgeting, promoting, serving food, determining prizes, staffing, looking for sponsors, planning entertainment, scoring, presenting awards, photographing, and everything else connected with the tournament.

In other countries, different sports are often favored for charitable tournaments. In Canada, volleyball tournaments help raise funds for disabled people. In the United Kingdom, soccer and squash tournaments are popular fundraisers for various charities.

To celebrate the year 2000, Tiger Woods hosted the Williams World
Challenge in Scottsdale, Arizona. The final rounds were played on
January 1–2, 2000. Even the last-place golfer won $120,000, but the real
winners were the inner-city children benefited by the Tiger Woods
Foundation and Target House at St. Jude's Hospital.

INTERMISSION

**What types of stories about athletes are the focus of media
sources, and why? What must an athlete consider to make
the charitable events successful?** Controversial stories receive media

attention because those stories attract readers. Athletes must consider the special

cause, location, and media coverage necessary for success.

FOUNDATIONS

PROMOTION

A **foundation** is an organization that is established to
maintain, assist, or finance other institutions or programs
that are of an educational, charitable, or social nature.
Olympic ice skater Peggy Fleming is a prime example of
an athlete doing her part. Fleming was the only U.S. athlete
to win a gold medal in the 1968 Winter Olympic Games in Grenoble,
France. Fleming's foundation associations include the Kidney
Foundation, the San Jose Valley Medical Center Foundation, the
Dermatology Foundation, and the National Osteoporosis Foundation.
Fleming has also become a spokeswoman for breast cancer awareness,
having survived the illness herself after a 1998 diagnosis.

GOING THE EXTRA MILE

Some athletes go beyond contributing to favorite charities and actually create foundations that continually aid their favorite causes. One example is Dallas Cowboys quarterback Troy Aikman. Aside from leading his team to three Super Bowl victories, Aikman is well known for his contributions to communities, and has been a finalist for NFL Man of the Year, a title given to a player for his contributions to society, for the past five years. He established the Troy Aikman Foundation to assist children's charities in the Dallas–Ft. Worth area. Proceeds from a children's book he wrote in 1995 went to his foundation. Also in 1995, his foundation contributed to "Aikman's Zone," a 2,500-square-foot playground and educational center for children staying at the Children's Hospital of Dallas.

Athletes in many sports have founded charities and foundations. Bonnie Blair, world-record holder and winner of many Olympic gold medals for speed skating, organized the Bonnie Blair Charitable Fund, which gives to numerous causes. Mia Hamm's Foundation supports women athletes and research into bone marrow diseases. The Tiger Woods Foundation helps inner-city children.

Dan Jansen, a gold medal winner in the 1994 Winter Olympic Games in Lillehammer, Norway, is another speed skater who established a foundation. The Dan Jansen Foundation solicits funds for charities including leukemia research and youth sports programs. Jansen chose

Dennis Rodman is to the NBA what the "bad guys" are to pro wrestling. Some fans continue to love him, while others are delighted that the LA Lakers opted to replace him. His replacement, A.C. Green, hasn't missed a game in 12 years and plans to become a minister when he retires. Many are disgusted by Rodman's flamboyant actions. However, few could deny that he is one of the top rebounders in NBA history.

Most of Rodman's publicity has centered on his on- and off-the-court antics. Rodman has a number of body piercings and tattoos. His hair color changes frequently. He seems to enjoy his controversial image and has capitalized on it in his books, *Bad as I Wanna Be* and *Walk on the Wild Side.* While he appears reckless, Rodman contributes much time and money to charities and other worthy causes. All the same, his controversies may have cost him his future in pro basketball. The Lakers waived Rodman in May 1999 after just one season. Rodman, who has played for a number of teams, left Chicago in 1998 and had trouble finding a team interested in hiring him.

THINK CRITICALLY

1. Why do you think that Rodman behaves as he does? Do you think it has helped or hurt him in his career? (Consider sports-related activities as well as his career as a pro ball player.)

2. If you were Rodman's public relations manager, what advice would you give him, and why?

Ongoing Assessment
Use the Intermission as an opportunity to conduct ongoing assessment of student comprehension of the lesson material.

TEACHING STRATEGIES
At-Risk Students
Go over the definition of community service and its benefits. Ask students to brainstorm possible community service projects and list the projects on the board.

TEACHING STRATEGIES
Auditory Learners
Give students examples of community service activities and ask them to associate a popular athlete with each event. Students should explain why they chose a particular athlete for each event.

Take a Bow
Sammy Sosa has the publicity from a record number of home runs two years in a row. Perhaps his greatest publicity comes from his generosity to youth in the United States and the Dominican Republic.

Think Critically
1. Fans admire Sosa for his baseball performance and his community service in the U.S. and the Dominican Republic.
2. He will be remembered for his record number of home runs and his generosity. Fans and community leaders may remember different things.

to focus on leukemia research after his sister died from the disease. One of his foundation's activities is the Dan Jansen Celebrity Golf Classic. His foundation has numerous sponsors, including Nissan, Hyatt Hotels, Midwest Express, and John Hancock Insurance.

Athletes are not the only celebrities who have created foundations to support charities. For example, television personality Jane Pauley and her husband, cartoonist Gary Trudeau, have a foundation. The Pauley-Trudeau Foundation contributed more than a quarter of a million dollars to charity in 1997.

INTERMISSION

What is a foundation? Give examples of foundations and charities supported by celebrities. A foundation is an organization that is established to maintain, finance, or assist other institutions or programs that are of an educational, charitable, or social nature. Examples will vary.

TAKE A BOW

SAMMY SOSA

Sammy Sosa is loved both for his athletic ability and for his humanity. He was just behind Mark McGwire's record for most home runs in 1998, and ahead of McGwire in August 1999.

Sosa was the fifth of seven children born to Juan Montero and Mireya Sosa. At the age of 14 he tried his hand at baseball, using a stick for a bat and a milk carton for a glove. In 1985, he was discovered by a scout, and the Texas Rangers signed Sammy when he was just 16. Sosa gave most of his $3,500 bonus to his mother.

A citizen of the Dominican Republic, he established the Sammy Sosa Foundation in 1998 to benefit underprivileged children in Chicago and the Dominican Republic. In August 1999, the foundation opened the Sammy Sosa Children's Medical Center for Preventative Medicine in San Pedro di Marcoris.

Sosa has given freely of his time and money to other humanitarian causes. In 1997, he organized a Sammy Claus World Tour to give away toys to over 7,000 children in the U.S. and the Dominican Republic. For every home run he hit in 1998, Sosa donated 40 computers to schools in his native country. He also created the Sammy Sosa Relief Fund to help hurricane victims in the Caribbean be provided with food, medicine, and supplies to rebuild their homes and schools.

THINK CRITICALLY
1. Why do you think that fans admire Sosa?
2. What do you think he will be remembered for, or do you think that depends upon who is doing the remembering? Explain.

UNDERSTAND MARKETING CONCEPTS

Circle the best answer for each of the following questions.

1. Why do athletes support charities and foundations?
   a. because they care about the causes supported by the organizations   d
   b. to raise public awareness about special concerns
   c. to help needy and ill children
   d. all of these

2. The news media   b
   a. avoids bad publicity for athletes
   b. often ignores athletes' connections with charities
   c. prefers to stick with sports statistics rather than personal interest stories
   d. both a and b

THINK CRITICALLY

Answer the following questions as completely as possible. If necessary, use a separate sheet of paper.

3. Discuss at least three reasons why an athlete would choose to sponsor a tournament or establish a foundation.

Help others in need.
_____

Promote a special cause.
_____

Create favorable personal publicity.
_____

_____

_____

_____

4. List five special causes for which foundations might be created and suggest a popular athlete to sponsor each. Explain the reasons for your choices.

Answers will vary.
_____

_____

_____

_____

_____

ASSESS
Reteach
Make sure to emphasize the importance of community service and its benefit to celebrities. Ask students to give examples of tournaments and foundations to make sure they understand the rationale for each.

Enrich
Ask students to design a T-shirt, sun visor, or other souvenir to give away at a charity tournament.

CLOSE
Re-establish the importance of celebrities taking an active role in the community by sponsoring tournaments and leading foundations for special causes. Ask students to list the advantages for the community and the athlete.

CHAPTER 6
LESSON 6.2

SPORTS CAMPS

GOALS

Explain why sports celebrity camps have become increasingly popular.

Define the importance of corporate and business contacts in the area where a sports camp will be held.

SCHEDULE
Block 90–135 minutes
Regular 2–3 class periods

FOCUS
Ask students if they have ever attended a sports clinic. What sport was it for? Was there a celebrity? What did the student(s) think of the experience?

OPENING ACT
Why do young people like to participate in sports camps during their summer vacations? Why do parents like the camps? What draws more attendance to the camp? How would you rate the advertising for camps when compared to what actually happens at the camp?

Answers for Opening Act Cooperative Learning
Answers will vary. A popular athlete might make the camp more interesting and worth the extra cost if the athlete is actively involved with the camp.

OPENING ACT

Students usually look forward to a summer break from their studies. It is an opportunity to devote more time to developing skills and interests for which there is less time when school is in session. According to the National Camp Association, there are about 10,000 summer camps in the U.S. alone, attended annually by over five million youths. Most camps include sports activities, and many are devoted to helping children increase their skills at a particular sport. Some of these feature popular college or professional athletes and coaches who add promotional power. Usually these camps need to charge more in order to pay these personalities. In turn, people are willing to pay more because they want to work out with the stars.

Work with a partner. Discuss whether you would like to attend a camp that included instruction from a top professional. Do you think it would be worth the extra tuition? Why or why not? Discuss advantages and disadvantages of attending.

POPULARITY OF CAMPS

Why would serious young athletes want to participate in a sports camp headed by a famous athlete or coach? Perhaps they believe the best players will be able to teach their sport the best. Perhaps they hope for a contact in the pro world, a way of "getting their foot in the door." Parents may think this is a way of helping their child climb the ladder of sports success. Whatever their reasons, and whether or not their hopes come true, more people spend sizable amounts every year for children and teens to participate in summer sports camps.

CAMP EXPECTATIONS

What can families reasonably expect of celebrity sports camps? Generally, lodging, food, and a specific schedule of planned activities are standard, but adults should read material from the camp very carefully to know just what is promised. For example, parents may send their child to a baseball camp expecting that he or she will have a personal lesson with the baseball superstar promoting the camp. In fact, the star may only give a short welcome speech, or he may only work with the most advanced campers. Worse yet, he may not be at the camp, having only agreed to endorse the camp.

Location is another important consideration. Sometimes working parents are just looking for a convenient camp where their children can safely learn the basics of a sport while they are at the office. Others may be willing to fly their children across the country just so they can learn advanced skills from their sports hero. Adults should at the least ensure that campers will have safe and adequate sporting facilities, well-trained camp coaches and counselors, and clean, comfortable lodging facilities. They will also want to consider where their children will feel most at ease. A camp can be located in a small rural setting or on a college campus near several other sports camps. Parents should also consider whether their children will be more comfortable with a smaller or larger number of other campers.

GOOD MARKETING AND MANAGING EQUALS SUCCESS

A camp that promises but doesn't deliver won't last long. Camps compete for motivated campers, and parents demand quality for their money. Good sports camps rely on reputable marketers and organizers to help them succeed. Promotional materials must be enticing, but they must also be accurate. Other professionals will target corporations to solicit for sponsorships. Many companies, such as Nike and Champion, recognize the promotional value of sponsoring children's sports camps. They receive positive advertising as they help groom the consumers of their products.

Still, to successfully engage such businesses in sponsorship, the camp executives will need a strong business plan and a detailed budget. Before presenting their plans, they will also need to research possible companies to target for sponsorships. Who might be interested in this kind of investment, and why? Producers of sporting equipment and sports stores are good targets, but local businesses looking to promote goodwill in the community in which the camp is held are also worth approaching. An effective presentation on just how the camp can benefit the community may convince local companies to support the project.

With the growth of the Internet, businesses ignore the benefits of advertising and promoting their products and services online at their peril. Camps are no exception. Type "camp" or "sports camp" into a popular search engine, and you may end up with thousands of entries.

See if the World Wide Web can help you find a sports camp you might like to attend. Try different sites—general camp search sites, such as athleticcamps.com, and specific sport camp sites, such as americasbaseballcamps.com.

THINK CRITICALLY
1. What kind of information do you find at the sites? What do you find appealing or unappealing?
2. Pick one site. What would you change about it to make it more attractive to a potential camper?

MARKETING-INFORMATION MANAGEMENT

The business will need to know just what the camp expects from its sponsorship and what it will receive in return by way of recognition. In general, a sponsor can expect

- a positive public relations campaign
- specific visibility and awareness of their sponsorship
- advertising space in the camp's publications
- the presence of sponsorship banners, posters, and fliers that create goodwill between the company and consumers
- potential sales of their products at the camp

INTERMISSION

How can a camp enhance its potential to be successful?

A camp can enhance its success with actual involvement of athletes, testimonials, and strong media coverage.

CAMP PROMOTION

PROMOTION

Once a location and sponsors are acquired, the work is well underway, but far from done. Organizers will need to hire camp staff, create an easy registration process, and get the word out about the camp. Sponsors will certainly want to publicize the camp and have brochures and registration materials available for their customers. Additionally, the promotional campaign should include a variety of media and methods, such as:

- radio announcements
- local TV ads
- contests (with the winner receiving a free week at camp, a free T-shirt, an item signed by the camp celebrity, or something similar)
- press releases to newspapers
- interviews and photos
- giveaways such as T-shirts, sunglasses, or visors by the camp's sponsors
- a community appearance by the camp's celebrity

The camp brochures should include details about the camp—goals, objectives, schedule, registration requirements (ages and skill levels), housing, dates, location, and costs. Once an application is processed and accepted, parents should receive a more detailed list of what campers should bring with them, schedule highlights, arrival and departure times, medical information, emergency release forms, and insurance forms.

ONGOING PROMOTIONS

The marketing doesn't end once camp is in session. A successful camp will work with public relations professionals to ensure that articles about camp and campers make the local papers during sessions. Personal interest stories, such as those that highlight a child who beat the odds to become successful at a sport, promote goodwill. Sponsors may choose to hold weekly drawings for one of their products or services in order to create ongoing promotions. Professional photographers should be hired to capture photos for the newspapers and next year's brochures, and camp personnel should collect quotes from campers to use in future promotional materials.

Follow-up materials to parents help to promote goodwill. Asking their opinions of the camp's services and their child's experience can help organizers improve the sessions for the following year, and they can help parents and attendees feel that they have a voice in improving the camp.

Successful marketers will also maintain a mailing list from all who attended the previous year. They may offer incentives for alumni, such as a discount for attending an additional year. Another successful marketing tactic is to ask enthusiastic campers to provide several of their friends' names and addresses, offering a bonus gift to those whose listed friends decide to attend the camp.

TIME OUT

Special Olympics offers "Unified Sports Camps" in many states. At these camps, Special Olympians and other athletes team up to learn and play sports. Corporate sponsors of these camps include America Online and Coca-Cola.

TEACHING STRATEGIES
Visual Learners
Show students a wide array of brochures from different camps and highlight two or three top features for each camp. This will strengthen the material covered in this lesson.

Ongoing Assessment
Use the Intermission as an opportunity to conduct ongoing assessment of student comprehension of the lesson material.

INTERMISSION

Name at least five ways in which camps can advertise their services.

Answers will vary. Possible answers: radio announcements, local TV ads, contests,

and community appearances by an endorsing athlete.

UNDERSTAND MARKETING CONCEPTS

Circle the best answer for each of the following questions.

1. **Marketing-Information Management**   Which answer best explains why youth attend summer sports camps? **b**
   a. They couldn't get into summer school.
   b. They want to improve their sports skills.
   c. Their parents don't know what else to do with them.
   d. It is the best way to become a pro sports athlete.

2. **Promotion**   What can public relations professionals do once camps are in session? **d**
   a. nothing, they've done their job
   b. collect positive quotes from campers to use in new brochures
   c. hire photographers to take pictures for next year's ads
   d. both b and c

THINK CRITICALLY

Answer the following questions as completely as possible. If necessary, use a separate sheet of paper.

3. **Geography**   List three good locations for a sports camp and explain which sports these locations are suited for and why. Also suggest suitable sponsors for each of the camps, and explain your choices.

   Answers will vary.

   _____

   _____

   _____

4. **Communication**   Research a local sports camp in your area. What sport is taught at the camp? What age groups does the camp cater to? Is the camp targeted toward beginning or advanced participants? How much does the camp cost? What is included in this fee? Do any sports stars participate in the camp? Is this a camp you would like to attend? Why or why not? Summarize your findings in a one-page report.

   Answers will vary. Help students locate websites or local information.

   _____

   _____

   _____

WORKSHOPS

Summer camp is great for children and teens who have time to spare, but training goes on year round, and many amateur adult athletes do not have the luxury of taking a week or more off to work on their sports skills. One-day or weekend clinics and workshops provide these people other opportunities to improve in less time, and usually for less money.

Work with a group. Discuss sports clinics. Have you attended a one- or two-day sports clinic? If yes, how would you describe it? In what ways do you think that a workshop would differ from a week-long camp experience?

Define the relationship between sponsorship and interest in one-day seminars.

Evaluate three methods of advertising workshops, and discuss the benefits of each.

TARGETING SPECIFIC SKILLS

Because sports camps are organized over a five- to fourteen-day time period, their schedules allow athletes to address a variety of skills used in the particular sport. For instance, at baseball camp, participants might be taught the mechanics of swinging the bat in a 90-minute session the first morning of camp, followed by a lecture on caring for a baseball glove, lunch, and a practice game in the afternoon. They may not return to another strategy session on hitting until later in the week, but they will have covered other aspects of the game.

CLINICS CONCENTRATE ON A SPECIFIC SKILL

In contrast, a one- or two-day clinic may be called "Secrets of the Swing" and concentrate only on that skill. The sessions are more intense and concentrated, and the number of participants must often be more limited than at a camp setting. Rather than hiring an entire staff of coaches and counselors to run the event, a seminar may only have one celebrity athlete in charge of the whole group. Someone who is especially interested in improving his or her batting abilities may be more interested in this clinic than in a more general week-long camp that works on all phases of play.

CLINICS INTRODUCE A SPORT

Short clinics also frequently introduce a sport to beginners. The agenda may include several short sessions about each basic element of the game. A beginners baseball clinic might open with a short lecture called "Rules of the Game" to help beginners understand the positions and plays. It could be followed by an interactive session on swinging the bat. After lunch, participants could have a session on pitching and catching. The day could conclude with a fun practice game.

SCHEDULE
Block 90–135 minutes
Regular 2–3 class periods

FOCUS
Ask students what their favorite sport is. Is there a skill they wish they could focus on so they could improve their performance?

OPENING ACT
Summer camps provide an outlet for young people to learn more about sports, but adults who have less time available take advantage of one- or two-day workshops to improve their knowledge or participation in a sport.

Answers for Opening Act Cooperative Learning
Answers will vary. A sports clinic focuses on one topic or skill; whereas, a workshop concentrates on more skills and allows more time to combine all skills into performance. A workshop introduces a sport and helps a participant improve a skill.

TEACH

Sports camps that continue for 5 to 14 days can offer a wide array of activities ranging from skill enhancement to speeches from famous celebrities.

Clinics are only one or two days in length and concentrate on one skill. Clinics do not require as many personnel as sports camps and they charge smaller fees.

Some clinics introduce a sport. The University of Nebraska has a clinic (class) to teach the fundamentals of football so the fan gains a better understanding of the game.

The bottom line for any business venture is profit. One- or two-day workshops only have to focus on the workshop and do not have to get involved with extensive lodging and food arrangements.

Sponsorships for workshops provide fees to bring in celebrities and add spark to the event. Sponsors not only receive the publicity of being involved but they can also advertise their merchandise in hopes of increasing sales.

Ongoing Assessment

Use the Intermission as an opportunity to conduct ongoing assessment of student comprehension of the lesson material.

LOWER COST

One- to two-day clinics do not have nearly the overhead costs associated with summer camps. For an overnight workshop, participants often arrange their own food and lodging. The athlete or team putting on the clinic need not worry about those expenses. If the workshop is held on a college campus, sometimes lodging is available in dorm rooms and participants can eat in the university cafeterias. Organizers can also arrange for blocks of rooms in hotels and promote these in their informational materials. Also, large staffs are not needed, reducing the cost of salaries.

WORKSHOP SPONSORSHIPS

Sponsorship is a major consideration for workshops. The featured athlete will need to be paid. Money is needed to lease the space for the workshop, and for a marketing budget. Sponsors can help keep participants' fees down, enabling more people to attend, and they can add interest to the event. In return, sponsors can promote their products and get to know their clientele better. Sponsors can send representatives to the clinic and talk to participants about their product and service needs. Often the sponsoring company is offered a time slot in the program to talk about its offerings. Those attending appreciate the sponsor's help in making the workshop possible, so they can be an attentive audience.

Sponsors will require details about the workshop—time, place, target audience, celebrity athlete involved, participant fees, and advertising budget. They will want to know just how the sports marketing firm will position their brand for name recognition. Successful marketers will include their sponsors in numerous ways, such as the following:

- All media advertising and informational print materials
- Onsite banners, fliers, and exhibitor booth space for the sponsor to market their products and services
- Spoken recognition at the event and time for the sponsor to discuss the company's products/services
- Licensing potential

Sponsors often contribute products to workshops. For instance, at a soccer clinic, Quattro Industries could offer free use of its soccer balls. The company could also give a free soccer ball to all who participate in the clinic. Other promotional items, such as pens with the company logo, could be distributed at the event.

INTERMISSION

What are the benefits of workshops to participants? Why would companies want to sponsor workshops?

A workshop introduces a sport or helps a student improve a specific skill. Sponsors

help keep fees down and the sponsors promote products and get to know their

clientele better.

ADVERTISING

MARKETING-INFORMATION MANAGEMENT

Sometimes well-planned workshops fail because they are insufficiently advertised. Successful sports marketers will conduct research in the area in which a workshop is being held in order to learn more about its demographics. They will answer questions such as:

• What do citizens in this town read daily? Are there free newsprint weeklies that have high rates of advertising success?

• Do the area schools have a high percentage of participation in this sport?

• Where do people who might be interested in this event tend to congregate in their leisure time? At which local sports facilities could posters and brochures be placed? What sports facilities are in the area in which posters and brochures can be placed?

• Which are the best radio stations to consider for promotional ads?

AVENUES FOR ADS

PROMOTION

Once the initial research is done, and enticing, well-written ad copy is created, it is time to get the information to the public. Marketers will also need to determine when to disseminate the information by calculating the planning and preparation time necessary for participants.

Newsprint Amateur athletes tend to follow professional activity in their sport through their local newspapers. As papers offer reasonably priced advertising opportunities, marketers can place large boxed ads to catch the interest of potential participants. Care should be taken to keep copy concise and attractive, using bold letters to draw a reader to the workshop opportunity itself and the main attractions of the event.

Other benefits of newspapers and weekly newsprint mailers are that they require little lead time to place the ad and that copy can be changed quickly, usually within 24 to 48 hours. Disadvantages include that they are not as targeted to the clinic's prospective attendees and they are

Exercise workshops designed to teach a new exercise or the latest craze in staying in shape are gaining popularity. Some nightclubs offer free lessons, prior to the night hours, to attract more business.

TEACH

Sponsors will want to know what they get for their financial commitment. Unless you can give them 5 or 6 advantages to sponsorship, you will not get them to sign the dotted line. Sponsors may donate products to the workshops to use as promotional giveaways.

Workshops fail when they have not received adequate advertisement. Also, the community must be studied to determine what workshops have greater potential for success.

Advertisements must be professionally produced and put in publications that will garner the greatest mileage.

The sports section of a newspaper is a good place for advertising workshops. A newspaper is a reasonable means for advertising an event but it has a short life span because it is thrown away quickly.

We're all familiar with hype in advertising, such as "This is the BEST seminar on the planet!" or "In one hour you'll punt like never before!" While such phrases are in-tended to draw participants to a seminar, they are misleading. How does one deter-mine "the best seminar on the planet"? Does punting "like never before" mean bet-ter, or just differently? And whenever you see the word "virtually" in an ad, you can substitute the word "not," because the word roughly translates to mean "in effect, but not actually; almost."

THINK CRITICALLY
Pay close attention to advertising for a day. Keep in mind that advertising include bill-boards, posters, radio spots, logos, and designer labels as well as traditional ads. How surrounded are you by advertising? How are some advertisements misleading?

usually thrown away quickly. Additionally, many sports are not given much space in the sports section regularly. Those who would be interested in workshops for sports such as gymnastics, skating, cycling, and equestrian sports may not see ads in the sports pages.

Magazines and E-Zines
Sports magazines, especially those targeting the specific sport that the workshop ad-dresses, are great places for promotional ads, especially if there is significant lead-time to promote the event. They will be more expensive than news-papers, but these publications tend to be read by enthusiastic athletes in the sports that are most likely to offer clinics. Additionally, web magazines and web sites that target the workshop's sport have similar advantages to print magazine promotion. They may also re-quire less lead-time. Costs for ad space vary widely.

Targeted Mailings and Brochures Marketing com-panies can both buy and create their own targeted mailing lists of people most likely to attend specific events. While direct mail is the most ex-pensive of advertising methods mentioned here, if it is sent to a well-researched group of customers, it can be the most successful method. The marketing letter can be personalized with the addressee's name, and the materials are more likely to be read by someone with an interest in the workshop. Collecting information from satisfied customers who have attended similar clinics is essential in developing good lists.

INTERMISSION

What questions should be asked when planning a work-shop? What are the advantages and disadvantages of the above-mentioned methods of advertising?

Is there a demand for the workshop? Who would be a good sponsor? What is the

best promotion? Advantages and disadvantages will vary.

UNDERSTAND MARKETING CONCEPTS

Circle the best answer for each of the following questions.

1. One- or two-day sports seminars a
   a. may target a specific aspect of a sport
   b. involve huge staff requirements
   c. are usually advertised on television
   d. are useless for beginners

2. Promotion Companies can benefit from sponsoring workshops because d
   a. they can learn from their consumers by talking with participants
   b. they can increase their brand recognition
   c. they can increase their public image among consumers
   d. all of these

THINK CRITICALLY

Answer the following questions as completely as possible. If necessary, use a separate sheet of paper.

3. Write a one-page proposal to convince a local sports store to promote a high school basketball clinic in which an NBA player has agreed to participate.

Answers will vary. Emphasize community involvement and the visit by the

celebrity. The sponsor receives publicity and has an opportunity to

advertise.

_____

_____

_____

4. An Olympic mountain biker who would like to present a workshop in your area four months from now has approached your marketing firm. How will you choose to advertise this one-day event? Explain your choices.

Answers will vary. There is enough time for a magazine advertisement. The local

newspaper raises awareness, but the magazine could reach a more specific

target market. Direct mailings could also reach a more specific target market.

_____

_____

CHAPTER 6 REVIEW

REVIEW MARKETING CONCEPTS

Write the letter of the term that matches each definition. Some terms will not be used.

__e__ **1.** company that helps to finance sports activities, camps, and workshops

__a__ **2.** sports activity often organized with the intent of donating proceeds to a charity

__b__ **3.** focus on a specific audience or skill

__f__ **4.** organization established to assist charitable groups and institutions

__c__ **5.** a one- or two-day event in which participants can develop sports skills

a. tournament
b. target
c. clinic
d. promotion
e. sponsor
f. foundation

Circle the best answer.

6. Sports stars may participate in clinics
    a. to increase their public appeal
d **b.** to earn additional money
    c. to help people improve their sports skills
    d. all of these

7. A business that donates money or products and services to an event in exchange for brand recognition and public relations is a(n)
    a. endorser
c **b.** promoter
    c. sponsor
    d. none of these

8. Summer sports camps are intended
    a. only for the kids who are excellent in their sport
    b. to help pro athletes warm up before their training camps
d   begin
    c. to turn amateurs into pros
    d. none of these

9. Athletes become involved in community service by
    a. running tournaments
d **b.** donating money to charities
    c. establishing foundations
    d. all of these

THINK CRITICALLY

10. List three negative stereotypes about professional athletes and tell how the athletes can create positive images for themselves.

Answers will vary.

_____

_____

_____

_____

11. For each of the following celebrity charity event, choose an athlete that you think would be a good host. Explain your answers.

golf tournament

Celebrities and explanations vary.

soccer tournament

_____

tennis match

_____

10K run

_____

punt, pass, and kick competition

_____

12. Using the Internet, locate a total of five camps and/or one- to two-day clinics promoted by successful athletes. Describe the main features of each of the web sites. Is the professional athlete an active instructor for the camp/clinic, or will he or she just be making an appearance during the event?

Answers will vary.

_____

_____

_____

REVIEW

MAKE CONNECTIONS

13. Mathematics Your sporting goods store donated eight pairs of brand-name roller blades as prizes at a one-day workshop on skating skills. In return, your store's ad will appear in all the promotional materials for the clinic, and you will have a booth at the clinic in which you can hand out information and sell skates and skating equipment. The skates retail for $325 a pair, but you buy them wholesale for $165. There will be 50 participants in the workshop, but adults are welcome to watch as well. How many pairs will you need to sell at the clinic to cover your donation? Do you think this sponsorship was a cost-effective and positive decision? Explain why, based on the costs of roller blades.

$325 − 165 = $160 profit per pair, $165 × 8 = $1,320; cost of donation

$1,320 ÷ 160 = 8.25, You would need to sell 9 pairs of rollerblades to cover the

donation. This might be considered a good promotion because you would only have to

sell skates to fewer than 20% of the participants in order to break even.

The *Sports and Entertainment Marketing* Teacher's Resource CD includes a spreadsheet

template to help students complete this activity.

Look for the file p140 Make Connections-Mathematics.xls Office Templates folder, or the

file p140 Conx.txt in the Text Templates folder.

14. Communications Outline the information for a web page to advertise a sports camp of your choice. Be sure to include dates, price, who is conducting the camp, description of the camp, and what items are included in the price. Either format this information attractively in a word-processed document or actually design a web page. If neither option is available, find appropriate photos or artwork that you would use for a home page and create a layout on poster board.

Answers will vary.

15. History Interview a grandparent or any older adult to learn about images of sports heroes of their youth and about ways in which children were taught sports and improved their athletic skills. How did they feel about sports heroes, and what do they recall about the celebrities that formed their opinions? Did they associate them with any charitable organizations or activities? Did children attend sports camps or workshops? Did they ever have opportunities to learn from pro players?

Answers will vary.

_____

_____

_____

_____

_____

_____

PROJECT EXTRA INNINGS

Assume that a famous athlete who is establishing a foundation has approached your marketing company. He or she needs to sign sponsors, create an ad campaign, and create a high-publicity event to announce the foundation to the public and get people involved with it.

Work with a group and complete the following activities.

1. Decide who the sports personality is and learn enough about the athlete to determine an appropriate cause for the foundation so that you are working with specifics. Research the cause for this foundation so that you can write necessary background information about it in promotional materials.

2. Determine appropriate individuals and companies to approach for sponsorships and explain your choices. Outline the approach you will take to convince them to become sponsors.

3. Help your sports star determine a promotional event as a kick-off for the foundation.

4. Determine an appropriate time and place for the event and choose the avenues through which you will promote the event.

5. Create promotional materials. Your advertising materials will vary for each kind of ad you decide to place. (For example, copy for a press release will be different from that for a radio ad.)

6. Design an informational brochure for the event that includes a registration form for participants.

EXTRA INNINGS
Answers will vary.

Example:
1. Mia Hamm (bone marrow research): Mia had a sibling affected by bone cancer.
2. Sponsors: Nike, Adidas, Umbro, Rawlings Soccer Balls; Approach: meet prospects at a major World Cup Soccer Tournament so they see the enthusiasm for the sport and Mia Hamm. Go over all the benefits of sponsorship. Give sponsors a sign-up bonus (more advertising time or space). Treat the sponsors with highest regard.
3. Promotional event: U.S. soccer tournament for youth (proceeds to go to bone marrow research).
4. Place: Los Angeles, New York, Houston or Chicago; Time: June, when kids are out of school.
5. Promotional materials will vary. (Look for the message and quality of the promotional materials.)
6. The brochure should highlight all important features of the event.

CHAPTER 7

SPORTS MARKETING

WINNING STRATEGIES

RACING TO THE FINISH LINE

From his start operating an ice cream stand and working at a gas station, Tom Cotter has built the highly successful Cotter Group that specializes in public relations and advertising for clients in the world of auto racing. A long-time fan of racing, Cotter got a break into the industry in 1983 with Performance Associates, Inc., in New Jersey. From there he took a job in public relations in Charlotte at North Carolina's motor speedway and was soon named the director. In 1989, he started Cotter Communications with only one partner, a one-room office in an old house, and a single client: Kraft Foods and its Country Time Drink Mix.

Ten years later, Cotter Communications employs over 50 people, serves over 20 clients, and operates out of a 14,000 square foot office near Lowe's Speedway, with satellite offices in New Jersey and Boston. Its success stories include Maxwell House Coffee, Sara Lee, John Deere, and Gillette, and Kraft continues to be a satisfied customer.

In addition to serving his clients, Cotter participates in numerous charitable activities, which won him the Myers Brothers Award for his involvement. He gives of his time and resources to the Wheelchair Roll-a-thon, Motor Racing Outreach, and Children's Miracle Network.

THINK CRITICALLY:

1. Why do you think that large corporations would want to sponsor the race car industry?
2. Learn more about the Cotter Group at http://www.cotter. How has the company enjoyed such success? How could someone go from selling gas and cars to promoting NASCAR racing and major corporations?

CHAPTER 7
LESSON 7.1

MARKETING FIRMS

Explain the role of a sports marketing firm.

Understand the importance of maintaining a positive image for sports owners and marketing firms.

OPENING ACT

If you look through any sports magazine, shop at any store from a department chain store to a specialized sports shop, or turn to any sports TV channel, and you will see the immense power of advertising in the sports world. Whether you see a teenage tennis star wearing multiple logos or a race car covered with detergent ads, you understand that advertising is the fuel that professional sports burn. Millions of dollars are spent every day by companies that want people to buy their products and use their services.

Work with a partner. How do these firms link up with teams or individual athletes? How does a sports figure find a company to sponsor him or her?

MARKETING SPORTS

Successful sports marketing firms have several important characteristics in common. The first is integrity. A strong sense of ethics and fair play exhibited over a long period of time builds confidence and trust among clients and helps to enhance a firm's reputation. Companies whose expertise is broad and varied have an inside track in the race for success. Knowledge of information technology is also essential for the success of any firm in sports marketing.

MARKETING-INFORMATION MANAGEMENT

How do sports marketing firms put their expertise, knowledge of information technology, and integrity to good use? They bring business sponsors such as Reebok, Pepsi, and Ford Motor Company, and

nonprofit sponsors such as the World Wildlife Fund, the American Cancer Society, and the United Steel Workers Union, together with sports teams, individual athletes, and coaches. The marketing firm then negotiates terms of a contract and manages the contract for the two parties. The most important part of the management phase is media marketing.

SERVICE SPECIFICS

Sports marketing firms match athletes and businesses for their mutual benefit. The business/athletic teams can range from a billion-dollar contract negotiation for NBC-TV to broadcast the Summer Olympics to an arrangement for a pro quarterback to appear at a grand opening. In the case of the opening, the pro player is paid a fee by the store. In return, the store uses the quarterback to attract shoppers to its new location. If enough people who come to the opening also shop in the store, they will more than pay the fee the store owes the athlete.

The phrase "sold out" doesn't always mean that every seat at a game is taken. Actually, the seats may be sold, but there may not be fans in them. Large corporations frequently buy blocks of seats and use them for incentives and gifts to give to major clients and to their best salespeople.

In newer stadiums, fancy and expensive seating areas are being built specifically for corporations. They are similar to first-class in an airplane: the fans in these seats have extra space and their food is catered. Corporations may also arrange for special transportation, such as limousine service, to and from the event for the people to whom they give these tickets.

THINK CRITICALLY
Do you think that large corporations should be allowed to buy large blocks of tickets to sporting events, thereby preventing individual fans from purchasing seats? Why or why not?

associated with a winner or someone with a positive image. Companies are constantly broadening their base of sports sponsorship. A sports figure uses a sports marketing firm to bring together an athlete and a business sponsor.

If NBC-TV gives $1 billion to a city that is hosting the Olympics, the city uses that money to help put on the games, which are extremely expensive. NBC can then sell advertising time to corporations that want to sell their products. If Coke pays NBC $1 million to run commercials, it expects to make much more than that in increased sales of its product. If everything works as planned, this is a win-win situation. The city puts on the games, NBC makes money selling advertising, and the companies who buy the commercial spots make money from increased sales. The sports marketing firm that puts this all together makes a good profit as well.

ROLE OF THE AGENT

Some marketing firms have a single agent owner, while others may have dozens of agents. An **agent** is a person responsible for making contacts with clients and sponsors. Some agents represent individual clients, such as a sports personality like Greg Maddux. Others represent businesses or organizations in order to expand their name recognition.

A good sports marketing firm can offer a "turnkey" operation. That is, the firm will handle everything from initial contacts to the final production. The firm's agents will analyze the needs of the sponsor and match them with a compatible client. Next they will negotiate a contract, bring both sides together to sign the agreement, handle all media details, and provide support for the venture until the contract is fulfilled.

PROVIDING INCENTIVES

Because the world of sports marketing is highly competitive, various incentives are often offered to encourage salespeople and to attract new clients and buyers. You have probably been induced to buy at some point through such campaigns. "Season clearance" sales are major enticements to buy, as is the pitch "Buy one, get one free." Customers are also persuaded to buy when there may be a prize as a result of their purchase.

Customers are not the only ones who may benefit from incentive promotions. Salespeople who sell the most products in a given quarter or month may win a financial bonus. Additionally, gifts may be offered to new clients that the salespeople bring into the company.

INTERMISSION

List three basic qualities that a sports marketing firm should possess to make it competitive. What are two services that sports marketing firms provide their clients?

Qualities: integrity, strong sense of ethics, fair play

Services: match athletes and business for mutual benefit; put together financial arrangements between a city, an event, advertisers, and commercials.

THE BIG PICTURE

Sports are expensive. Costs to amateur athletes include equipment, practice, and coaching. Events have costs that include paying for host space and paying employees to sell tickets, manage crowds, and referee the event. Building sports facilities is costly. Over $2 billion has been spent in the last 10 years on stadium construction in the U.S. and Canada alone. Athletes are demanding sky-high salaries. For example, after the advent of free agency in the NBA, Shaquille O'Neal negotiated a contract with the Los Angeles Lakers for $120 million.

THE IMAGE OF OWNERS

Fortunately for the sports world, numerous games are popular, and fans are willing to pay high prices for tickets, refreshments at a game, sports merchandise, camps, fan clubs, lectures, weekend seminars, and workshops. However, fans are affected by the image of professional team owners, who they often perceive as self-seeking big businessmen. These owners have the same problem that their top players have: how to demonstrate to the public that they are hard-working business leaders who want to provide the public with the sports entertainment they seek and who are willing to donate some of their proceeds to charitable causes.

PRO BONO

"Pro bono" is a Latin term that means, literally, "for the good." It refers to jobs that a sports marketing firm may do for free. That is, it will take no money for the services it performs. The Exordium Group, a sports marketing company in California, uses the motto "Doing Well by Doing Good," and describes its philosophy on its web page: " ... we include nonprofit organizations in our projects whenever possible .... [We] have an ongoing commitment to assist at least one nonprofit organization per year on a pro bono basis."

Many professional athletes, especially those who are "superstars," command respect and admiration from countless fans, especially children and young adults. Some pro stars, however, have committed felonies—being charged with assault, weapons infractions, drug use, and illegal gambling.

Pete Rose, star infielder for the Cincinnati Reds, produced more base hits than any player in the history of baseball, but was banished from baseball for gambling. He was found guilty of betting on professional sports. This was a serious breach of ethics and has kept Rose from being elected to the Baseball Hall of Fame.

THINK CRITICALLY

1. Do you think Pete Rose should be in the Hall of Fame?

2. Would you use Pete Rose as a pro sports figure to help advertise your new business? Why or why not?

In 1998, The Exordium Group did pro bono work for FEMBOT, an organization that gives cyber concerts to raise awareness for women's issues. The company also worked with Richard Drobaugh's World Ride Against Cancer.

Companies, large and small, retail, wholesale, manufacturing, and service oriented, all want to increase their market share. Sports teams—large (such as professional baseball and football) and small (bicycle racing and equestrian)—and individuals (such as ice skaters and gymnasts) need revenue to succeed. The sports marketing firms, with their agents and expertise, bring the two groups together and work out programs that will help both. It may be General Mills or Procter & Gamble, but it could also be Bob's Furniture Store or Big Mike's Used Cars that would like to use an athlete or an auto racing team to help put a name before the public. Sports marketing firms get this done.

INTERMISSION

Explain why sports are so costly and why it is both difficult and important for owners of sports teams to maintain a positive image. Why would a company that is in business to make money do some work for free?

Sports are costly because of necessary facilities, equipment, athletes, training, and

services for the event. A negative image can be eliminated based on good work

performed for free.

ASSESS
Reteach
Re-emphasize the importance of developing and maintaining good relationships between sports and business. Sports marketing agents must have the savvy to maintain these relationships.

Enrich
Ask students to determine two "pro bono" activities for a sports marketing firm to perform in their community. What impact will free services for these events have on the community?

CLOSE
Wrap up the lesson by asking students to make a list of incentives that a sports marketing firm can offer athletes and businesses. What is the purpose of these incentives and are they profitable for the sports marketing firm?

UNDERSTAND MARKETING CONCEPTS
Circle the best answer for each of the following questions.

1. **Marketing-Information Management** A sports marketing firm would do all of the following except **a**
   a. find a pro tennis player who would agree to advertise a brand of sport shoe
   b. draw up the contracts between the athlete and the shoe company
   c. provide salespeople to work in the company's shoe store
   d. coordinate photographers to take pictures of the tennis star wearing the shoes

2. **Promotion** A good sports marketing firm would want to do pro bono work because **b**
   a. it could make twice as much money as doing regular work
   b. it could improve the firm's reputation
   c. its employees would get more sick time
   d. the firm could let some workers go and still make money

THINK CRITICALLY
Answer the following questions as completely as possible. If necessary, use a separate sheet of paper.

3. **Communication** Would it be a good business concept to put a famous athlete who had been in prison for assault with a firearm, but had later been cleared of the charge, on a box of breakfast cereal? Defend your answer.

   Answers will vary. This idea is probably not good because consumers will

   remember the athlete's bad reputation.

   _____

   _____

   _____

4. List 10 athletes that you can find on products sold in stores or on the Internet. Pick one and write a brief account of how a sports marketing firm may have helped him or her.

   Answers will vary.

   _____

   _____

   _____

   _____

THE GLOBAL MARKET

GOALS

Describe sports that have become popular internationally.

Describe ways in which sports marketing has increased international awareness of sports.

Explain some challenges in marketing the Olympics and women's sports.

SCHEDULE
Block 90–135 minutes
Regular 2–3 class periods

FOCUS
Why do students think that some games are more popular in one country than another?

OPENING ACT
At one time sports were very regional throughout the world. A free world has been good for marketing sports around the globe. Sports have been imported and exported from other countries throughout the world.

Answers for Opening Act
Cooperative Learning
Answers will vary.

Exported: Basketball, baseball, American football

Imported: Soccer, luge, martial arts

OPENING ACT

Before World War II, sports were relatively static on the world stage. Baseball and football were played in the United States, while soccer ("futbol") held the attention of nearly the rest of the world. South and Central America, Europe, and the Soviet Union played soccer, while Asia and sub-Saharan Africa had nothing in the way of big market sports. Other sports were played, of course, but nothing on the scale of baseball, soccer, and American football. During the 50 years since the end of World War II, the popularity of major and minor sports and sports marketing has increased, and have snowballed since the breakup of the Soviet Union.

Work with a partner. Think of some examples of sports that have been both imported to and exported from the United States. Take a poll: Who do you think is the most famous athlete in the world? Now imagine you are conducting this poll in Germany or Japan. Do you think the answer would be the same? Try the Internet to see if you can find some answers there.

THE MIGRATION OF SPORTS

Sports marketing goes hand in hand with the various sports. The state of world sports at the end of the twentieth century has much to do with the political history of the past 50 years. When the United States ended its occupation of Japan after World War II, it left an interesting legacy: bubble gum, baseball caps, and the sport of American baseball. The Japanese took to baseball with a passion. Leagues were formed, both amateur and professional, and soon Japanese children were mesmerized by the diamond, the outfield, and the double play.

OTHER INTERNATIONAL SPORTS TRENDS

Americans also carried volleyball to distant parts of the world. In return, Americans became familiar with Asian martial arts, especially judo and karate. Baseball spread from America to Cuba and other Caribbean nations. The strengthening of the Olympic games elevated all sports to a new level, and sports marketing came into its own. Africa and Asia became involved in international competition as well. Also, soccer is now very popular in the United States in recent years thanks to global influence.

Advances in communications and transportation allowed international audiences to see games from all over the world. Teams could travel quickly around the world, increasing international competition and international sports sponsorship.

In Korea, Japan, and the Philippines, baseball reigns. In the past 20 years, international teams have dominated the Little League World Series held in Pennsylvania. This is one of the results of the strong growth of American sports outside the U.S.

INTERMISSION

How has the spread of American sports to other countries evolved? How have technological advances increased the popularity of sports?

The spread of American sports evolved through historical events, the Olympic

Games, and technology that allows people all over the world to see games and the

best athletes.

WORLD SPORTS 2000

Sports at the turn of the century are certainly changing and crossing international boundaries at a quick pace. The National Hockey League (NHL) was traditionally comprised of American and Canadian players. Since the fall of the Berlin Wall, the NHL has attracted dozens of Eastern European players. African and Eastern European players find their way to the NBA. Japanese and Dominican athletes play in American baseball. The American sports marketing system has made playing here very lucrative, and, in general, athletes earn more money in salaries in the United States than in any other nation.

SCOUTING FOR TALENT

In order to find top international players of U.S. sports, teams pay **scouts** to travel the world to locate the best athletes in their respective sports. After finding these international stars, they hope to entice them to come to America to play. Scouts are allowed to offer predetermined salaries, bonuses, and other incentives to bring in new players.

TEACH

Marketing sports throughout the world has been greatly influenced by political history. A free world dependent upon international trade has opened opportunities for worldwide sports.

Countries can learn a lot about other parts of the world by participating in sports and learning new sports.

International competition and international sports sponsorship have increased due to television coverage of sports throughout the world. Competition crossing state borders has now become competition crossing national borders.

Not only are sports crossing national borders but major college and professional teams are recruiting athletes from all around the world. This diversity builds excitement in sports throughout the world.

Scouts travel around the world to find the best athletes. They often times offer special incentives to encourage athletes to sign the dotted line. What would be good examples of legal incentives to offer athletes?

Communication has become so sophisticated that people around the world can watch the Super Bowl or Olympics at the same time. Teams have traveled throughout the world to build interest in American football, baseball, and basketball.

The more the world is different, the more it is alike in the wide world of sports.

Popular athletic gear representing favorite teams in different sports can be seen around the world.

Ongoing Assessment

Use the Intermission as an opportunity to conduct ongoing assessment of student comprehension of the lesson material.

One of the most popular sports teams in the world is Manchester United, a top English soccer team.

SPREADING THE WORD

Fans around the world are able to watch dozens of sporting events via satellite, but nothing beats the real thing. To that end, American teams play many exhibition games in other countries. Presenting college football in Japan, college basketball in Australia, and pro football games in England and Germany creates an interactive marketing tool that engages new spectators and interests young athletes in participating.

Marketing American sports in other countries is paying off. Italy and Switzerland have women's softball teams. In Germany and Holland, fans can hear the crunch of pads as football teams scrimmage. Italian and Croatian players are finding their way to the NBA. Baseball teams are springing up in Russia.

GLOBAL MARKETING

There are other American sports marketing strategies as well. Connected with the European teams and games are the sales of sports-related items, just as in the United States. You can see young boys on the streets of Milan, Italy, and all over Europe, dressed in baggy shorts, high tops, Chicago Bulls jerseys, and Nike caps, appropriately worn backwards. America's marketing and advertising imprint has gone global.

Soccer, known as "football" in many European and Latin American countries, is the world's most popular sport. International marketing has raised the level of interest in this sport in the United States in recent years. The U.S. hosted the men's soccer World Cup in 1994 and the women's World Cup in 1999. There is now an American professional soccer league. There are a number of American players now in the English Premier League, considered one of the world's best and most competitive soccer leagues.

INTERMISSION

How has marketing made sports teams more international? What are some of the signs that U.S. sports have become global?

Marketing has created awareness and raised interest in sports around the world.

Players from all over the world are being recruited for premiere sports.

INTERNATIONAL MARKET NICHES

Sports today are big business. Often earnings drive the industry more than wins. Personal and team triumphs and setbacks occur in international play, and these elements keep crowds coming back for more. Money is the greatest factor that fuels the competitions. One major example of financing taking priority over the sports themselves occurred in

1994 when the International Olympic Committee voted to no longer hold the Winter and Summer Olympic Games during the same year. By staggering the events by two years, winter and summer sports would no longer be competing for advertising dollars. This major change in timing allowed the two sets of games to achieve record profits.

The international competition of so many sports in the Olympic games probably creates the biggest sports marketing opportunity of them all. Not only fans, athletes, and sponsors, but also towns, diplomats, and even federal governments must be organized to handle so many international visitors in such a small area. For example, the federal government helped provide 2,000 buses to move spectators to events for the 1996 Summer Olympics. This resource saved the Olympic organizing committee over $12 million. The competitive world of international sports marketing analyzes facilities, potential government cooperation, and financial resources to determine where events will occur. In the case of the Olympics, it takes six to seven years of preparation in order for 17 days of competition to take place successfully.

MARKETING WOMEN'S SPORTS

Sports marketing has seriously neglected women's sports until recently. While many fans would turn on their TVs twice a year to watch women's figure skating and women's gymnastics, these competitions were mostly amateur, and while marketing was involved, it was limited.

When the U.S. Women's Soccer Team won the World Cup Soccer Tournament in 1988, it barely made the sports pages. Ten years later, due to their continued success and to the international popularity of the game of soccer, fans closely watched the U.S. team, including a half million that attend the games. Women, as much as men, have made this sport popular in the United States.

Sheryl Swoopes and Cynthia Cooper are superstars in the Women's National Basketball Association (WNBA), founded in 1996 after unsuccessful attempts to form leagues in previous years. The teams and their stars have a strong following, averaging 10,000 spectators per game during the 1998 season. Their robust web site keeps fans up on players, sponsors, schedules, and the latest WNBA items for sale.

The growing popularity of women's sports adds new female fans to the market, many of whom were uninterested in the traditional men's major league games. Women also have different interests than men, and a new frontier of marketing sure to become lucrative for creative marketers is the production of sports-related items that will appeal to this new category of fans.

INTERMISSION

How do women's sports create new challenges for sports marketers?

Women's sports are relatively new and have just recently attracted substantial interest.

Marketers need to determine target markets and the needs for women in sports.

UNDERSTAND MARKETING CONCEPTS

Circle the best answer for each of the following questions.

1. **Distribution** The sports world has become more international in nature due to **d**
   a. historical changes in the world
   b. advanced technology
   c. increased opportunities for sales
   d. all of these

2. The Summer and Winter Olympics **d**
   a. have increased international awareness of sports
   b. have made it more difficult for companies to become sponsors
   c. are staggered to increase sponsor participation and sales
   d. a and c

THINK CRITICALLY

Answer the following questions as completely as possible. If necessary, use a separate sheet of paper.

3. Look at sports magazines and web sites for evidence of four international players entering American sports leagues. List your findings and describe how they have contributed to their sports.

   Answers will vary.

   _____

   _____

   _____

   _____

4. Write down evidence of four sports not originally associated with the United States that have become popular in the U.S. Explain why you think these sports appeal to Americans.

   Answers will vary. The sports selected might appeal to Americans because they

   give people additional opportunities to participate in sports.

   _____

   _____

   _____

CAREERS IN SPORTS MARKETING

CHAPTER 7

LESSON 7.3

You may be a good athlete or someone who enjoys watching and following sports. Maybe you take interest in one or two sports or simply enjoy sporting activities in general. If you would like to explore the possibilities for a career in the sports industry, you will need to make a plan and act on it in order to gather the information that will be helpful in making a decision. In addition to professions that deal directly with the athletes, coaches, and leagues, there is a wide range of indirectly related jobs linked to sports.

Work with a group. What are some of the different aspects of a sports marketing career? What skills do you need?

GOALS

Identify numerous sports marketing careers.

Describe skills and personal characteristics necessary for a career in sports marketing.

SCHEDULE
Block 90–135 minutes
Regular 2–3 class periods

FOCUS
Now that students have learned something about sports marketing, ask students if they are considering a career in sports marketing.

OPENING ACT
There are a wide array of careers available in sports marketing; however, competition for these careers is fierce and only the best laid plans will help you land a career in sports marketing.

Answers for Opening Act Cooperative Learning
Answers will vary.

Sports Marketing: careers in professional, college sports public relations, legal agreements, sports apparel/equipment

Skills needed: human relations, communications, negotiations, public relations, creativity

A WIDE WORLD OF CAREERS

Many sports-related careers are available as the field of professional sports continues to expand in the U.S. One of the most interesting and exciting is sports marketing. Jobs range from careers in professional sports and the college and amateur ranks to positions in related fields in a variety of businesses, such as sports apparel and equipment.

TWO ROADS TO SUCCESS

Marketers divide sports marketing opportunities into two general categories. The first deals with activities such as matching clients, formulating contracts, designing programs for clients, overseeing projects, and providing follow-up evaluations. The second is involved with technical services, such as media, graphics and photography, and video production.

When the Carolina Panthers entered the NFL, they had much to do before their first game. Marketing firms handled everything from designing the team logo to sending players for personal appearances to planning promotions.

Besides tickets to the events, hot dogs are perhaps the biggest sellers at major sports games. One major university reported that a stadium averaging 75,000 fans will sell between 40,000 and 60,000 franks at a game.

Sports marketing has found a niche in Internet marketing. Browse through sports marketing sites. Take notes on sites that you find well presented and interesting. What separates these sites from the rest?

THINK CRITICALLY
Look up five teams or individual athletes on the Web. Find out if they have items for sale on the website. How are the items presented and packaged? Which site makes it easiest to purchase an item? Explain.

Watch a NASCAR event, and you begin to realize the massive amount of work that marketing plays in professional stock car racing. Every race car is covered with ads for products. Every one of the logo ads involved presentations, contracts, and price negotiations.

Many other sports rely heavily on marketing relationships as well. Figure skating competitions feature ads covering the walls around the ice. Professional cyclists form teams that are identified by their corporate sponsors. Sporting arenas are often named after companies who pay large fees to the arena owners.

OTHER MARKETING AVENUES

DISTRIBUTION

One of the best places to find examples of sports marketing is in the bookstore of any college or university. You will find hundreds of items that depict the school's teams and mascot. From T-shirts, caps, jackets, and athletic shorts to lamps, wastebaskets, blankets, and mugs, every item markets the school and its athletic teams. All along the line, from production to placement on shelves at the bookstore, someone in a sports marketing career is involved.

Not every job in sports marketing is directly related to advertising and sales of items. For example, "Funnybone the Clown" works every home game at Turner Field, home of the Atlanta Braves baseball team. First contracted as part of a marketing campaign to build fan loyalty just after the baseball strike of 1996, she paints faces, makes balloon animals, and talks to the kids in Turner Town, a special room just for children, which is decorated with cartoon characters. This performer and those involved in contracting her are all involved with sports marketing.

INTERMISSION

List five general activities with which a sports marketing firm would be involved. Pick one sport with which you are familiar, and name five different places where you see marketing activities that are associated with this sport.

Activities: presentations, contracts, price negotiations, monitoring and follow-up, and

designing programs. Answers will vary.

FOCUS ON CAREERS

One of the largest career areas in sports marketing is media. Under the broad umbrella of media marketing, you will find four focus areas: print, radio, television, and the Internet. Sports marketers must have some knowledge of each area in order to feel comfortable dealing with people and situations in each medium.

Just as the Internet has its own jargon—language that refers to Internet-specific functions—radio, TV, and print media also have special vocabularies to make communication more concise. Future sports marketers can benefit from apprenticeships in media. The skills and terminology learned in these areas give a potential sports marketer a solid foundation to work in public relations.

Other public relations skills are needed as well. The abilities to meet people, talk with them in a relaxed manner, and speak confidently and persuasively before a group are essential sports marketing skills, as is the ability to use the Internet efficiently and effectively.

OLD-FASHIONED HARD WORK

Drive, persistence, and hard work are fundamental to a successful career in sports marketing. A teenage girl in Dallas knew she wanted to work with the Dallas Cowboys in some capacity. She wrote letters, filled out applications, and followed up with phone calls to check the status of her requests. Although she was only requesting part-time work or even an unpaid internship, she was not interviewed. The Cowboys only hired college students. After more letters, calls, and a personal appearance at the human resources department, she finally received a call: "Could you come in for a few hours each week during the summer?"

At first the work merely involved answering the phone and sorting mail. But Amy handled it with such zeal and efficiency that her supervisor took notice. Soon she was handling more demanding work and was asked to return during summer vacations while in college. Solid basic skills in writing and speaking, combined with a desire to succeed, opened the

door for her. Organizational skills and the determination to complete tasks allowed her to be recognized as the type of team member her employer wanted.

INTERMISSION

Why can it help a potential sports marketer to do some work first in the media? In what other skills should a sports marketer have a background?

Experience in a particular field adds to your value in that field. Skills include public

relations, Internet, organization, and persistence.

TAKE A BOW

MIA HAMM

The scene: the Rose Bowl in Pasadena, California. It is the 1999 Women's World Cup Soccer Championship. On the field are some of the best female athletes in the world. One stands out. For 12 years Mia Hamm has held court in the fast-growing world of women's soccer. In 1987, at the age of 15, she played for the United States World Cup Team, the youngest female ever to do so. She led the University of North Carolina to four NCAA champi-onships and left school with the records as all-time leading scorer in goals, assists, and points.

As the recipient of the Women's World Cup MVP in 1995 and 1997, and the U.S. Soccer Female Athlete of the Year for an unprecedented five years in a row (1994–98), Mia Hamm has become a true superstar. Her book, *Go for the Goal,* is subti-tled *A Champion's Guide to Winning in Soccer and Life.* It is inspirational and gives young athletes sound advice as they work toward successful soccer

or sports careers.

In her busy schedule, Mia finds time to do important chari-table work. She has formed the Mia Hamm Foundation to sup-port research in bone marrow diseases and to encourage young women athletes. In 1998, it raised over $150,000. Hamm has successfully landed major sports marketing sponsors for this venture: Nike, Gatorade, and Mattel, as well as sports photographers.

While many sports figures are seen by the public as somewhat self-absorbed, Mia Hamm shines as an example of what a super-star can be.

THINK CRITICALLY
1. Go to a library or bookstore and find Mia Hamm's book *Go for the Goal.* If possible, read it and share it with a friend. Compare your thoughts on the book with others who have read it.
2. Consider ways in which sports marketing is involved in Hamm's career.

UNDERSTAND MARKETING CONCEPTS
Circle the best answer for each of the following questions.

1. Which of the following is *not* an aspect of sports marketing? c
   a. matching clients and sponsors
   b. overseeing marketing projects
   c. teaching new employees basic writing skills
   d. working with the media

2. **Promotion**   Which of the following skills are needed for a successful sports marketing career? d
   a. media skills
   b. organizational skills
   c. writing and speaking skills
   d. all of these

THINK CRITICALLY
Answer the following questions as completely as possible. If necessary, use a separate sheet of paper.

3. Assume you are on a committee to plan the senior class trip. You want to hold a fundraiser to help with expenses. Construct a scenario in which you invite a popular sports figure to host an event. How could a sports marketing agent help you put on this event successfully?

Answers will vary. The agent can bring you and the athlete together, draw up the

plan for hosting the event, oversee the event, and take charge of the media,

graphics, and photography of the event.

4. Imagine that you can enter the world of sports as a sports marketer. What type of situation would you choose? What are some of the things you would enjoy doing? What would you need to study to prepare for this career?

Answers will vary. Necessary skills include human relations, writing, negotiation,

public relations, creativity, and awareness of legal concepts.

ASSESS
Reteach
Make sure to emphasize that there are a wide array of marketing careers for students to consider. Where there is a will, there is a way to get involved in those careers.

Enrich
Ask students to select their favorite sport. What career would they choose in sports marketing to be more involved with this sport? How will they get their start in the selected career?

CLOSE
Ask students to define sports marketing careers and list at least ten different careers that would be classified as sports marketing. Students should also outline a plan for success when entering a sports marketing career.

ASSESS
Reteach
Ask students to make a list of the responsibilities that sports marketing firms have when marketing a sport internationally. How does pro bono work play a role in marketing sports?

Enrich
How large a role can ethics play in marketing sports internationally? For example, how would you market an international competition to two different countries that have a history of warfare and strife?

CLOSE
Wrap up the discussion about sports marketing by having students list all of the sports they can think of. Then have students try to prioritize the list into what they would consider the top ten most popular sports. What makes these ten sports so popular? Ask students to name a promotion, an ad, a logo, or other marketing strategy that may have helped contribute to the popularity of these sports.

CHAPTER 7 REVIEW

REVIEW MARKETING CONCEPTS

Write the letter of the term that matches each definition. Some terms will not be used.

__e__ **1.** language specific to a professional industry

__f__ **2.** person responsible for making contacts with clients and sponsors

__b__ **3.** gifts or bonuses designed to motivate buyers, sellers, and sponsors

__d__ **4.** providing services for free; "for the good"

__a__ **5.** meeting people comfortably, speaking effectively, persuading successfully

a. public relations skills
b. incentives
c. speakers' bureaus
d. pro bono
e. agent

Circle the best answer.

6. Sports marketing firms
    a. market athletes
    b. market ideas
    c. solicit sponsorships
    d. all of these

d

7. A prize inside a cereal box is an example of
    a. a promotion
    b. an incentive
    c. a sweepstakes
    d. pro bono.

b

8. Which of the following is not true?
    a. Soccer is the world's most popular sport.
    b. Some firms do "bono fide" work, donating their products and services for special causes to enhance their public image.
    c. The number of international sports competitions have increased in the past 50 years.
    d. Women's sporting events are gaining popularity.

b

9. Sports careers
    a. don't require any professional training or skills
    b. don't last long, because only young people are successful at them
    c. encompass a vast array of job possibilities
    d. are diminishing as sports become less popular

c

THINK CRITICALLY

10. Think of an incentive to get more consumers to buy skis at your sporting goods store. Explain your rationale.

Answers will vary.

_____

_____

_____

_____

_____

_____

11. Design a magazine ad and a radio ad to promote the Women's National Basketball Association to European countries.

Answers will vary. Ads will need to create excitement and desire to attend a professional

women's game.

_____

_____

_____

_____

_____

12. Suppose that you are a scout and have just spotted a top-rated college soccer player. Your job is to promote a national men's soccer team for the U.S. Devise a plan to entice this young man to become a new member and strengthen the team.

Answers will vary.

_____

_____

_____

_____

_____

_____

CHAPTER 7 REVIEW

MAKE CONNECTIONS

13. Mathematics   Assume that you are in charge of ticket sales for a major stadium. It recently added 10 luxury boxes that each hold 20 fans. The construction cost for each box was $350,000. Cover the cost of these boxes within five years. How much will you charge per box on an annual basis, assuming that a box costs you $5,000 per year to maintain? Will you hold any of the boxes to be available on a game-by-game basis? Why or why not? To whom will you market these boxes, and why?

$350,000 × 10 = $3,500,000 total cost of boxes; $3,500,000 ÷ 5 years = $700,000 per year;

$700,000 ÷ 10 boxes = $70,000 per box per year to construct; $70,000 + $5,000 = $75,000

per box per year to construct and maintain; Answers will vary.

The *Sports and Entertainment Marketing* Teacher's Resource CD includes a spreadsheet

template to help students complete this activity. Look for the file p162 Make Connections-

Mathematics.xls Office Templates folder, or the file p162 Conx.txt in the Text Templates folder.

14. Communications   Research possible sports careers in which you may be interested. Find a company that offers this kind of career opportunity. Write a letter to the company's personnel direction in which you explain why she should choose you to become a summer intern.

Answers will vary. The letter should tell about the student's skills, determination, and

sincere interest in sports marketing.

15. History   Research the history of one of your favorite sports. Discover the country in which it originated and other countries to which it has spread. Why do you think the sport has grown to involve participants in other countries, if indeed it has? If it has not, why not?

Answers will vary.

16. Communications Create a poster that advertises a company's pro bono work in an upcoming sporting event. Include specific information on the poster.

Answers will vary. Students should emphasize how the company is contributing to the

community for free.

_____

_____

_____

_____

_____

_____

_____

_____

_____

PROJECT EXTRA INNINGS

You are on a marketing team that has been asked to promote international volleyball competitions. As part of that venture, you have chosen a team to travel for one month during the winter holidays, playing at various venues.

Work with a group and complete the following activities.

1. To whom will you go for sponsorships to pay for the players' equipment and travel expenses? What will be your marketing strategy?

2. Perform research to find other countries in which volleyball is popular, or at least played by older teens and young adults. You may want to consult the Internet or call universities with volleyball teams to find this information. Based on your findings, create an itinerary that is manageable over a month's time.

3. Create an advertising campaign to create advanced interest in the games.

4. Draw up a list of businesses, companies, and town committees that you might need to reach before finalizing your schedule. What kinds of information would you need to discuss and organize prior to the games?

5. Determine the kinds of follow-up you need to implement in order to develop a market for the international volleyball competitions.

EXTRA INNINGS
Break up the class into different groups. Have each group work through the activities. Have one representative from each group present the group's marketing plan. At the end of the discussion, ask students what some elements of a successful sports marketing campaign are.

CHAPTER 8

ENTERTAINMENT INDUSTRY

LESSONS

WINNING STRATEGIES

BECOMING AWARE OF AWARE RECORDS

Aware Records is a small, independent record label that fills the unique slot of finding tomorrow's rock bands today. Begun in 1993 by Gregg Latterman, Aware uses a grassroots promotion strategy and seeks intriguing ways to market its artists. It is one of the few independent labels that sponsors a tour.

Aware got its start by compiling and marketing the music of several different bands who were not yet widely known and who had not yet signed recording contracts. Aware has been very successful in identifying up-and-coming bands. Aware Tours now feature more than 15 bands playing more than 40 venues throughout the United States.

In 1997, Aware signed a joint label deal with Columbia Records that provides Columbia a small label for developing artists and gives Aware a major distribution channel. Aware is positioned to become a major player in the music business, but Latterman wants to maintain the integrity of an independent label.

THINK CRITICALLY
1. Why might Aware want to remain an independent label rather than associating fully with a large company?
2. Why do you think Aware has grown so quickly?
3. What risks might Gregg Latterman have encountered during his release of the first compilation?

TEACHING RESOURCES
❏ CNN Video, Chapter 8
❏ CD-ROM Resources, Chapter 8

Winning Strategies
Think Critically
1. Aware might want to stay independent because the company can stay flexible, react more quickly, and maintain control with current and original staff.
2. Aware has grown quickly due to finding the right bands and grassroots promotion.
3. Some risks are loss of time, effort, and money invested.

ENTERTAINMENT PROFITS

Explain profit and cost-cutting strategies in the motion picture industry.

Calculate film revenue, and discuss the importance of foreign markets for movies.

Describe financing in auto racing.

SCHEDULE
Block 90 minutes
Regular 2 class periods

FOCUS
The history of the movie industry starts with the growth of the large studios and their control of the industry. Independent moviemakers are creative in finding ways to get their movies to an audience. Talk with students about low-budget movies. Does a low budget always mean a bad movie?

OPENING ACT
To prepare the students for this lesson, discuss control of movie content by foreign governments such as China.

Answers for Opening Act Cooperative Learning
Lack of financing and support limit success due to lack of the promotion, quality production, and distribution contacts.

OPENING ACT

Independent filmmakers create their works without the financing and huge staff of major production studios. The government of France requires broadcasters to use independent film producers for 75 percent of the films produced or bought for television. There is no such requirement in the United States, so smaller filmmakers often have a hard time getting their movies out. In the U.S., a few major corporations take home most of the profits from entertainment marketing.

Discuss ways that lack of financing and support staff can limit the success of independent filmmakers. Discuss independent films you have seen that succeeded despite these restrictions.

THE PROFIT MAKERS

Despite record audience attendance, only two of the seven major Hollywood movie studios turned profits in 1998. Paramount Pictures, a unit of Viacom Inc., and Twentieth Century Fox Film Corporation, a unit of News Corp., were both profitable, thanks mostly to the blockbuster *Titanic,* which sold more than $1.8 billion in tickets worldwide. The remaining five studios apparently suffered from the continuing high costs of the production and distribution of movies.

IS BIG BEST?

FINANCING

Large studios appear to be taking on the role of financial manager in an effort to spread the economic risk of making a movie. Studios are seeking out partners to help produce, promote, and distribute films. Future studios may be lean and mean, with very little money tied up in studio facilities or ongoing personnel costs.

Titanic was the first movie to earn more than $600 million in North America. Its promoters never missed a promotional opportunity, and they succeeded at each and

every try. While most movies are long gone from theaters by the time they are released for video sales, *Titanic* was still showing in 502 theaters the weekend prior to its video release. Stores all over the country stayed open after midnight to accommodate customers who lined up to purchase the video when it was released at 12:01 a.m. Millions of video copies were sold over the next few weeks.

COST-CUTTING STRATEGIES

To control distribution costs, major studios frequently cut the number of wide release movies. A **wide release** is a movie released in more than 2,000 theaters at one time. Between 1997 and 1998, the number of wide releases dropped from 151 to 139, according to EDI, a box office tracking firm. This was the first decrease in five years. The number of tickets sold in 1998 increased by 93 million, possibly because of this strategy.

Low-budget movies have little money for advertising, so their creators sometimes capitalize on the promotional budget of major multimillion-dollar movies by using a similar theme in their title. An example is a low-budget movie titled *Carnosaur,* which came out two months prior to the *Jurassic Park* movie. The book *Jurassic Park* had already been a best seller, and the movie was being talked about everywhere. The *Carnosaur* promoters made every association possible to get people to connect the two movies.

MARKETING MYTHS

In the past, Hollywood producers may have thought that the more money spent on a movie, the more money it would earn. That philosophy was proven wrong in 1999 with the release of *The Blair Witch Project.* This independent film was made in just five days for less than $50,000. Due to extraordinary pre-release publicity created by its makers, *Blair Witch* was expected to bring in as much as $500 million, including domestic and foreign ticket sales and video sales.

THINK CRITICALLY

1. Research the pre-release marketing strategy of *Blair Witch.* Explain the difference between the marketing strategy of *Blair Witch* and traditional film marketing strategies.
2. Will movies of the future be able to capitalize on the *Blair Witch* strategy? Explain.

INTERMISSION

Name three ways in which movie studios can cut costs.

Answers will vary. Circulate fewer movies in wide release, cooperate with other

companies to promote and distribute, recruit talented unknowns to star or direct.

Toy Story was the first purely computer-generated feature length film to earn $200 million at the box office. *The Lion King* was the first animated film to reach that level.

The top five highest grossing movies as of 1999 are:

Titanic, $601 million

Star Wars, $461 million

Star Wars: The Phantom Menace, $418 million

E.T., $400 million

Jurassic Park, $357 million

PROFIT AND OPPORTUNITY

A film's profit is the money that's left after all the bills have been paid. The profit from an American film depends largely on the popularity of that film overseas.

GENERATING FILM REVENUE

To figure their profits, moviemakers look at several elements of the whole process. They look at the ratio of tickets sold to the cost of production, for example. They also look at income from merchandising, soundtracks, relationships to theme parks, and global releases, as well as ticket sales in the United States and abroad. After all costs are paid and all income is calculated, the profit is then clear. For *The Blair Witch Project,* profits came soon. Made for less than $50,000, the movie grossed $36 million in ticket sales during its first three weeks in theaters.

CULTURAL OPPORTUNITIES FOR PROFITS

DISTRIBUTION

Worldwide distribution revenue is critical to bringing most movies into profitable territory. News Corp.'s Fox Unit sold nearly $2 billion in movie tickets outside the United States in 1998 with such hits as *Titanic, There's Something About Mary,* and *The X Files.* The income from an international release of a movie can increase the box office take by 50 to 100 percent over domestic ticket sales. Most films generate less than 25 percent of their final income from domestic ticket sales alone.

Films made in the United States may find it harder to make a profit in some overseas countries in the future. For example, in India in early 1999, theater owners and movie distributors in the state of Maharashtra, which includes the capital Bombay, indicated they would no longer show dubbed versions of English-language films. They said this action was to prevent corruption of Indian taste. A more likely reason is a desire to make theaters available for Indian-made films.

The Chinese government's China Film Co-production Corporation began seeking ways to co-produce movies with U.S. studios and independent producers in 1999. With 1.3 billion people, the Chinese market is a promising new potential audience. Currently the Chinese government must approve the content, filming location, and distribution of any films released in China. Chinese officials require films to avoid political topics and religion as part of the content criteria for doing business in China.

INTERMISSION

How can studios generate a profit besides ticket sales in the United States? How might the movie distribution system differ in countries other than the United States?

Studios generate profit through merchandising, theme park relationships, sound-

tracks, and global releases. Foreign governments might have restrictions that would

keep American films from being released in their countries.

FAST MONEY

FINANCING

The difference between entertainment and sports is determined by the viewer. Movies are definitely entertainment. However, some people consider stock car racing to be entertainment. Stock car racers face the same financing problems that film producers do. Racing groups have come up with two primary ways of securing the financing for their expensive form of entertainment.

First, a new mutual fund, the StockCar Stocks Index Fund, has been created. It is made up of stocks in firms that sponsor National Association for Stock Car Auto Racing (NASCAR) drivers. Investment stocks from companies such as Home Depot and Sara Lee are included with about 50 other sponsors' stocks. Fund managers plan to capitalize on the popularity of racing as entertainment. Seventy-two percent of racing fans consciously look for goods of NASCAR sponsors, according to a survey conducted by Performance Research.

Second, racers use a variation on the traditional sponsorship style. In NASCAR, one sponsor works with one individual racer and pays for that racer's car and its upkeep. If the sponsor cancels for any reason, the driver is, in effect, stalled until another sponsor comes along. Racing drivers and fans are concerned about the prohibition of tobacco advertising in sports. Tobacco companies have been major sponsors of racing for more than two decades, and some are worried that tobacco's huge financial contribution cannot be replaced. However, a racing crowd of 155,000 (at the Pepsi 400 in Brooklyn, Michigan, in August of 1999) is sure to draw the attention of nontobacco sponsors.

INTERMISSION

In what ways is the sponsorship of stock car racing different than that of other entertainment? Why would a food company sponsor a race car?

A single sponsor takes on a single racer in NASCAR and tobacco sponsorship could

hurt NASCAR more than other forms of entertainment. A food company might

sponsor a driver to take advantage of NASCAR fans' known brand loyalty.

Jeff Gordon is one of the top drivers in NASCAR races today. NASCAR fans bought more than $50 million in Jeff Gordon memorabilia in 1998.

UNDERSTAND MARKETING CONCEPTS
Circle the best answer for each of the following questions.

1. Selling Which of the following are ways to generate profits from a movie? **d**
  a. sales of related licensed merchandise (ancillary rights)
  b. relationships to theme parks
  c. sales of soundtracks
  d. all of these

2. Promotion A wide release of a movie is releasing it in **d**
  a. 200 to 500 theaters
  b. 500 to 1,000 theaters
  c. 1,000 to 2,000 theaters
  d. more than 2,000 theaters

THINK CRITICALLY
Answer the following questions as completely as possible. If necessary, use a separate sheet of paper.

3. How are future major movie studios likely to become more like independent studios of the present?

Answers will vary. Major studios are likely to adopt a number of cost-cutting

strategies like those used by independent studios.

_____

_____

_____

_____

4. Communication Research three sponsors of NASCAR. Explain which segments of the NASCAR audience each sponsor wants to reach.

Answers will vary.

_____

_____

_____

_____

_____

DISTRIBUTION OF ENTERTAINMENT

CHAPTER 8

LESSON 8.2

GOALS

Understand the different kinds of entertainment distribution.

Discuss promotional strategies for motion pictures.

DISTRIBUTION OF ENTERTAINMENT

In the early days of television, there were three television networks from which to choose. Now there are many more entertainment distribution systems. Traditional television broadcasting is still powerful at the beginning of the twenty-first century, but cable, satellite, and Internet distribution of programming are quickly grabbing shares of the market.

CABLE MANIA

DISTRIBUTION

In the late 1990s, the number of cable television networks, especially those with digital channels, increased greatly. The original cable channel space was limited, but digital technology allowed more channels to be added.

Cable television programs at stations throughout the country are picked up by a master antenna and delivered to homes though cables. Homeowners subscribe to a service that includes installation of the equipment (a separate one-time cost) and a monthly fee. Fees start around $7 for a small package of only local channels and go up as the packages offerings increase.

Cable programmers promote their newest shows at the Western Cable Show in Anaheim, CA, each year in December with the hope of getting their new shows into the viewer packages offered by cable operators. The new channels also target specific demographic markets. For example,

the Fox Family Channel offers the *girlzChannel* and the *boyzChannel* aimed at the junior-high-age market. In July 1999, Cabletelevision Advertising Bureau reported that 80 percent of American homes had cable hook-up, and that cable viewing had surpassed traditional network viewing.

SATELLITE TELEVISION

Satellite TV competes with cable in areas where cable is available, but it is the only way for people in rural areas to receive many or sometimes any stations. Consumers who want satellite access must buy a dish, starting around $130, and then subscribe to a monthly service. That cost begins around $20 and increases with the number of channels added.

The satellite industry is predicted to grow to 40 million households by 2007. Offering more than 200 channels and reaching viewers cable cannot reach, satellite TV is another valuable avenue for marketers. Consumers who live far from shopping areas can learn about products through television and then buy through the Internet or by phone or mail. One drawback of satellite TV is that the dishes often cannot pick up transmissions from local stations.

INTERNET ENTERTAINMENT

SportsPrize Entertainment Inc. is a web-based company that markets sports information, interactive games and tournaments, chat rooms, and sports-related merchandise online. Revenue is generated through advertisements and retail sales of merchandise as well as through merchandise auctions. Selling through the Internet is called **e-commerce.**

One goal of SportsPrize.com is to create a community of sports fans on the Internet. Its primary audience is 25-to-54-year-old males who are college graduates with a household income of more than $70,000. SportsPrize.com maintains a strict privacy policy, but with the permission of the site user, gives the user's interests to marketers. Marketers then prepare advertising campaigns geared toward those users. With 320 million Internet users expected by 2002, and 55 million of those being Internet shoppers, the Internet is becoming the most valuable place to advertise.

T he Federal Communications Commission recently approved a device called the V-chip. The V-chip allows consumers to screen TV programs based on a rating system. All new sets come with a V-chip.

Television networks have a system for rating programs. It begins with TV-Y for young children and ends with TV-MA for mature audiences only. Parents can set the device to block out certain rated or unrated programming, which could include news, sports, and local commericals.

THINK CRITICALLY

1. What would be the impact using the V-chip to cut off commercials?
2. Should TV ads be rated? Explain why or why not.

MEGA-DISTRIBUTION

Broadcast webs (not the World Wide Web) are groups (called *affiliations*) of television networks, production studios, and related entertainment firms that produce shows inhouse for their group. This kind of business structure, in which one company controls several different areas of the same industry, is known as **vertical integration.** Vertical integration is a change from previous distribution systems through which the networks aired shows developed by independent producers.

USA Networks may become a model for media companies in the twenty-first century. USA Networks merged with Lycos, a major Internet search engine. The merger allied those two corporations with subsidiary firms Ticketmaster-CitySearch Online, Home Shopping Network, Internet Shopping Network/First Auction, and Ticketmaster. The new company, USA/Lycos Interactive Networks, is worth more than $1.5 billion. The merger brings together 70 million television-viewing homes and 30 million Internet users. One of the goals of the merger was to create "cross-promotional opportunities." These opportunities allow the television giant to advertise online and the Internet provider to advertise on the television network. Most media companies depend on advertising sales to generate profits, but now USA Networks will have as much income from direct selling through the Internet as from advertising. Providing an Internet window to its related businesses makes USA Networks a front-runner among the media giants. The merger of USA Networks and Lycos has created a company with the ability to market both advertising and entertainment to the world through television, telephone, and the Internet.

INTERMISSION

What are the three major sources of entertainment distribution?

Cable television, satellite television, and the Internet

MOVIE MARKETING

Movies shown in theaters and movies rented from the video store include advertisements for other movies. These ads are called **trailers** or **previews.** Trailers are critical to attracting an audience. Trailers are rated and much attention is paid to what is shown in the few seconds they're allowed.

A well-coordinated promotional plan can wring out the last drop of consumer interest. Video retailers report that pay-per-view promotions for a movie tend to increase interest in the rental. The movie *Titanic* had fallen off the Video Business Top 40 Renters chart when a pay-per-view

Making products associated with a successful movie is not always a successful strategy. *Star Wars: Episode 1—The Phantom Menace* topped the opening day box-office record and the single-day record when it opened in 2,970 theaters in 1999. Hasbro purchased the rights to distribute Star Wars-related merchandise for $600 million. A month after the opening, Hasbro was disappointed in sales of the merchandise and prices for some items were slashed.

THINK CRITICALLY
Work with a partner. Discuss the promotional strategies used to market a well-known film and related merchandise prior to release. Share your thoughts with the class.

advertising campaign began. The movie jumped back onto the chart and then to number six in video sales for the week. Paramount further increased interest by introducing TV advertising aimed at Christmas gift-giving of the video and also a new point-of-purchase display at video stores.

In a brilliant promotional strategy, the producers of *The Blair Witch Project* developed a web page that made the story look like a real news story. Film awards and the Internet site caused word to spread quickly about the quirky movie. Prior to release of the movie, the producers updated the web page periodically and added short, intriguing trailers. The per-screen revenue for *Blair Witch* was over $56,000 compared with *Eyes Wide Shut,* the number one movie at that time, which had a per-screen average of $9,000.

A trend in the "kidvid" promotion is to bypass releasing movies in theaters and go directly to rental and sales of video. Family movies released directly to video include *The Lion King II: Simba's Pride,* which generated almost $10 million in sales with no theater showings.

SEE IT AT HOME
Movie fans no longer have to travel to first- and second-run theaters to see their shows. Videos are available for purchase at mass-market retailers, such as Wal-Mart. These retailers generally dominate the sales numbers through sheer volume. To help stimulate sales in music and video specialty stores such as Blockbuster or Hollywood Video, distributors often may provide **point-of-purchase (POP) displays.** The POPs are set up by the checkout area and are an effective promotional tool.

Changes in technology cause changes in the format of a movie offered for sale or rental. Movies, once available to the public only in 16-mm film at considerable cost, are now available in new formats at lesser cost. Digital videodisc (DVD) players, for example, have gone down in price, and their sales have gone up. Also, the selection of movies available in the DVD format has expanded with the sales of players. Sales of DVD players may have caused the sales of videotapes to take a downturn in 1998.

INTERMISSION

Describe several ways movies are marketed.

Answers will vary. Trailers, pay-per-view, POP display, direct-to-video releases,

TV commercials, web sites.

UNDERSTAND MARKETING CONCEPTS

Circle the best answer for each of the following questions.

1. Technology Satellite dishes are particularly convenient for TV viewers in a
   a. rural areas
   b. downtown areas of large cities
   c. large subdivisions with underground power lines
   d. none of these

2. Selling through the Internet is called c
   a. cyber selling
   b. electronic retailing
   c. e-commerce
   d. none of these

THINK CRITICALLY

Answer the following questions as completely as possible. If necessary, use a separate sheet of paper.

3. You are a retailer who wants to target both boys and girls ages 10 through 13. You sell video games, movie videos, CDs, and other forms of entertainment technology. You are considering advertising on cable TV, satellite TV, and the Internet. State where most of your advertising dollars will go and why.

Answers will vary.

_____

_____

_____

_____

_____

4. Communication Write two paragraphs explaining which of the following entertainment sources you use most: TV, video rental, Internet, or movie theaters. Explain why. Discuss any promotions you remember from your last viewing.

Answers will vary.

_____

_____

_____

_____

_____

ASSESS
Reteach
Ask students to turn to a partner and discuss how audio-video entertainment gets to viewers. In other words, what are the distribution channels?

Enrich
Have each student write a multi-paragraph forecast of what entertainment distribution will be like in twenty years. Look for individualized entertainment delivered directly to the viewer wherever and whenever they want it. Look for original thoughts.

CLOSE
Ask students if they learned anything that was completely new to them in this lesson.

CHAPTER 8
LESSON 8.3

MARKETING MUSIC AND THEATER

Understand the promotion of rap music.

Explain two kinds of theater promotion.

Discuss the legalities of music distribution.

SCHEDULE
Block 90 minutes
Regular 2 class periods

FOCUS
Music, concerts, theater, and the arts are the focus of marketing in this lesson.

OPENING ACT
From its beginnings in black America, rap music is the music of youth beginning the 21st century.

Answers for Opening Act Cooperative Learning
Rap is promoted through sampling, which means that part of a new song will be included on a CD with a top seller. Cable TV and radio are used to promote rap. Cable TV and radio were added as rap became mainstream.

TEACH
Ask students if they listen to rap music. Allow them to discuss their favorite artists.

OPENING ACT

Rap and hip-hop are now the top-selling music in the United States, outpacing country by 9 million CDs, tapes, and albums in 1998. The musical style credits its beginnings in the early 1970s to Clive Campbell, known as Kool Herc. Kool was dubbed the original "break-beat deejay" because he was the first to recite rhymes during the instrumental part or "break" of records he was playing. Joseph Saddler took Kool Herc's creation further by inventing "scratching"—spinning a record back and forth to create a scratchy sound.

Work with a partner. Discuss how rap music is promoted. How has promotion changed as rap's popularity has grown?

TODAY'S TOP MUSIC

Hip-hop, the culture of rap music, took 20 years to become mainstream, but between 1997 and 1998, the sales of rap increased by 31 percent over previous years. This growth compares to a 9 percent increase in the music industry as a whole. Today's hip-hop culture has expanded from its African-American beginnings and now appeals to white, Latino, and Asian youth.

MARKETING RAP

Rap's use of sampling as a form of promotion has helped it become a huge commercial success. **Sampling** is the inclusion on a CD of excerpts from the music of other artists. Often sampling is used to achieve a desired artistic effect in a piece of music. However, sometimes sampling can be compared to a trailer in the movies. For example, Master P, founder of New Orleans music label No Limit, promotes material from new artists on each of its new CDs in the hope of gaining buyers from the samples. Sean "Puffy" Combs, creator of the Bad Boys music label, uses *intuition* to decide what is marketable. Puffy is credited with helping move hip-hop toward mass appeal.

MAINSTREAM RAP

Just as Hollywood is the home of movie production in the U.S., Madison Avenue in New York is the home of American advertising. Madison Avenue marketing firms like the revenue-oriented spirit of rap and have financed rap's move into mainstream America. Hip-hop singers and dancers were featured in television ads for such products as The Gap's khaki trousers and Coca-Cola's Sprite.

Sarcastic or political messages were the original focus of rap, but the content has moved away from revolutionary statements and toward entrepreneurship and social activism. Lauryn Hill, originally with the Fugees but now a solo star, walked away with an armload of Grammys in 1999. The acknowledgment of worth indicated by these awards helped rap move further into a commercially successful genre and away from consideration as an alternative form of music. Rap has come so far that Wyclef Jean, the lead singer of the Fugees, sang a solo at the memorial mass for John F. Kennedy, Jr. As rap artists focus more on messages that bigger record labels can accept, they are increasingly touching the hearts and wallets of consumers.

INTERMISSION

What change caused the hip-hop culture to become more appealing to a mass audience? Why do artists want mass appeal?

Sampling and a change in lyrical content helped hip-hop become more popular. Mass

appeal validates their work and leads to larger pay-offs.

The top five longest-
running shows
on Broadway and
the number of
performances as of
May 1999, were:

Cats: 6,949

A Chorus Line: 6,137

Oh! Calcutta!: 5,962

Les Misérables: 5,031

*The Phantom of
the Opera:* 4,734

PROMOTING THEATER

Broadway, "legitimate theater," has long used the traditional promotional strategies of advertising on billboards, radio, and television, and in up-scale or theater magazines and other publications. But two more unusual avenues are helpful in marketing the product—word of mouth and a class sponsored by Duke University.

LET ME TELL YOU ABOUT. . .

Word-of-mouth continues to be a major source of promotion for Broadway shows. New Yorkers who are excited about their city like to show it off, and tourists who have enjoyed their trip like to tell about it. For example, a Russian immigrant who drives an airport limousine once described his taking every opportunity to cruise down Broadway after dark. Millions of people share his fascination with the lights and the people on one of the most famous streets in the world. During his conversations with passengers, he recommends Broadway shows, and his passengers often take his advice. Additionally, talk show host Rosie O'Donnell is credited with increasing sales of Broadway tickets because of her endorsements of Broadway shows on her own TV show.

DO I GET A GRADE FOR THIS?

In an unusual promotional move, the Metropolitan Opera of New York (The Met) is generating its own new customers by getting non-fine arts majors to think about the arts. Offered through Duke University in Durham, North Carolina, and the Met, the program is aimed at college students who are pursuing careers in law, medicine, business, and government. The semester-long course meets in New York and includes attending 15 operas, 20 plays on and off Broadway, half a dozen dance performances,

PROMOTION

TEACH
The principal theater district in Manhattan is located on Broadway, between 42nd Street and 59th Street. Theaters located in this principal district are considered the premier sites for theatrical production in the U.S. Discuss live theater productions that are presented in your community or school.

Ask students why college students would pay for a course that promotes the arts. Would other students enjoy such a course?

New York Philharmonic rehearsals and performances, visits to museums, and talks with actors, producers, directors, and singers. Having potentially influential people gain knowledge of and appreciation for the arts helps build the future market for the arts. And, in a further unusual turn, students pay for the promotion!

INTERMISSION

Describe ways "legitimate theater" is promoted.

Word of mouth, university arts appreciation classes, posters, TV ads, newspaper ads.

DISTRIBUTING MUSIC

In the 1990s, concert booking and music distribution channels are transforming the ways music reaches consumers. Concert bookings as well as distribution channels for music are in a state of change.

CONCERTS

Prior to 1994, booking concert tours for rock groups was handled in one of two ways. In the traditional way, major concerts involved a three-part deal that included the agent, the promoter, and the artist's manager. The promoters understood that the United States was divided geographically, with each of a dozen promoters covering a different region. In the nontraditional way, there were "wildcat tours" that cut out the agent and combined the promoter and manager jobs. By the mid-1990s, Robert F. X. Sillerman bought out most of the regional promoters. Mr. Sillerman's company, SFX, now produces almost 98 percent of the major concerts in this country.

MP3

DISTRIBUTION

Marketing music to paying customers now competes with quality music copied for free—but often illegally—from the Internet. The pirating is done with a free software program called MP3 (Mpeg Layer 3). The $12-billion-a-year music industry is taking a hard

The copyright laws that apply to records, tapes, and CDs apply equally to MP3. Before downloading an MP3 file to listen to it, make sure the owner of the copyright has given permission for listeners to download MP3 versions of the song.

Take a Bow
Gloria Estefan has moved from refugee status to become a major star. Her popularity has led the way for new top stars such as Ricky Martin.

Think Critically
1. Gloria Estefan illustrates the universal appeal of music by having hits in Europe and Latin America.

2. Look for the design of the promotional campaign to include appeals to the audience in multiple languages if appropriate and multiple media.

3. Estefan risked alienating both Cubans and people from the U.S. by trying both kinds of music.

Ongoing Assessment
Use the Intermission as an opportunity to conduct ongoing assessment of student comprehension of the lesson material.

look at its way of doing business. The packaging of music, whether on a cassette or CD, or over the Internet, is a changing method of marketing. Many musicians are bypassing record companies to market directly to their fans through the Internet.

The practice has been for musicians to release CDs every year or so with a group of songs. On the Internet, musicians can release one song at a time. Musicians are setting up a new relationship with fans. Making money using this new marketing technique will be the challenge.

INTERMISSION

What are some ways of distributing music?

Concerts, MP3s, CDs, cassettes, CD singles, cassette singles, TV concerts, videos.

TAKE A BOW

GLORIA ESTEFAN

Gloria Maria Fajardo—now Gloria Estefan—escaped from Cuba to the United States with her family when she was a year old. Her family was running from the takeover of the government by Fidel Castro.

Estefan began singing for her father when she was a child. In 1975, she met her husband Emilio and joined his group, the Miami Sound Machine. The group was a hit in Central America and Puerto Rico. The group was not successful in the U.S. until one of their songs had hit the top spot on the European charts. After that point, their concerts were sell-outs.

In 1990, Estefan broke her back when a truck hit the tour bus in which she was riding. Many believed her career was over. But, in less than a year, she was performing again, as well as she ever had before.

Estefan has been influential in bringing notice to Latin music. She sold eight million copies of her 1993 all-Spanish album, "Mi Tierra." That and a later album, "Abriendo Puertas," were hits in Europe and Latin America. She has been criticized as "being too Latin for the Americans, too American for the Latinos," but she responds, "But that's who I am. I'm Cuban American."

THINK CRITICALLY
1. How has Gloria Estefan illustrated the universal appeal of music?
2. How would you design a promotional campaign for someone who is fluent in two different styles of music?
3. What risks did Estefan take when she tried both "Cuban" and "American" music?

UNDERSTAND MARKETING CONCEPTS
Circle the best answer for each of the following questions.

1. **Promotion** Which of the following is a promotional technique associated with rap artists? **a**
   a. sampling
   b. print media ads
   c. television ads
   d. sales pitches at concerts

2. **Promotion** A new and unique way of promoting the performing arts is through **a**
   a. college classes
   b. seasonal tours to New York
   c. Internet ads
   d. none of these

THINK CRITICALLY
Answer the following questions as completely as possible. If necessary, use a separate sheet of paper.

3. **Technology** Find a print media advertisement for a concert or play. Find an ad from the Internet for the same or a similar type of concert or play. Write a paragraph about the differences between the two ads. Write a second paragraph about the similarities between the two ads. Hand in a copy of the print ad and the URL of the Internet ad.

   Answers will vary.

   Differences include: Internet ads can include animation but are limited to the

   user's screen size. Print ads are static but can be very large.

4. **Technology** How can musicians make money if their music is free on the Internet? Explain your ideas in a paragraph.

   Answers will vary. An example is an artist selling ad space on the page where

   the music is available.

CHAPTER 8
LESSON 8.4

AWARDS AND ANNUAL EVENTS

Explain the promotional value of entertainment awards.

Discuss ways in which entertainment is distributed.

SCHEDULE
Block 90 minutes
Regular 2 class periods

FOCUS
As students enter the room, ask them to answer the following question in writing: what does it mean financially for a movie to be nominated for an Academy Award? After a few minutes, begin a discussion by asking students if just being nominated influences potential ticket sales. Introduce students to trade shows, another type of annual event. Ask students if they are familiar with trade shows in other types of businesses.

OPENING ACT
Awards ceremonies are a promotional tool for entertainment and a way of recognizing achievement in the profession.

Answers for Opening Act Cooperative Learning
Look for reasons such as fans continue to watch, sponsors continue to buy ads, generates lots of publicity, and adds a level

OPENING ACT

Annual entertainment award shows on television compete for the attention of viewers. The MTV Video Music Awards, CableACE Awards, Rock and Roll Hall of Fame inductions, Screen Actors Guild Awards, and Country Music Association Awards are just a few of the ceremonies with uncertain marketing value. The big four—the Grammys for music, the Tonys for Broadway shows, the Emmys for TV, and the Oscars for movies—overshadow all of these awards.

Work with a group. Discuss why the number of award ceremonies continues to increase.

AWARDS INFLUENCE SALES

Recognition by one's peers is a high level of honor in any industry. In the entertainment industry, recognition also brings money, current acclaim, and increased potential for future success.

THE OSCARS

The most famous and prestigious of the entertainment awards are the ones given by the Academy of Motion Picture Arts and Sciences. The 5,000 members determine each Academy Award, also known as the Oscar. An Oscar nomination is a promotional bonanza for a motion picture, director, studio, and star. A nomination creates exciting media coverage and significantly increases the number of ticket buyers. Many people want to see the nominated movies before the awards, and many others wait to see which films and stars have won. Nominations are also important because they're rare. No more than five nominations are made for each category of award each year.

Academy Award winners are almost always pictured the day after the award ceremony on the front pages of major newspapers. Both winning an award and getting a nomination have promotional value that money cannot buy.

PROMOTION

The Oscars have the second-highest TV viewership after the Super Bowl. The ABC network has purchased broadcast rights to the Academy Awards through the year 2008. In 1999, ABC moved the Awards from Monday night to Sunday night because Sunday is the biggest TV-watching night of the week. Now, perhaps following the precedent set by the Super Bowl, the Oscars program is preceded by a "preshow" that includes shots of stars arriving and spot interviews. In 1998, ABC charged $915,000 per ad minute during the Oscars.

The popularity of the Oscars ceremony and its ability to draw a major audience have secured the show a number of major sponsors, such as Pizza Hut and oil producer Atlantic-Richfield.

Marketing movies around the Oscars works two ways. Consumer attention is drawn by the excitement of pre-award publicity. The movie producers and studios themselves also advertise their films to the members of the Academy, through trade publications and the talk-show circuit. For several weeks prior to Awards night, studios spend as much as $15 million on publicity and marketing. A movie that wins Best Picture is likely to bring in an extra $100 million in ticket sales plus prestigious publicity for all concerned with it.

Best Picture winners that were also box office hits include:

Titanic, 1997
Forrest Gump, 1994
Dances with Wolves, 1990
Rain Man, 1988
Gone with the Wind, 1939

of status to the entertainment receiving the nomination or winning the award.

THE GRAMMYS

The National Academy of Recording Arts and Sciences (NARAS) is an association of more than 13,000 musicians, producers, and other recording professionals. The NARAS is internationally known for the annual Grammy Awards. Nominated by a committee, the winners are selected by a vote of the membership. There are 92 categories in the Grammy Awards.

A Grammy does bring a lot of attention to a musician, but it does not guarantee success or sales. Some winners in the Best New Artist category are never heard from again. For example, in 1989, the Best New Artist award went to Milli Vanilli. The prize was later revoked when the group admitted that they did not sing one note on their prize-winning album.

As with the Oscar, the accompanying publicity that comes with winning a Grammy cannot hurt the marketability of the winner. Just winning does not guarantee that fame and fortune will follow.

THE EMMYS

The Emmy is an award given by two branches of the same 8,000 member organization. The Academy of Television Arts and Sciences presents the Primetime Emmy for excellence in nighttime television, and the National Academy of Television Arts and Sciences presents awards for daytime television.

Emmy Awards, like all the other awards, bring significant attention to television shows, and the viewing audience can be expected to increase for shows that win or that have winning stars. For example, it is likely that ABC's late-1990s show *The Practice* picked up a significant number of viewers when Camryn Manhiem won an Emmy and dedicated it to "all the fat girls." Her surprise speech became publicity for a topic that had long gone unacknowledged, and it has brought excellent attention and a marketing boost to size-oriented publications, such as *Radience,* and clothing distributors, such as Lane Bryant and *Mode* magazine.

Alanis Morissette was just 21 when her album *Jagged Little Pill* won a Grammy for Album of the Year in 1995.

Michael Jackson won the most Grammys in one year (eight) in 1983. Seven were for his album *Thriller,* and one was for *E.T., the ExtraTerrestrial.*

Entertainer
Rita Moreno is the
only person to win an
Oscar, an Emmy, a
Tony, and a Grammy.

THE TONYS

The Tony Awards are named after Antoinette Perry, who served as the head of the Board of the American Theatre Wing. The awards are given to professionals in theater for distinguished achievement and not for "best" in any category. Since 1976, Tony Awards have also recognized regional theaters that have contributed to artistic achievement and growth of the theater. The ceremonies have been televised nationally in the U.S. since 1967. The Tony Awards are more of a special-interest award than the Oscars or Emmys because of the travel and expense involved in getting audiences to the plays in New York.

In the hope of increasing the television audience for the 1997 and 1998 airings of the Tonys, the organizers invited popular talk-show host Rosie O'Donnell to be the host. Ratings were the best they had been in ten years, and she was credited with having drawn new viewers. When she did not host the 1999 awards, the ratings dropped significantly.

INTERMISSION

What are the four major entertainment awards? Why are entertainment awards important?

Oscar, Emmy, Tony, and Grammy. Award winners achieve greater sales, attendance,

or viewership.

TO MARKET, TO MARKET

Getting potential customers together in one location so they can hear and see promotional information about products is the purpose of trade shows. Digital distribution of movies is one of the new technologies to have come out of trade shows. Annual events draw unique markets of their own.

TRADE EVENTS

Trade shows focus on businesses that are related. Studio executives, directors, producers, and stars from more than 40 different countries attend ShoWest, the world's largest annual gathering of motion picture industry professionals. ShoWest includes a trade show, seminars, and awards. The ShoWest Awards were first broadcast live in 1997. In addition to the

awards, the broadcast features previews of soon-to-be-released films that are a promotional gold mine for the upcoming films. Hundreds of press credentials are issued to journalists who will write about the new films and technology advances introduced at the convention. News articles are free promotion, or publicity.

Digital Distribution   One of the major advances in equipment that premiered at the National Association of Theatre Owners' meeting at the 1999 ShoWest was the digital projector. Current technology still requires movies to be mounted in film form on huge, heavy reels that are sent to theaters. Showings of the movies are limited by the number of copies a theater is provided. A theater could lose ticket revenue, for example, if it had only one print of a wildly popular movie, but had the auditoriums and patrons to show three showings at a time. *Titanic,* for example, often showed in at least two theaters in the same complex.

Digitized movies can be distributed via satellite, fiber optics cables, special discs, or, someday, the Internet. Digital projectors will allow theaters to show the same movie in several theaters at once. This, in turn, will create opportunity for larger audiences.

A drawback to the digital projector is its cost of about $100,000. This is compared to $30,000 for a traditional projector. Since the movie studios currently pay for making prints and distributing them, the theater owners want the studios to share in the costs of conversion to digital projectors. In May 1999, the movie *Star Wars: Episode I, The Phantom Menace* became the first film sent via satellite to four digitally equipped theaters.

Seasonal or Theme Events   Seasonal or theme events are centered in geographic areas. They market directly to the people who will attend them. In Edinburgh, Scotland, the Fringe Festival is a combination trade show and seasonal event. Started as a small show operating on the fringe of the Edinburgh International Festival, the Fringe has become the main attraction. In August of each year producers, agents, directors, and critics attend to see the new artists and productions that shape the direction of international theater for the coming year. As they shop for acts, they plan new products to promote. The actors and playwrights are selling their product. The Fringe has grown into one of the most significant annual promotional events for the world theater stage.

INTERMISSION

What is the difference between a trade show and a seasonal or theme event? How will digital distribution increase revenue for theaters? Trade shows focus on related business while

seasonal or theme events focus on the locality near the event. Digital distribution

makes it possible to show a single movie in several theaters at the same time.

UNDERSTAND MARKETING CONCEPTS
Circle the best answers for each of the following questions.

1. **Promotion** Entertainment awards are an important form of c
   a. distribution.
   b. information management.
   c. publicity.
   d. product/service planning.

2. Trade shows are promotion for a
   a. what's new in an industry.
   b. nominees for entertainment awards.
   c. special annual events.
   d. none of these

THINK CRITICALLY
Answer the following questions as completely as possible. If necessary, use a separate sheet of paper.

3. **Communication** Has winning one of the "Big Four" awards caused you to then see a movie, buy a CD, watch a TV show, or see a play because of the awards show? Explain why or why not.

   Answers will vary.

   _____

   _____

   _____

   _____

4. **Communication** Name and discuss the last nonschool annual or entertainment event you attended. How did you learn about it? Why did you go? Would you go again? Why or why not? Name any event sponsors you can remember.

   Answers will vary.

   _____

   _____

   _____

   _____

   _____

ENTERTAINMENT MARKETING CAREERS

OPENING ACT

The entertainment marketing business is much like any other business except that it is extremely difficult to enter. Applicants for positions generally always far outnumber the positions open.

Work with a group. Find an entertainment marketing job announcement on the Internet or in print media. What are the educational qualifications for the position? Does the position require prior work experience? Discuss what you would do to prepare for this job.

Discuss the preparation needed for a career in the entertainment marketing field.

Comprehend the skills needed for specific jobs in entertainment marketing.

GETTING THERE FROM HERE

Breaking into entertainment marketing is not easy, but there is always room at the top for people who are willing to prepare themselves, continue learning, take advantage of internships and other opportunities, and work smart.

MARKETING YOU

PRODUCT/ SERVICE MANAGEMENT

As is true with landing any job, acquiring an entertainment marketing job is a matter of marketing yourself. The first step is planning the product—you. This means knowing what you want to do and what it takes to get that job. Gathering the information about a group of jobs and using it to make decisions can give you the edge you need. Knowing the educational background, experience, and skills required is a must.

HOW TO PREPARE

Before you can market yourself for any job, you must first decide what you want to do for at least several years of your life. Then you must research the jobs that exist in that area. Knowing about the companies that provide those

SCHEDULE
Block 90 minutes
Regular 2 class periods

FOCUS
Discuss with students the level of difficulty they may face in finding entertainment marketing jobs. Can this class help them get ahead of the competition?

OPENING ACT
Discuss supply and demand in the job market as it relates to entertainment marketing. Ask why there are often more applicants than jobs.

Answers of Opening Act Cooperative Learning
If the Internet is not available to students, have printed information available regarding entertainment marketing jobs. For preparation for the entertainment marketing jobs, discuss volunteering to help related groups like public radio or TV stations or a community theater groups.

Finding a career in the film industry requires clever promotional strategies. One current strategy is to make a short film (just a few minutes) for only a few hundred dollars, duplicate these "shorts," and give them to agents and developers to pass on to studio executives. The shorts are an easy way to gain entrance to the film industry, and some studios are finding new talent through this promotional process.

jobs will help you decide whether that sort of work is for you. The Internet offers great opportunities to conduct research about companies that employ people in jobs that interest you. Other sources of information include:

- people you know
- company annual reports
- business directories such as Standard and Poor's *Register of Corporations, Directors, and Executives*
- college placement offices
- recent news articles

INTERMISSION

What do you need to do to prepare for a job?

Gather information about the job, take appropriate courses in school, "market yourself."

MARKETING JOBS

MARKETING-
INFORMATION
MANAGEMENT

The *Occupational Outlook Handbook,* a publication of the Bureau of Labor Statistics, provides an excellent overview of different marketing-related jobs. According to the *Handbook,* opportunities for marketers, advertisers, and public relations specialists will be among the fastest-growing in the nation at least through the year 2006.

The number of consumers who attended at least one live performance or art exhibit increased from 41 percent in 1992 to 50 percent in 1997, and similar increases are expected to continue. As the number of con-

sumers rises, so will the number of artists, performers, and staged performances. This naturally leads to a rise in the number of entertainment marketers and public relations specialists needed. Public relations specialist positions are expected to grow by 27 percent in the next ten years.

A general background in marketing, advertising, or public relations can turn into a focus on entertainment with some ease.

PUBLIC RELATIONS SPECIALISTS

Public relations specialists build and maintain positive relationships between their employer and the public. In a sense, a public relations specialist is anyone who looks out for the best interests of another. Public relations specialists' responsibilities include keeping the media and consumers aware of the company or person they represent. In the entertainment business, specialists might include actors' agents, studio press agents, and even an office worker who secures a contract for her film-site catering company.

The average workweek of public relations specialists is listed as 35 to 40 hours, but, as with many other jobs today, that can easily increase, with or without pay. Flexibility with daily schedules and the ability to travel are necessary. The best opportunities for PR specialists are in larger cities.

Most employers prefer a college degree combined with experience, but the experience can be gained through a college internship. Government statistics show that median (middle) earnings were about $34,000 in 1996.

MARKETING AND ADVERTISING MANAGERS

Even with the rapid increase in marketing and advertising jobs in the near future, competition is expected to be intense. The potential to earn high salaries exists, but long hours, including weekends and evenings, are common, as is the need for substantial travel.

Marketers may find themselves doing work they studied to do or work they never dreamed of doing. Their jobs are dictated by consumer interests at the time. Responsibilities of market research, strategic planning, sales, advertising, pricing, and product development may be included.

A wide range of educational backgrounds is acceptable, but many people get into marketing after acquiring experience in related positions. Salaries for marketing majors graduating in 1997 averaged about $29,000 for entry-level positions. The median salary for experienced marketers in 1996 was $46,000.

In the late 1990s, employers began posting open positions on the Internet. One Dallas search firm reports receiving about 100 e-mailed resumes per day. These numbers are expected to increase as use of the Internet increases.

While many companies have invited applicants to respond by e-mail, human resources personnel are annoyed to find electronic resumes to be sloppy and impersonal. Some job applicants do not include cover letters and fail to customize the resume or follow traditional rules for job application.

THINK CRITICALLY
Find a job posting on line. Then prepare an electronic resume and present it to the class. Write a paragraph explaining how applying for a job over the Internet might be different than applying through traditional routes.

SKILL REQUIREMENTS

In recent years, employers have begun to work with high schools to prepare students for the workplace. The three skills most desired of young employees are math, communications, and interpersonal skills.

Communications skills are critical in marketing-related jobs, and interpersonal skills are not far behind. In almost every marketing job ad posted, the job seeker will find the notice, "ability to communicate persuasively, both orally and in writing, is vital; ability to work as part of a team is critical."

Other skills needed on a daily basis in marketing jobs are:

- creativity
- initiative
- good judgment
- problem-solving/research skills
- outgoing personality/self-confidence
- understanding of human psychology
- enthusiasm for motivating people
- maturity
- resistance to stress
- flexibility
- decisiveness

INTERMISSION

What are the top skills needed in marketing careers? How can you learn and refine those skills?

Communications skills and interpersonal skills. You can learn and refine these skills

through high school and college courses and workplace experience.

UNDERSTAND MARKETING CONCEPTS
Circle the best answer for each of the following questions.

1. **Promotion** Keeping the media and consumers aware of a company or individual is the job of c
   a. an advertiser
   b. a marketer
   c. a public relations specialist
   d. none of these

2. **Marketing-Information Management** Which of the following are important for success in a marketing job? d
   a. communications and interpersonal skills
   b. psychological understanding and creativity
   c. self-confidence and enthusiasm for motivating people
   d. all of these

THINK CRITICALLY
Answer the following questions as completely as possible. If necessary, use a separate sheet of paper.

3. **Communication** Write two paragraphs explaining why understanding psychology is important in an entertainment marketing job.

   Answers will vary.
   _____
   _____
   _____
   _____
   _____

4. **Communication** Work with a group of three or four. Carry out mock interviews for entertainment marketing positions. What are some questions for both the interviewer (the employer) and the interviewee (the job applicant) to ask?

   Answers will vary.
   _____
   _____
   _____
   _____
   _____

ASSESS
Reteach
Ask students to discuss the personal characteristics needed to succeed in entertainment marketing. Talk about ways to enhance those characteristics through internships and volunteer work.

Enrich
Ask students to conduct an Internet search for entertainment marketing job openings. Determine the following for at least two jobs:

❑ firm name

❑ career title

❑ career description

❑ educational requirements

CLOSE
Ask students to list the personal characteristics that are critical to success in entertainment marketing careers. Look for communication skills, interpersonal skills, self-confidence, creativity, initiative, maturity, good judgment, and problem solving.

CHAPTER 8 REVIEW

REVIEW MARKETING CONCEPTS

Write the letter of the term that matches each definition. Some terms will not be used.

_f_ **1.** advertisements that accompany videos or movies shown in theaters

_b_ **2.** enables music downloads from the Internet

_a_ **3.** getting customers together in one place to hear promotion about products

_c_ **4.** people who develop products, sales strategies, and pricing for products

_d_ **5.** movie studios' decreasing the number of wide releases

a. trade show
b. MP3
c. marketing managers
d. cost-cutting strategy
e. satellite TV
f. trailers

Circle the best answer.

6. An example of e-commerce is
    a. buying a book through the Internet.
    b. downloading music from the Internet.
    c. researching the day's stock quotations through the Internet.
    d. none of these

a

7. Calculating film revenue includes looking at income from
    a. ancillary rights and ticket sales in the United States.
    b. merchandising and global releases.
    c. soundtracks and relationships to theme parks.
    d. all of these

d

8. Sponsorship of stock car racing is different from that of other entertainment and sports because
    a. stock car racers have only one sponsor.
    b. tobacco sponsorship is prohibited.
    c. racing fans tend to buy products from the stock car sponsors.
    d. none of these

a

9. Contributing to the "softening" of rap music was/were
    a. the murders of two primary stars.
    b. the loss of audiences who could not identify with the rap message.
    c. the influence of Madison Avenue on mainstreaming rap.
    d. all of these

c

THINK CRITICALLY

10. Name three benefits to the viewer/consumer of a television show or channel devoted entirely to that person's market segment. For example, what benefits, both in entertainment and marketing, do the boyzChannel and the girlzChannel provide?

Viewer becomes familiar with products intended for his or her use. Viewers' tastes in

programming are catered to. Viewers' time is not wasted on ads for products they will

never use.

11. Some movie theaters now run ads for local businesses before the movies start. Would you advertise this way if you had a business? Why or why not?

Answers will vary.

12. Parents in every generation are shocked by the music of their children. What might your parents find shocking about your favorite music? Prepare a one-page promotional piece to persuade your parents that your music has value and that will make them want to buy the music.

Answers will vary.

CHAPTER 8 REVIEW

MAKE CONNECTIONS

13. Mathematics   A local band with five members has the following expenses: renting a recording studio for $2,400; release of a song over a web site for $5,000; duplication and packaging of a CD at $50,000 for 20,000 copies; advertising and distribution costs of $62,000; agent and songwriter fees of 10 percent of all gross sales. If the CD sells for $15.00 per copy, how many copies will have to be sold in order to clear $10,000 for each member of the band?

$10,000 × 5 band members = $50,000; $2,400 + 5,000 + 50,000 + 62,000 = $119,400

total costs; $119,400 + 50,000 = $169,400 needed to clear; $15 × 0.1 = $1.50 per copy

in agent and songwriter fees; $15.00 − $1.50 = $13.50 gross profit per CD

$169,400 ÷ 13.50 = 12,548.15; The band will need to sell 12,549 copies to clear

$10,000 per band member.

The *Sports and Entertainment Marketing* Teacher's Resource CD includes a spreadsheet

template to help students complete this activity. Look for the file p194 Make Connections-

Mathematics.xls Office Templates folder, or the file p194 Conx.txt in Text Templates folder.

14. Communication   Describe what you think are the most important changes taking place in the early twenty-first century in movie marketing. Cite at least two sources of information.

Answers will vary.

Examples will include film festivals and promotion via the Internet

15. Communications   Use the Internet to research MP3. Write an "antipromotional" piece about it. That is, write a one-page paper advertisement that will persuade people not to use MP3 technology.

Answers will vary.

16. Technology Research the impact of direct broadcast satellite on TV broadcasting. Write a one-page paper summarizing your research. Include information about how marketing of TV programs has changed due to direct broadcast satellite and the impact on local advertising. Discuss the potential impact of the Internet on TV programming.

Answers will vary.

_____

_____

_____

_____

_____

_____

_____

PROJECT EXTRA INNINGS

Choose one entertainment marketing career to research. Using the Internet and/or library for your research, write a story about what your life would be like upon graduation from high school if you were to prepare for and actually work in that career.

Work with a group and complete the following activities.

1. Describe the education or post-secondary training needed to secure an entry-level position.

2. Discuss the outlook for the job as far as expected increase or decrease in number of openings.

3. Discover the city or state where the most job openings will be available.

4. Find out the current entry-level salary range and the salary range for experienced workers.

5. Research living expenses for the city to which you'll need to move.

6. Learn what you will do during a routine workday.

7. Learn about non-routine workdays.

8. Present the information to the class in a three-minute presentation. Use presentation software such as PowerPoint to develop your presentation.

EXTRA INNINGS

Students will need access to the Internet and/or library to successfully complete this project. Students will need access to the software program PowerPoint to use in making the presentation. Students may need some review of how to use PowerPoint.

Students will need time to develop the presentation. Setting up checks along the way may help some get started and stay on track. Set interim deadlines for when the following are due:

❑ Career to be researched

❑ Outline of topic

❑ Preliminary PowerPoint presentation

❑ Date of final presentation

The _Sports and Entertainment Marketing_ Teacher's Resource CD includes a presentation template to help students complete this activity.

Look for the file p195 Extra Innings.ppt in the Office Templates folder, or the file p195 XInn.rtf in the Text Templates folder.

CHAPTER 9

MARKETING ENTERTAINMENT

LESSONS

9.1 CUSTOMIZED ENTERTAINMENT

9.2 ENTERTAINMENT TECHNOLOGY AND MARKETING

9.3 WORLD ENTERTAINMENT MARKETING

THE MOUSE VERSUS THE REMOTE

Until 1999, the Internet was not considered a serious threat to television. Viewing video online was too slow and often frustrating. But Digital Entertainment Network (DEN), taking advantage of new technology, launched an entertainment network on the Internet. DEN offers a variety of programs that last six minutes and that are accompanied by 15 minutes of interactive content. DEN's goal is to replace TV as the main entertainment medium.

DEN attracted sponsors such as Ford and Pepsi by offering product placement in the shows as well as endorsements from the program stars. Ford vehicles are promoted throughout the programming. The team working with this revolutionary network includes former Disney president David Neuman and former Ladies Professional Golf Association commissioner Jim Ritts. The rest of the staff is a fusion of programmers, actors, and writers. DEN plans to keep the cost of production of a program episode to as little as $15,000. An episode of a popular TV show such as ER can cost millions.

DEN programming uses a format called narrowcasting. The program content is directed toward niche audiences rather than toward age groups as is most TV programming. The shows are archived for later viewing and are offered in multiple languages.

THINK CRITICALLY

1. What challenges face Digital Entertainment Network in achieving continued success?
2. To what demographic group is DEN targeted?
3. Name some products that might be advertised at DEN's web site.

WINNING STRATEGIES
Ask students if they believe the Internet will replace TV.

Think Critically
1. Among the challenges that face DEN are producing ads that are as interesting as the shows, the lack of technology in people's home, the time it takes on older computers to download video, getting the attention of potential audiences, and standing out from other web sites.

2. DEN is focused on young people aged 12 to 30.

3. DEN's web site will advertise Pepsi and Ford as long as they are sponsors. Students should look for non-competitors of Ford and Pepsi, but whose products appeal to the age group.

CHAPTER 9
LESSON 9.1

CUSTOMIZED ENTERTAINMENT

GOALS

Explain customizing entertainment products for a market segment.

Describe customized entertainment marketing for Baby Boomers.

OPENING ACT

For more than a decade, regional corporations have been replacing neighborhood movie theaters with cineplexes containing as many as 30 screens. Magic Johnson, a retired basketball legend, created Magic Johnson Theaters as a way of counteracting this trend. Johnson chooses the locations of his theaters based on the economic needs of minority neighborhoods. By January 2000, four theaters were to be open, one each in Atlanta, Los Angeles, Houston, and Washington, D.C. Johnson wants his theaters to be community centers, focused on distribution of a personalized service to a market segment. Customizing allows marketers to promote to a small segment of the population.

Work with a group. Discuss marketing information Magic Johnson would need to determine locations for more theaters.

CUSTOMIZING PRODUCTS

MARKETING-INFORMATION MANAGEMENT

A **market segment** is a group of people who have the ability and the desire to purchase a specific product. One of the first steps in developing the market mix for a particular entertainment product is to collect marketing information about the largest market segment for that product. Once adequate information is learned about this segment, product marketers can customize products or services to the tastes of the target audiences. **Customizing** is changing a product to fit the needs or wants of a particular market. For example, in the late 1990s, CBS television cancelled shows popular with families and women, and replaced them with western drama and sports series in an attempt to attract a greater share of the young male television audience.

LOCAL TV AMERICAN STYLE

PRODUCT/ SERVICE MANAGEMENT

Current product planning for the majority of national television shows takes place in Los Angeles. Planning and production of these shows are expensive and require a large audience to pay the costs. Local television programming, on the other hand, is generally considered of amateur quality and of no interest to viewers nationally. In contrast, Barry Diller, head of the USA Networks, which owns the Home Shopping Network, cable TV's USA Network, and TicketMaster, wants to customize services to market segments.

Diller has begun a new format of locally produced programming featuring talk shows with ties to local sports, newspapers, and magazines. This experiment began in Miami, Florida, on one of Diller's UHF stations. The shows are made at a fraction of the cost of nationally produced shows and are customized to the local market. The reduced cost requires a much smaller audience to make a profit, and simplifies financing. If the locally produced show is a hit, it can be duplicated in other localities or sold nationally.

LOCAL TV—CHILEAN STYLE

A locally produced hit among viewers in Santiago, Chile, has become popular throughout that country. The Catholic University Television Channel—TucV in Santiago—produces *Amandote* (Spanish for *Loving You*). The customized soap opera, starring local talent, takes place in easily-recognized restaurants and other popular locations across the city of five million and features shots of the city. *Amandote* might be of little interest in other markets, but it attracts a large local market segment of young adults.

MARKETING-INFORMATION MANAGEMENT

For local programming to succeed and attract advertisers, knowledge of the interests of a market segment is required. Management of the marketing information about potential customers provides the direction for the entertainment.

TEACH
Changing a product to attract a specific group to buy the product is customizing for a market segment.

Mass market TV production has been centered in Los Angeles.

Local TV connects to local celebrities and interests.

Young adults in Santiago, Chile, like to watch a local soap opera starring local talent and filmed in local settings.

Having access to data about the audience helps focus programs.

Ongoing Assessment
Use the Intermission as an opportunity to conduct ongoing assessment of student comprehension of the lesson material.

INTERMISSION

What are some benefits of marketing entertainment to a small audience rather than to the masses?

Answers will vary. It is easier to know and please a small audience than a large one.

MARKETING TO BABY BOOMERS

One of the best-known market segments is the Baby Boomers—the generation born in the United States between 1946 and 1964. These 76 million people will reach their peak spending level at age 46. The surge in Boomer spending began in 1993 and will continue to grow into the year 2008 when the number of 46-year-olds begins to decline. The impact on leisure time activities, such as entertainment, will continue the major consumer economic surge started in 1946 with diapers and baby formula.

BOOMERS WON'T RETIRE

Baby Boomers are expected to soften the line between complete retirement and work. Many will continue to work beyond normal retirement age, and others will serve as volunteers or will work part time. Some will do both since Boomers are expected to remain active throughout their lives. These people enjoy recreational activities, personal fitness, and all types of entertainment, from concerts and shows to the fine arts. Most important, these consumers have the discretionary income to pay for the pastimes, products, and services.

SEGMENTING THE GROUP

Marketing plans for an entertainment product are developed after careful examination of available data and research about the market segment. Knowledge of the customers' preferences, spending habits, incomes, occupations, and areas of residence can provide the marketing information needed to focus the marketing message.

MARKETING-INFORMATION MANAGEMENT

Marketers and product and service planners must be careful to create target or niche markets when dealing with a group as large and varied as the Baby Boomers. For example, those Boomers born in 1946 are starting to think about retirement. Those born in 1964 are worrying about how to get their children through college. According to the U.S. Census Bureau, the average age of the United States population in 1994 was 34; in 2000, 35.5; and in 2035 it will be 39.1.

The United States has a long history as a "melting pot" that welcomes all immigrants. However, for marketing purposes it has primarily been viewed as a white, Anglo-Saxon nation. This will be changing if the latest studies by the U.S. Census Bureau prove to be accurate.

The Bureau estimates the fastest growing segment of society to be Hispanic. This group is expected to contribute 32 percent of the nation's population growth from 1990 to 2000; 39 percent from 2000 to 2010; 45 percent from 2010 to 2030; and 60 percent from 2030 to 2050. By 2010, the Bureau estimates Hispanic spending in the United States will be nearly $200 billion.

THINK CRITICALLY
What does this information tell entertainment marketers and marketers in general?

UNDERSTANDING ALL PARTS OF THE GROUP

You must take care not to exclude a part of the group you want to reach. To assume that all the people in a large group have the same tastes in entertainment is a major mistake. The Baby Boomers are as diverse in opinions as they are large in number. The marketing message aimed at a subgroup of Boomers must be fine-tuned to meet that groups' needs.

Baby Boomers offer a huge potential customer base. Boomers will continue through 2020 to be a major target of entertainment marketing.

INTERMISSION

Why are Baby Boomers important to entertainment marketers?

Baby Boomers are important because there are so many of them and they have large disposable incomes.

TAKE A BOW

CRISTINA SARALEGUI

Cristina Saralegui is the host of the premiere Spanish-language talk show, *El Show de Cristina.* Seen on Univision Television, her show boasts 100 million viewers each day. Univision attracts 90 percent of the Hispanic households in the United States and its cable network, Galavision, has 10 million subscribers. *El Show de Cristina* has held the number one position in its time slot since 1989. Saralegui is a gracious host who puts guests at ease and encourages them to talk. She allows no rude language or outlandish behavior. Saralegui also has a radio commentary show, *Cristina Opina,* produces a monthly magazine, *Cristina la Revista,* and has published an autobiography, *My Life as a Blonde.*

As did so many others during the early 1960s, Saralegui escaped from the Castro government in Cuba with her family. In the United States, Saralegui had to fight for an education because her father thought girls' futures held only marriage. Eventually Saralegui secured a position with *Cosmopolitan* magazine, and formed a Spanish version called *Cosmopolitan en Espanol* that became one of the best-selling magazines in Latin America. Now, Cristina is a leader in United States-based Latin American television, and her future seems to hold anything she wants.

THINK CRITICALLY

1. Why should product planners and marketers take notice of Cristina Saralegui and Univision Television?
2. What marketing information can be gained from a study of Saralegui's audience?

UNDERSTAND MARKETING CONCEPTS

Circle the best answer for each of the following questions.

1. **Marketing-Information Management** An advantage to customized entertainment over entertainment for the masses is b
   a. more people will buy it
   b. it costs less to produce
   c. no information is needed about the customers
   d. none of these

2. **Marketing-Information Management** People in the Baby Boomer generation are important to entertainment marketers because they d
   a. have discretionary income
   b. are interested in leisure-time activities
   c. are expected to be active throughout retirement
   d. all of these

THINK CRITICALLY

Answer the following questions as completely as possible. If necessary, use a separate sheet of paper.

3. If Baby Boomers in the age group of mid-thirties to mid-fifties are the largest group in the nation, why is so much advertising aimed at the age group of 12 to 24?

   Answers will vary. People in the 12–24 year old group tend to have parents who

   are in their mid-thirties to mid-fifties who tend to purchase items their children

   want.

   _____

   _____

4. Break the Baby Boomers down into four different niche markets based on age and gender. Name two products or services to market to each niche.

   Answers will vary. Students must justify the selection of products or services.

   _____

   _____

   _____

   _____

ASSESS
Reteach
Ask students to use each of the highlighted words from the lesson in a sentence describing what they have learned.

Enrich
In pairs, discuss how marketing to Hispanic Baby Boomers may be different than non-Hispanic Baby Boomers. In what ways are they similar? Join with two other pairs and compare your answers.

CLOSE
Ask students to compare marketing to a segment and marketing to the masses. Ask them how technology affects these two marketing strategies. Look for answers to include differences in the content of the entertainment, the general appeal of mass entertainment, and segments entertainment as being more on the edge and newer.

ENTERTAINMENT TECHNOLOGY AND MARKETING

GOALS

Explain the impact of technology on entertainment.

Describe the need for balance between privacy and marketing information.

OPENING ACT

Companies doing business related to the Internet are estimated to have a combined revenue of over $1.3 trillion. Businesses that sell products online account for more than $102 billion of the total revenue and employ almost 500,000 workers. Online retailers include fee- and subscription-based companies, advertising agencies, and travel providers. Entertainment via the Internet is also expected to be an important market.

Work with a group. Discuss how Internet-based entertainment can advertise to attract potential consumers. Present your ideas to the class.

INTERNET ENTERTAINMENT

The rush to get brand identification for entertainment programming on the Internet looks like a Los Angeles freeway at 5:30 p.m. Everyone is there and going in the same direction—but very slowly. High-speed Internet connections are provided by few companies, and product planning for the limited slots available for entertainment is starting to be competitive. Successful video events that attract millions of viewers are finally taking place on the Internet. However, the entertainment is ahead of the technology. The Internet as a system for the distribution of entertainment is still being created, and consumers will determine its future.

COMPUTER-VISION

Televisions, telephones, and computers are converging into one communication delivery system. The information revolution is changing the rules of the communications business.

DISTRIBUTION

Bandwidth is the technical term for the capacity of communication channels. Improvements in fiber optics cable and use of telephone and electrical lines are expanding bandwidth. Expanded bandwidth and frequencies for digital television allow broadcast networks to deliver the Internet to every home that has a television. This is changing the distribution system for entertainment as much as moving pictures did one hundred years ago.

With increased bandwidth, users will be able to personalize television in the near future. Swiping a card on your computer/television set will customize what you interact with, see, and hear. An item seen during a show will be available for purchase on a parallel channel. Entertainment and product promotion will blend together. Hybrid retailers will offer entertainment that includes shopping and advertisements.

MORE ABOUT THE INTERNET

The Internet is an international network of computers. These computers provide access to information on practically every subject. In a sense, it is the world's largest library. It does not offer exhaustive information on every topic, but it is a good place to go for a broad view.

In order to enjoy the Internet, you must have an Internet service provider (ISP) such as America Online (AOL) or Microsoft Network (MSN). These fee-based companies make it possible for you to "surf the Net." ISPs, on their opening pages, also give you quick access to news, weather, sports, entertainment, health, shopping, and music. However, these are just a few of the services ISPs offer.

Full-length movies eventually will be offered on the Internet and will be shown on large screens. As Internet companies rush to make deals for movie rights and film libraries, video-on-demand distributed through the Internet will become available. The convergence of different technologies will require great imagination about their future uses in distributing entertainment.

JUDGMENT CALL

While in its infancy, Internet film piracy, a copyright violation, is a growing legal problem for the film industry. Internet film piracy occurs when an individual attending a commercially-produced film in a theater records the film with a digital camcorder and then uploads the film to an Internet site. This problem occurs most often on college campuses where state-of-the-art equipment may inspire experimentation. The equipment owned by most people does not have enough speed or memory to carry a full-length motion picture.

As the capacity of home PCs grows to accommodate super-fast connections to the Internet, the problem may spread. The Motion Picture Association of America is taking action to stop the activity before it grows. Infringement cases are turned over to the FBI as quickly as they are discovered.

Illegally digitized films will eventually damage legitimate distribution over the Internet. Deals between filmmakers and Internet service providers to stop illegal distribution are in development stages now.

THINK CRITICALLY
Discuss how Internet piracy can negatively impact movie fans.

INTERMISSION

How is technology changing the distribution of entertainment?

Internet portals offer instant access to information. Personalized programming will soon be available through the Internet also.

TECHNOLOGY

The Internet is a key component in changes to the entertainment marketplace. As the number of online consumers continues to increase, electronic commerce and promotion of entertainment-related businesses will see increasingly dramatic changes.

As companies move to merge TV and the Internet, viewers will frequently use programs that combine the two. ABC used television and live interactive Internet programming in its first sports event in January 1999. The Tostitos Fiesta Bowl included data, scores, and games from ESPN.com. Fans could log on to their computers, watch the game on TV, and, between the two, receive more information about the game and player statistics than had ever before been available in a standard game broadcast.

A major issue in the development of the Internet as a media for entertainment marketing is protection of privacy. Other changes in computer technology, including the use of cookies, are also affecting the development of entertainment.

Seeing-stars.com is a web site targeted to people's interests in entertainment. The site is promoted as a guide to celebrities and Hollywood. It provides travel information for people who will visit Hollywood as well as information about stars.

THINK CRITICALLY
Visit seeing-stars.com or a similar site on the Internet. Who are the advertisers and what are they selling? Discuss the niche market of this web site.

COOKIES, ANYONE?

From their web sites, electronic marketers gather such information about visitors as where the visitors go within the site and which ads and pages they see. **Clickstream data** is collected at each mouse click within a web site. A **cookie,** a small data file placed on the hard drive of the web site visitor, collects the data. Internet marketers consider the information they gather about consumers key to attracting the advertisers who pay the bills. Knowing customers' interests allows companies to focus on what customers want and who makes up the companies' market segments. Consumers must assume responsibility for protecting their own personal information. Cookies can be blocked or deleted from a computer after a site is visited.

CONSUMER PRIVACY

The privacy of customers and their right to know how their information is being used is an issue that must be addressed by the industry. If it is not, it will be addressed by federal legislation. There is a great deal of concern about marketing information gathered from children. Security of credit card information is also a concern for Internet shoppers. Despite these concerns, use is growing at a tremendous rate. The uses of the Internet for marketing will be limited only by the marketers' imaginations.

MOVIES OR TOY COMMERCIALS?

Changes in technology are blurring the line between movies and commercials. Recent children's movies have produced huge sales of related toys and other merchandise. *Toy Story* and *The Lion King,* for example, were toy-promotion bonanzas. The promotional plans for the toys were finished before the scripts for the movies were completed. More recent movies use 3-D, computer-generated animation and

graphics to integrate toys and plastic puppets with living actors. The technology to accomplish these high-quality special effects is improving at a tremendous speed.

In the summer of 1998, DreamWorks Studios released the movie *Small Soldiers.* DreamWorks executives coined a new word "toyetic" to describe the opportunity for merchandising toys related to the movie.

PROMOTION

Can you sell large numbers of toys and merchandise related to a movie that is not a hit? According to industry watchers, this is not possible. Making a good movie is the key to promotion. Kids have to like the movie characters and convince parents to buy. Parents will vote for or against a movie's popularity with the dollars they spend on the related toys and merchandise. A successful movie will invoke pressure from children for parents to spend earnings on the popular items. Giving personalities to inanimate objects through technology piques the imagination of children who are a valuable niche market.

INTERMISSION

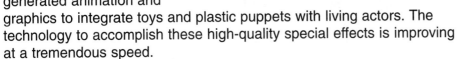

Discuss how technology can be a threat to consumer privacy. How do children's toys and movies serve as promotion for each other?

Data collected from consumers through the use of cookies is used by companies,

often without consent of the consumers. Toys can encourage children to want to see

a movie, or the movie might encourage children to want a toy.

TEACH
Ask the students to give other examples of entertainment and advertising that has merged. Look for infomercials from TV and products shown in movies.

DreamWorks is the movie studio formed by Steven Spielberg, Jeffery Katzenberg, and David Geffen. The promotional plans for the toys were done before the script for the movie was complete.

Cross promoting the movie and the related merchandise is a major revenue stream for the movie producers.

Movies are focused on a marketing segment and promotion is directed toward that segment.

Ongoing Assessment
Use the Intermission as an opportunity to conduct ongoing assessment of student comprehension of the lesson material.

UNDERSTAND MARKETING CONCEPTS

Circle the best answer for each of the following questions.

1. **Marketing-Information Management** A cookie is a a
   a. small data file placed on the hard drive of a web site visitor
   b. technical term for the capacity of communication channels
   c. collection of mouse-clicks within a web site
   d. none of these

2. **Promotion** The opportunity for merchandising toys related to movies has been termed c
   a. distribution
   b. a promotion bonanza
   c. toyetic
   d. none of these

THINK CRITICALLY

Answer the following questions as completely as possible. If necessary, use a separate sheet of paper.

3. **Technology** List at least four technology-related changes in the entertainment industry in your lifetime.

   Answers will vary. Examples include cable TV, satellite TV, HDTV, stereo TV,

   CDs, DVDs, and the Internet.

   _____

   _____

   _____

   _____

4. **Communication** Should the story idea for a movie or the merchandising plan for related items come first? Choose one of the two sides and write a paragraph about your opinion.

   Answers will vary.

   _____

   _____

   _____

   _____

   _____

   _____

WORLD ENTERTAINMENT MARKETING

OPENING ACT

In 1997, Viacom's Paramount Pictures produced *Titanic,* the number one movie in the U.S. Sumner M. Redstone is Chairman and CEO of Viacom, Inc. Redstone believes there are billions of dollars waiting around the world for American entertainment and information. Under Redstone's leadership, Viacom is seeking a worldwide audience through Viacom's varied "power" shows and movies. He believes there is little difference in the likes and dislikes of people throughout the world.

Work with a group. Discuss whether you agree with Sumner M. Redstone. Are people's tastes similar enough that one leisure entertainment product will sell well all over the world?

Examine the global marketing of entertainment.

Understand global distribution of entertainment.

GLOBAL MARKETING

DISTRIBUTION

Entertainment is distributed throughout the world. A Singapore newspaper features a story about a film festival in Scotland, and a TV entertainment feature in Chile talks about a musician's performance in Germany. The Public Broadcasting System (PBS) in the United States shows weekly British TV programs. One of Viacom's brand-name channels, MTV International, is distributed to more than 300 million subscribers, with 59 million in Asia and 57 million in Europe.

CROSSING THE OCEANS

The British television show *Teletubbies,* seen on PBS, reaffirms Sumner M. Redstone's thought of world tastes being similar. A hit in the United Kingdom with adults and preschoolers, *Teletubbies* was first aired in the United States in April 1998.

Teletubbies was planned as the first television show for one-to-two-year olds. *Teletubbies* features the comical antics of four fuzzy, pear-shaped creatures. The stars, who speak baby talk and have TV antennas on their heads, attracted 2.5 million U.S. preschoolers during the show's first week on the air.

Talking Teletubbies dolls sold well from the start. Other merchandise promotions include Tubby slippers, backpacks, pajamas, books, puzzles, and home videos. Itsy Bitsy Entertainment Company is promoting the show in the United States. It estimates retail sales of related items at $2 billion. Teletubbies is an entertainment media culture promoted to very young children. The Tubbies also have a diverse following among parents, teens, college students, and others in both the U.S. and the United Kingdom.

GLOBAL CHALLENGES

Uncertainty about government policy in some countries occasionally chills the spark of interest in selling entertainment products in those countries. Although marketing information may show that the audience exists for a product, many countries want to develop their own entertainment industry. International products are discouraged through tariffs that make pricing exorbitant. France is particularly protective of its culture in the film and television industry. The European Union tries to reserve at least half of its TV programming for shows with a European origin.

The United States has no formal barriers to the import of audiovisual entertainment, but demand for foreign-produced entertainment is not strong. U.S. consumers show low interest in movies that have the original sound dubbed into English. Demand for U.S.-made movies dubbed into other languages is generally high, but U.S. creative property is not freely allowed into all European countries.

INTERMISSION

What does a global market mean for the entertainment industry? Why would European countries keep U.S. programming off TV channels in Europe?

A global market can mean greater profits because of wider distribution. European

countries might keep U.S. programming off their channels to support their own enter-

tainment industries and to limit the influence of American culture.

GLOBAL DISTRIBUTION

Today's marketplace is definitely global, and the trend is toward erasing the national boundaries that limit trade. Entertainment and sports events are becoming the universal language.

DISNEY IN EUROPE

Walt Disney took advantage of worldwide markets as early as the 1930s. However, World War II interrupted the growth of his international business. In 1949, Disney set out again to capture the European market for his cartoons and related products. He hired Armand Bigle, from France, to run the Disney distribution operations in Europe. Bigle's challenge was to convince merchants that using the Disney characters would improve their sales. Today, merchandise with Disney characters can be purchased in virtually every corner of the earth.

ELVIS IN ISRAEL

Popular U.S. entertainers have frequently enjoyed worldwide fame and marketability. Elvis Presley was one such entertainer, and the late star's marketability has continued after his death in 1977. Every other year, hundreds of Israelis gather at the Elvis Inn, a restaurant and gas station southwest of Jerusalem. The site serves as a shrine to the musician. The appeal of an icon such as the "King of Rock and Roll" offers a wide variety of opportunities to promote music and related products to people of many ethnic groups.

COUNTRY ALL OVER THE WORLD

American country music is popular all over the world. Nearly 400 million people watched the 1998 Country Music Association (CMA) Awards in countries as far apart as the United Kingdom, Australia, and Japan.

Also in 1998, the CMA tracked nearly 700 appearances by country stars in 29 countries outside North America. The top countries for appearances are the United Kingdom, Netherlands, Ireland, Germany, and Australia. The Kumamoto Country Gold Festival in Japan drew a crowd of 25,000, and Garth Brooks brought in 100,000 fans at the Barretos rodeo in Brazil. LeAnn Rimes was the first country artist to appear on Europe's favorite TV show, *Wetten Dass.* Her audience was 16 million strong.

INTERNATIONAL MUSIC

Many musicians from outside the U.S. achieve great success in America and around the world. The Eurovision Song Contest is a televised European popular music competition held each year since 1956. With over 300 million viewers worldwide each year, Eurovision is one of the largest live musical events in the world.

The contest is a stepping stone for many artists wanting to achieve worldwide success. Among the winners of the contest are international superstars like Celine Dion and ABBA. At one point in the late 1970s, ABBA was Sweden's largest export, topping car makers Volvo and Saab and appliance maker Electrolux. Katrina and the Waves were best known for their 1985 hit "Walking on Sunshine." They were able to revive a failing career by winning in 1997. Dana Rosemary Scallon, the 1970 winner, is now a prominent politician who ran for President of Ireland in 1997.

INTERNATIONAL SHOWCASE

Showcasing entertainment with an appeal to international movie audiences is the target of The Cannes International Film Festival. The event is held in Cannes, France. Cannes is well known around the world as a resort town on the Mediterranean coast known as the French Riviera. The Cannes Festival is managed by a nonprofit group, Festival International Du Film, and is sponsored by the French Ministry of Foreign Affairs and the Ministry of Culture and Communication. The purpose of the festival is to promote the film industry worldwide.

Producers and sellers of films from throughout the world come together with purchasers of films at Cannes. The event has been held for more than 50 years, and thousands of films are screened each year. The Marché International du Film (MIF) serves as the organizer for the festival. The Cannes Film Festival Board appoints a jury of prestigious film industry representatives. The jury reviews films selected by a committee whose members are also selected by the Board. The films are chosen from those submitted for consideration after being screened by the committee.

Cannes Awards are presented for feature films and short films, among others. Winning an award at Cannes can be a bonus to promotion of an otherwise unknown film. Although the awards and glamorous parties get the most media attention, the real purpose is film promotion to an international audience. Release of U.S.-made movies outside the United States continues to be a major source of revenue, constituting more than 40 percent of motion picture and TV revenues. Cannes provides U.S. buyers an opportunity to preview the best international films.

INTERNATIONAL SPORTS

The NFL Europe League is almost a decade old, and it seems here to stay. The NFLEL has six teams, one each in Spain, Scotland, and the Netherlands, and three in Germany. The teams play in Amsterdam, Barcelona, Frankfurt, Berlin, Dusseldorf, and Edinburgh. Nearly 48,000 fans turned out for the 1998 World Bowl in Frankfurt.

Television coverage of the NFLEL games is expanding both in Europe and the United States. In the United States, for example, Fox aired every regular-season game in 1999, as well as the World Bowl, live.

Among NFLEL's sponsors are Gatorade, Adidas, Sprint, and Kellogg. Expansion of sports and entertainment throughout the world is an exciting and lucrative new marketing channel.

INTERMISSION

Why are U.S. firms interested in foreign markets for entertainment?

Foreign markets contain additional consumers and thus additional potential revenue.

UNDERSTAND MARKETING CONCEPTS

Circle the best answer for each of the following questions.

1. The British TV show *Teletubbies* is an example of d
   a. entertainment that attracts all demographic groups.
   b. entertainment revenue that is possible in the world market.
   c. world TV viewing tastes being similar.
   d. all of these

2. **Distribution**   Entertainment created in the United States is sometimes hard to market in other countries because a
   a. other countries want to develop their own entertainment.
   b. citizens of other countries do not like American shows.
   c. other countries resent U.S. barriers against foreign shows.
   d. none of these

THINK CRITICALLY

Answer the following questions as completely as possible. If necessary, use a separate sheet of paper.

3. **Communication**   In two paragraphs, describe what you have learned about foreign-made television shows or movies. What are some possible strategies for promoting foreign-made television and movies?

Answers will vary.

_____

_____

_____

_____

_____

4. In two paragraphs, give your opinion on tariffs or other restrictions set by other countries that reduce the chances of U.S. entertainment being shown in those countries.

Answers will vary.

_____

_____

_____

_____

_____

CHAPTER 8 REVIEW

REVIEW MARKETING CONCEPTS

Write the letter of the term that matches each definition. Some terms will not be used.

__d__ **1.** international network of computers providing access to a collection of information

__c__ **2.** tries to reserve half of TV programming for shows with a European origin

__a__ **3.** collected at each mouse-click within a web site

__e__ **4.** changing a product to fit the needs or wants of a particular market

__b__ **5.** one of the best-known market segments

a. clickstream data
b. Baby Boomers
c. European Union
d. Internet
e. customizing
f. cookies

Circle the best answer.

6. A form of American entertainment popular in other countries is
    a. classical music by American composers
b **b.** country music
    c. swing music
    d. none of these

7. Fee-based companies that provide access to the Internet are
    a. bandwidths
b **b.** Internet service providers (ISPs)
    c. search engines
    d. none of these

8. Internet users must be conscious of and protective of
    a. unsolicited e-mail
    b. Internet advertising
c **c.** consumer privacy
    d. none of these

9. A group of people who have the ability and desire to purchase entertainment is a
    a. local audience
    b. sampling
a **c.** market segment
    d. none of these

THINK CRITICALLY

10. Think of the businesses in your town or neighborhood. Choose one that could market its products globally. Make a short outline of creative promotional ideas that would appeal to an overseas audience.

Answers will vary.

11. Argue either for or against designing a movie around the potential to sell related toys to children.

Answers will vary.

12. Explain how a TV program might benefit from a simultaneous Internet program.

Answers will vary. Sports viewers can find additional statistical information.

Advertisements on the web site can increase the show's revenue.

CHAPTER
REVIEW

Make Connections

For exercise 13, the *Sports and Entertainment Marketing* Teacher's Resource CD includes a spreadsheet template to help students complete this activity.

Look for the file p216 Make Connections-Mathematics.xls in the Office Templates folder, or the file p216 Conx.txt in the Text Templates folder. For those without access to spreadsheet software, there is a short cut. Students can add together all of the exchange rates and multiply that sum by the £50,325 to get the answer in dollars.

MAKE CONNECTIONS

13. Mathematics Businesses that market entertainment internationally may be paid in the currency of the foreign country. Assume you sell entertainment products in the United Kingdom. Assume the product you sell will always earn £50,325 per month at the end of each month. Assume also that your contract is for 12 months. Calculate your income in dollars for the year if the exchange rates (in dollars per pound) are the following: Jan.–1.655; Feb.–1.663; Mar.–1.672; Apr.–1.662; May–1.653; Jun.–1.649; Jul.–1.641; Aug.–1.632; Sep.–1.615; Oct.–1.629; Nov.–1.647; Dec.–1.659.

Earnings in dollars is calculated by multiplying the earnings in pounds by the exchange

rate in dollars per pound for each month and adding all the months together.

$50{,}325 \times 1.655 + 50{,}325 \times 1.663 + 50{,}325 \times 1.672 + 50{,}325 \times 1.662 + 50{,}325 \times$

$1.653 + 50{,}325 \times 1.649 + 50{,}325 \times 1.641 + 50{,}325 \times 1.632 + 50{,}325 \times 1.615 +$

$50{,}325 \times 1.629 + 50{,}325 \times 1.647 + 50{,}325 \times 1.659 = 83{,}287.88 + 83{,}690.48 +$

$84{,}143.40 + 83{,}640.15 + 83{,}187.23 + 82{,}985.93 + 82{,}583.33 + 82{,}130.40 + 81{,}274.88$

$+ 81{,}979.43 + 82{,}885.28 + 83{,}489.18 = \$995{,}227.50$

14. Communications In teams of two, research a movie made in the United States that was more successful financially in another country than it was at home. Write a one-page discussion of why the movie made more money in the foreign market. Discuss marketing strategies if you can find them. Be sure to cite your sources.

Answers will vary.

15. History Research the rock and roll "British Invasion" of the United States in the early 1960s. Name the first three hit groups. Describe how the groups were promoted to their target market(s). Discuss television and radio appearances, interesting elements of concerts, and ticket prices. Would their marketing strategies work for new groups today? Why or why not?

Answers will vary. Some groups included The Beatles and the Rolling Stones.

Promotional strategies include radio, TV talk-show appearances, and posters. Target

market was teenagers and young adults.

16. **Technology**   Use the Internet or recent magazines in the library to research Internet cookies. Write a one-page report that includes an explanation of cookies, including their pros and cons. Give an example or two of how companies use cookies to customize advertising to you.

Answers will vary. Cookiecentral.com is a good website for information about cookies.

_____

_____

_____

_____

_____

_____

_____

PROJECT EXTRA INNINGS

Each country has its own standards of acceptability for the contents of motion pictures. Imagine that you work for the marketing director of a new, but up-and-coming film studio. Your job is to research standards in a country and then advise your director on films the studio might make that would be both permitted and popular in that country.

Work with a group and complete the following activities.

1. Have each group choose a different country to research for movie marketing.

2. Find the addresses (e-mail or regular mail) for specific organizations or contacts who can provide information on entertainment content standards.

3. Write a letter or e-mail to an information source. Ask for information to be mailed to you about cultural factors or laws that would determine acceptable content for movies in that country.

4. Individually, make a list of three types of information a company would need to gather before attempting to market entertainment in another country. Then, discuss your lists as a group, and choose the six most important things you need to know. Use the Internet, library, or other sources to find the information. Be sure to cite your source for each piece of information.

5. Your group should make a five-minute presentation to the class about marketing entertainment in the selected country. Use computer presentation software, if possible, to enhance your presentation.

PROJECT
Extra Innings
Students may be given a list of countries from which to choose or allowed to select their own country to research. Products include:

❑ a letter or e-mail, which should be graded on standard letter format, found on the CD

❑ six types of information that the group will research about the country selected (the list should be pre-approved by the teacher before the research begins)

❑ sources of the information found in the research

Students should give a group presentation providing information about the country and the country's standards that might affect movie content. The group presentation should include all group members. A scoring rubric for the presentation may be found on the CD.

CHAPTER 10

RECREATION MARKETING

LESSONS

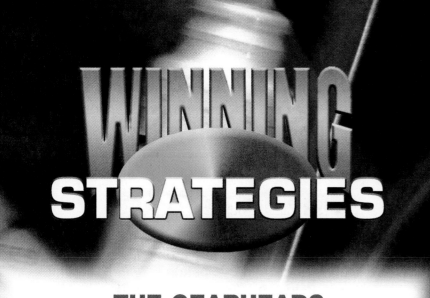

WINNING STRATEGIES

THE GEARHEADS

Started by friends in Seattle, WA, Gear.com is an online sporting goods e-tailer that sells sporting goods such as bicycling shoes, outdoor clothing, and golf clubs at 20 to 90 percent discounts. Gear.com works directly with manufacturers to sell the manufacturers' closeouts.

The staff at Gear.com has a passion for sports, and they test the gear before posting it on their web page. The president, Ken Blue, was in traditional retailing prior to helping launch Gear.com. He has a bachelors degree in outdoor recreation education and a minor in business administration. His interests beyond Gear.com include sailing, cycling, golfing, and mountain climbing.

Gear.com has no printed catalogs and no locations for customers to visit except the web site. This lack of overhead helps keep their prices low. Gear.com does have a constantly changing inventory of closeouts. Selected from manufacturers' overproduction or cancelled orders, closeouts do not include the latest items. Gear.com is in the business of providing quality recreational sports gear at very competitive prices.

THINK CRITICALLY

1. What pricing strategy does Gear.com successfully use?
2. What do you observe is different about Gear.com from other sporting goods retailers?
3. What risks does Gear.com have that traditional retailers do not have?

TEACHING RESOURCES
❑ CNN Video, Chapter 10
❑ CD-ROM Resources, Chapter 10

Winning Strategies
Questions to ask: Is Gear.com focused on a specific segment of potential customers? Why would people buy merchandise that is not completely up-to-date?

Think Critically
1. Gear.com uses low prices on closeout merchandise.
2. Gear.com is different in that it does not have a store or a catalog, only a web site.
3. Gear.com has the risk of buying merchandise that it cannot sell or return to the vendor.

RECREATIONAL SPORTS

Examine marketing strategies based on changing demographics.

Apply market information to recreational events.

SCHEDULE
Block 90 minutes
Regular 2 class periods

FOCUS
Why is a great deal of recreation marketing focused on Baby Boomers and older people? Answer—they have the time and money for recreation.

OPENING ACT
Ask the students if they know people in their 80s who are still active. Are the people in their 80s using the Internet? Mrs. Rothrock sends e-mail and buys airline tickets online.

Answers for Opening Act
Cooperative Learning
Look for answers that include traditional media like TV and newspapers and fitness magazines.

TEACH
Balancing the needs for recreational spaces and other interests such as protection of the wilderness or allowing housing to be built is a constant give and take.

OPENING ACT

Dorothy Kelly Rothrock, octogenarian, defies the rocking-chair image of her age group by walking, weight training at one health club, and participating in water aerobics at another club. "I belong to two different health clubs. I like the people at one, and the equipment at the other," states Rothrock. She frequently invites her water aerobics class to her home for lunch and a swim in her pool.

Work with a group. Determine what promotional strategies you would use to promote recreational facilities to active octogenarians.

FITNESS AND FUN

Health, leisure time, and money all drive the recreation business. Most people want to remain active and healthy all their lives. One challenge of recreational marketing is to motivate people to take action on their interests. Over the long term, high costs may reduce people's interest in professional sports. Smart marketers will fill in this gap by finding and promoting recreational sports that are affordable and attractive to the mass market. Traditional lifelong sports and fitness activities, such as golf, have the added challenge of attracting and keeping young participants.

FACILITIES VERSUS WILDERNESS

PRODUCT/
SERVICE
MANAGEMENT

As part of their regional planning process, community leaders must recognize the need for recreational space for local residents, comparing financial viability and demand for adequate facilities. They must also consider the environmental impact of recreation. Outdoor experiences such as backpacking, off-road driving, and rock climbing are potentially destructive to wilderness areas. Somehow, leaders and citizens must balance the two needs.

MANAGING CUSTOMER INFORMATION

Participation in recreational sports is related to household income. Families with higher incomes are more likely to take part in recreational activities than are families with lower incomes. Two reasons are the prices of needed equipment and ease of access to good facilities.

Managing information through a customer database is critical to the growth of any recreation-oriented business. Once pertinent information is recorded and analyzed, product planning and promotion can be geared to

MARKETING-INFORMATION MANAGEMENT

current and potential customers. Direct mail notices of equipment sales can be sent to current customers. A health club might purchase a sports equipment catalog mailing list and send the people on the list flyers promoting the club's introductory offers.

IS FITNESS A TREND?

Changing demographics are impacting the interest in recreational sports. For many people over 40, fitness has become a passion. The 1998 space flight of John Glenn brought recognition to the health and fitness interests of this age group. The Seventy-Plus Ski Club, in Schenectady, New York, has 14,000 members, and 400 of them are over age 90. The 1999 Senior Olympics, for athletes over 50, had more than 15,000 participants.

PROMOTION

More youngsters than ever before are participating in both school- and community-sponsored sports. One reason is the passage of Title IX, which prohibits discrimination against females in school sports. The NFL is attracting young fans to pro football by financially supporting youth organizations that include football in their training. Most professional sports want to increase the interest of fans in related games as a way of promoting high interest in the sport. The National Hockey League actively supports roller hockey and street hockey among youth and young adults, especially in warmer climates, in an effort to build a strong fan base. Marketing of recreational activities and equipment will remain a challenge through the next century, as recreational and sedentary activities compete for consumers' disposable incomes.

JUDGMENT CALL

Manatees are large water mammals that live in warm waters. Sizeable populations live in and around Florida.

In the last several years, many manatees have been injured or killed by recreational boaters, fishers, or polluters. More than 90% of manatee deaths are caused by boat propellers. Controversy over the rights of manatees versus the rights of recreation seekers finally became so heated that the federal government stepped in with endangered-species laws.

THINK CRITICALLY

Is federal intervention for protection of wildlife a limitation on the right of human beings to "life, liberty, and the pursuit of happiness"? Explain your reasoning. How would you market Florida's manatee areas?

INTERMISSION

How will changing demographics in the U.S. affect product planning and promotion of recreation?

Marketers will target the elderly and women more, as these groups grow in size and

in their penchant for recreational activities.

"When you're over the hill, you pick up speed," is the motto of the 6,500-strong Over The Hill Gang International (OTHG), a ski and adventure club for people over 50.

In addition to standard ski trips, OTHG offers adventure trips of bicycling, hiking, and whitewater rafting in several countries—but you can't go until you're old enough.

EVENT MARKETING

Businesses that include sponsorship of events as part of their advertising budgets must carefully consider the payback for dollars spent. Community leaders, educators, and the media who are involved in a recreational event can become influential customers.

Deciding which events to sponsor and the extent to which the company will be involved requires careful planning. Consideration must be given to the image projected by the event and how that image will influence current and future customers. A conservative investment-banking firm, for example, probably would be wasting time and money by sponsoring a local skateboarding event. Contributing a significant amount of time and money to an event should result in new customers or sales for the company.

THE FUTURE IS HERE

Getting ahead of trends is another formidable task facing fitness and recreational marketers. Thirty years ago, none of today's fastest growing sports existed. Inline skating, mountain biking, and snowboarding have evolved in the last two decades.

Promoting virtual adventure and fitness is a vital component of selling recreation in the twenty-first century. *Futuresport*, an ABC movie set in 2025, features air-cushioned skateboards. Today's high school students have designed disks on which adults can sit and propel themselves along with air jets.

SNOWBOARD MADNESS

As measured by equipment sales and visits to snowboarder resorts, snowboarding continues to grow as a recreational sport. In the past, snowboarding's growth was limited by geography and climate, but that is now changing faster than the weather. Snowdomes—indoor snowboarding facilities—are popping up all over the world. Tamworth SnowWorld, located near Birmingham, England, has a 150-meter slope inside its dome for year-round use. Two snowdomes were expected to open in the United States in 2000—the Gotcha Glacier in Anaheim, California, and

SnowValley in South Windsor, Connecticut. SnowValley has a construction budget of $300 million and will feature the longest and highest slope in any dome so far. Marketers are looking forward to thousands of customers—beginning with children as young as five—to lucrative equipment sales, and to a snowdome in every major urban area in the United States within a decade.

DISTRIBUTION

Marketers looking for new areas for snowboarding have found Santiago, Chile. Five million people live in and around this metropolis, which is surrounded by mountains and ski resorts. Chile's economy has been expanding for years, making it a prime choice for this new sport.

Although Santiago initially seems perfect for expansion by U.S. recreation marketers, there are some problems to be solved. One is the reversal of seasons in the Southern Hemisphere, which means off-season trade shows in the U.S. take place during the winter in Chile. Another is the local customs and regulations, which might be unfamiliar to marketers in the U.S. Marketers often hire local distributors to sell their companies' wares to local retailers, thus overcoming this problem.

INTERMISSION

Why is it important for sponsors and events to have something in common? How can marketers make developments in foreign countries easier? Without anything in common, a sponsor's

participation in an event is unlikely to increase the sponsor's sales. Marketers can

ease foreign development by educating themselves on the country and its customs

and working with local distributors.

The SnowWorld snowdome in Zoetermeer, near Amsterdam and Rotterdam, Netherlands, draws 400,000 snowboarding fans a year.

ASSESS
Reteach
Ask students to discuss recreational activities they participate in or in which they would like to participate. What attracts them to this activity?

Enrich
In groups, have students do research to discover an emerging recreational activity. What segment is it aimed toward and in what geographic locations? What would be the media for promoting the activity?

Close
Ask students to discuss why people enjoy recreational sports.

UNDERSTAND MARKETING CONCEPTS

Circle the best answer for each of the following questions.

1. **Marketing-Information Management**   A good recreational marketing plan for people over 40 would consider their d
   a. desire for health and improved appearance
   b. generous amount of leisure time
   c. discretionary income
   d. all of these

2. **Product/Service Planning**   Responsible recreation marketers must also note the need for c
   a. participation in big league-sponsored activities
   b. the inclusion of senior citizens
   c. the protection of remaining wilderness
   d. none of these

THINK CRITICALLY

Answer the following questions as completely as possible. If necessary, use a separate sheet of paper.

3. **Communication**   Write a one-page promotional piece about the creation of new soccer fields in your community. Be sure to discuss the destruction of ten acres of woods that must occur first. You must sell this project to all members of the community.

   Answers will vary.

   _____

   _____

   _____

   _____

4. **Communication**   Think of five billboards or TV commercials you've seen recently that either promoted recreational sports or used the sports as support for another product. What were the sports? What were the products being advertised? What were the target markets?

   Answers will vary.

   _____

   _____

   _____

TRAVEL AND TOURISM

CHAPTER 10
LESSON 10.2

OPENING ACT

Stop in any bookstore or visit an online bookseller. The number of travel guidebooks available is overwhelming. To promote the books to buyers, writers sometimes focus on specific groups of readers. For example, some books are aimed at niche markets, such as African-American travelers, who spend an estimated $25 billion a year on trips.

   Work with a group. Discuss why guidebooks often focus on specific groups of readers. Share the discussion with the class.

GOALS

Understand how technology has changed travel marketing.

Comprehend the magnitude of modern travel.

TRAVEL TECHNOLOGY

Technology is changing the travel industry. In the late 1990s, online travel sales were expected to liberate travelers from predatory pricing, particularly from airlines. This has not materialized because airlines set up their own web sites and capped commissions.

E-TICKETS

SELLING

Airlines offer rewards and discounts to encourage their best customers to use the airlines' web sites to book their own travel tickets—called **e-tickets**—rather than buy them through a travel agent. Airlines do not want travel agents to steer customers to better deals at other airlines. Most airlines have also capped the commissions they will pay online travel agents. The cap in late 1998 was five percent, or $10 maximum per ticket. Online agencies report a cost of around $21 for writing the average ticket. Online-only agencies must change if they are to survive.

LEAN TIMES FOR TRAVEL AGENCIES

Traditional, small, independent travel agencies with overhead costs of offices and staff are expected to lose profits because of the limits on commissions set by the airlines. The limits were set during a time when the general economy was running well and airlines were fully booked. Airlines may reconsider how they sell tickets if the economy falters in the future. In 1997, airlines paid $72 million to end a lawsuit by travel agents that had been harmed in the first wave of commission caps in 1995. Some sort of compromise may be better than long, drawn-out lawsuits.

   Despite the incentives to book online, 80 percent of all airline tickets are sold by travel agents. Travelers continue to prefer convenience and experienced, informed guidance in planning trips. People who travel

SCHEDULE
Block 90 minutes
Regular 2 class periods

FOCUS
Has the airplane changed the world's market for travel and tourism? What can you imagine that would be another major transportation-related change in travel? Has the Internet impacted travel? Yes, with the purchase of tickets online and trip planning.

OPENING ACT
Travel books are becoming very specific.

Answers for Opening Act Cooperative Learning
Guidebooks are like TV channels that are designed for specific segments of the market.

TEACH
Airline tickets are dominating ticket sales online.

Airline web sites are competing with online-only agencies for sales of tickets to customers.

TIME OUT

Some of today's popular, do-it-yourself Internet travel sites are bestfares.com, priceline.com, travelocity.com, and travelzoo.com.

If your travel plans allow you to be flexible, try these sites before you commit to dollars elsewhere.

PRODUCT/ SERVICE MANAGEMENT

frequently on business still want an established relationship with a travel agent, because agents save them time. One call to the travel agent can take care of airline, hotel, car rental, and dinner reservations. As airlines learn to sell on the Internet, they will learn to partner with hotels, car rental companies, and restaurants. When travel agents sell a complete vacation package, including airfare, hotel, and other add-ons, airlines still pay 10 to 15 percent commissions to the agent.

Despite loyal customers, though, the number of full-service travel agencies dropped more than five percent in the late 1990s. A one-stop web page where a traveler can conveniently book a package deal could deliver another devastating blow to many full-service agencies.

PRICE VERSUS CONVENIENCE

One online service attempting a one-stop web site is priceline.com. Priceline.com offered its stock publicly for the first time in early 1997. Its price opened trading at $16 a share and closed at $67 a share. That increase is a gain of more than 300 percent and an amazing vote of confidence by the public.

Priceline.com does not compete with travel agents because its focus is low prices, not convenience. Shoppers are asked to name their own price for airline tickets, hotel accommodations, and car rentals. The price may be right, but con-

venience cannot be a factor for the shopper. For example, to book a hotel room, the shopper is asked to name the city and dates for the stay. The shopper may not select the hotel, the location within the city, or ask for specifics such as a king-sized bed. Charges for the room reservation are immediately made to the shopper's credit card. When price is the major factor, priceline.com is worth a try, but the company will find it difficult to attract business travelers whose companies pay their expenses and for whom convenience is still a major issue.

INTERMISSION

Why do airlines operate their own web sites for ticket sales? How can travel agents attract customers away from web sites? Airlines operate their own web sites in order to encourage their

customers to buy from them. Travel agents can attract customers by being friendly

and offering complete travel arrangements, rather than just airplane tickets.

SMALL WORLD

PRICING

In 1998, international tourists spent $445 billion, not including airfares. The economy throughout the world impacts travel and tourism. For example, a good time to take a trip to Hong Kong is when its economy is down. Low prices in a country offer travel marketers a prime opportunity to sell to new customer segments. People who would not spend $5,000 for a trip to Hong Kong might take advantage of a lower-priced tour. A strong U.S. currency hurts domestic tourist trade by decreasing the number who choose to spend their limited time and money in the United States. In 1998, the United States dropped from second to third behind Spain and France in the total number of foreign tourists.

THE BUSINESS TRAVELER

SELLING

Airlines and hotels cater to business travelers, who buy last minute, high-priced tickets. They are a major source of profit for the travel industry, with business fares making up 60 percent of the airline fares. Business travelers are expected to pay the major portion of the increased costs as a result of the commission fee limits imposed by airlines on travel agencies. In attempts to promote to the business traveler, airlines have member-only clubs in most major airports. The clubs have membership fees in the range of $300 per year. Among other benefits, the clubs offer business travelers an office workspace and a quiet area away from the main terminal.

THE TOURIST

Family vacations are a booming business. The Travel Industry Association of America says 108.4 million U.S. adults took two vacations during 1998. Four out of ten vacationers travel 100 miles or more to a family reunion every five years. Fifteen percent of all U.S. adults travel to family reunions annually. Family reunions are a major incentive for the travel industry to market to adults.

Two other big sellers for travel marketers whose clients are adults are self-indulgence and culture trips. **Self-indulgence travel** includes luxurious surroundings and gourmet meals. **Culture travel** highlights historical, natural, or other special resources of an area. St. Lucia is one of the Windward Islands of the Lesser Antilles, located midway down the Eastern Caribbean chain. Inhabited long before colonial times, St. Lucia and its cultural treasures are a delightful mixture of past and present. This country's environmental conservation efforts are reflected in the stunning beauty of the location. The St. Lucia Tourist Board makes great effort to promote both historical and natural resources to tourists.

Additionally, travel marketers have a future with **activity tours**—travel centered around recreational

Youth hostels are particularly popular for young people who have little travel money. Overnight fees range from $8 to $17 per person.

MARKETING MYTHS

Many travel marketers believe they are helping the economy and benefiting the people
of an area where they send tourists.
Frequently, however, hotel profits do not stay
in the area, but are sent back to headquarters in another state or country. According to
Megan Epler-Wood, founder and executive
director of The Ecotourism Society:

"It is important for Americans to realize that
our travel choices make a tremendous difference to citizens throughout the world.
Entering into the travel industry is a special
responsibility, because you are not just selling travel, you are selling interactions between people, cultures, and environments.
When you market ecotourism or any form of
travel you are helping to educate consumers
about the wonderful diversity of our planet."

THINK CRITICALLY
How might ecotourism "begin at home"?
Discuss how you can practice principles of
ecotourism on your next trip.

activities. For example, Zephyr Inline
Skate Tours offers inline skate trips
to areas as diverse as Amish country
in Pennsylvania, San Francisco,
New York, and The Netherlands. All
ages and skill levels are welcome.
And for vacationers who want to
"rough it," a travel marketer can
arrange a cattle drive. Ranches
throughout the American West offer
trips back in time to an age of
horses, lariats, and food cooked over
an open fire. Such tours are a creative mix of recreation and travel.

ECOTOURISM

PRODUCT/
SERVICE
MANAGEMENT

Promoting ecotourism is
one of the fastest grow-
ing segments of the
travel industry.
Ecotourism is more
than nature tours during
which visitors enjoy the outdoors or
observe wildlife. The goal of ecotourism is "responsible travel to natural areas that conserves the
environment and sustains the well-
being of local people" (Epler-Wood,
1999). Ecotourism attempts to minimize the negative impact of visiting
sensitive environments and cultures
while helping the people of the host
country. Ecotourism involves local
people in planning the product that will
attract tourists. The use of locally owned lodging benefits the local people,
as opposed to a major corporation located elsewhere.

   Promoting ecotourism is a matter of educating the travel industry as
well as tourists. Protection of the areas to which tourists are attracted is
also self-preservation for the travel industry.

INTERMISSION

**Why does the economy around the world affect tourism
pricing? In what areas does the future look bright for travel
marketers?** Foreign economies affect currency exchange rates, which in turn

affect the price of tourism. Travel marketers have a bright future in business travel,

family travel, and ecotourism.

UNDERSTAND MARKETING CONCEPTS

Circle the best answer for each of the following questions.

1. Buying the right to a seat on an airplane through the airline's web site is called a(n) b
   a. Internet sale
   b. e-ticket
   c. web purchase
   d. all of these

2. The majority of travel agents' business comes from c
   a. Internet sales
   b. people traveling to Europe
   c. business travelers
   d. none of these

THINK CRITICALLY

Answer the following questions as completely as possible. If necessary, use a separate sheet of paper.

3. **Technology** Travel agents are facing declining business due to travelers making their own reservations through the Internet and to commission caps mandated by airlines. Name some traditional and creative ways agents can not only stay in business but also flourish.

   Answers will vary.

   _____

   _____

   _____

   _____

   _____

4. Where are two self-indulgence travel destinations in your region of the country? Who goes there? What are some of the expenses at these destinations? How are these locations marketed?

   Answers will vary.

   _____

   _____

   _____

   _____

Ongoing Assessment
Use the Intermission as an opportunity to conduct ongoing assessment of student comprehension of the lesson material.

ASSESS
Reteach
Have students look at Internet sites or travel magazines for travel destinations and determine if the site is an ecotourism site or not. Discuss reasons why or why not.

Enrich
Ask students to research what sustainable ecotourism means and to develop a promotional campaign that would raise public awareness of the importance of sustainable travel choices. Submit the campaign to the Ecotourism Society by regular mail or by e-mail to: ecomail@ecotourism.org

CLOSE
Discuss why people in the travel business should care about the preservation of locations where they send people.

CHAPTER 10
LESSON 10.3

RESORTS AND THEME PARKS

GOALS

Understand the importance of partnerships between airlines and recreation destinations.

Discuss the popularity of halls of fame as destinations.

Explain the difference between theme parks and resorts and their marketing strategies.

SCHEDULE
Block 90 minutes
Regular 2 class periods

FOCUS
Ask students if any have visited a theme park, resort, or hall of fame. Ask students about how they would travel to a destination that was more than 500 miles away if they had limited time for the trip. Is there a connection between success of a destination and transportation?

OPENING ACT
Ask students if they think Atlantis be could be considered an ecotourism site. Atlantis is not an ecotourism site.

OPENING ACT

In a fantasy recreation of the mythical lost continent of Atlantis, South African Sol Kerzner created a Caribbean island resort. Atlantis may be the largest island resort in the world. Located on Paradise Island in the Bahamas, it covers 600 of the island's 800 acres. Kerzner added a 1,208-room tower giving the resort three hotels, 100,000 square feet of gaming, dining, and entertainment and 38 restaurants. The newest hotel, Royal Towers, is two towers joined by a two-bedroom Bridge Suite that costs at least $25,000 per night.

The resort has a $20 million promotion budget. Articles began appearing in travel magazines and newspapers as travel writers rushed to view the $480 million expansion. In an effort to ensure construction of the resort, the Bahamian government provided subsidies in the form of tax breaks and the construction of a bridge that connects the resort with an airport.

Why did the travel writers start writing about the resort? Why was the government interested in building the bridge? Discuss the answers as a class.

TRAVELING TO DESTINATIONS

At the same time Atlantis opened, American Airlines cut flights to the Caribbean, announcing that it was dropping 20 out of 60 daily flights due to a shortage of planes plus robust action in high-fare business travel. Tourists usually purchase tickets months ahead, while business travelers give the airlines less lead time. Business travelers pay more for airline tickets and are more profitable customers. Airlines will often make decisions that benefit business travellers at the expense of tourists.

GETTING THERE IS HALF THE FUN

DISTRIBUTION

Some of the Caribbean Island resorts offer incentives of up to $1 million to airlines to keep air service at a reasonable level. Promotion of a resort is wasted if tourists cannot find transportation. Resorts and theme parks depend on airlines as a segment of their distribution system to bring customers to them. To this end, they frequently form partnerships to coordinate efforts.

RESORT TECH

Resorts and theme parks are following the lead of airlines and developing their own online sales of travel. At Disney.com, travelers can purchase travel packages for Walt Disney World. The web site connects to other Disney properties, airlines, and car rental agencies. The site has long sold T-shirts, videos, and other related Disney merchandise, but the direct sales of tickets and hotel rooms to consumers is a more aggressive push into electronic commerce. Other resorts and theme parks will soon follow this model.

INTERMISSION

Why do local governments, resorts, and theme parks cooperate with airlines? What is the advantage to resorts and theme parks of selling tickets and reservations online?

These partnerships are formed because increased air travel to a location is likely to

result in increased revenues for business in that area.

HALLS OF FAME

PROMOTION

As a travel destination, a hall of fame can serve as a basis for promoting tourism. Sports halls of fame cover every recreation from lacrosse to jousting, and from chess to marbles. The halls also include a multitude of nonsports interests, including the Rock and Roll Hall of Fame and Museum in Cleveland, the U.S. Astronaut Hall of Fame in Titusville, FL, and the National Museum of Racing and Hall of Fame in Saratoga Springs, NY.

A HALL IS NOT ALWAYS A HALL

Since there are no specifications for setting up a hall of fame, the sites can range from a simple display of information and pictures to a major complex. Attracting visitors is critical to keeping the hall alive. Getting a traveler to turn off the interstate and into the parking lot requires the perfect marketing mix—the right theme for the site, located at the right exit, promoted in the right way at the right places, and priced just right. Finally, everyone who visits must have a good time. Word of mouth is an excellent source of promoting to future customers.

A COMPLETE DESTINATION

The World Golf Hall of Fame in St. Augustine, Florida, is a golfer's paradise. It boasts 75,000 square feet of space, 32,000 feet of which are exhibits. Firms specializing in the design of halls of fame planned the building, and a firm known for premier exhibit designs created the display spaces. The developers considered the interests of golfers and nongolfers in planning this family destination. The World Golf Hall of Fame is surrounded by golf courses, resort hotels, an IMAX theater, shops, and residential areas. The Liberty Mutual Legends of Golf Senior PGA tournament selected a World Golf Village course for tournament play in 1999.

TIME OUT

In 1999, Louise Smith was inducted into the International Motorsports Hall of Fame in Talladega, AL. Smith began her 11-year racing career in 1945, won 38 races, and was the Hall's first female inductee.

Induction ceremonies into the World Golf Hall of Fame are conducted annually following this tournament. The World Golf Village is promoted as a vacation destination packaged with something for every member of the family.

INTERMISSION

Why are halls of fame popular destinations? How can halls of fame attract more visitors? Halls of fame are popular because the sports and entertainment they feature are popular. Halls can attract more visitors by forming partnerships with airlines and local businesses and creating exhibits the whole family can enjoy.

RESORTS AND THEME PARKS

Resorts and theme parks are also popular tourist destinations. Theme parks are thought of as family-oriented destinations, while resorts are aimed at adults rather than children. Theme parks generally have activities, rides, and other attractions centered on celebrities, characters, or entertainment that are well known to children. Resorts, on the other hand, frequently focus on a single recreational sport such as golf or other relaxation activities with or without the celebrity connection and children's activities.

Promoting theme parks means catching the attention of children, who have a major influence on the choice of destination. One major promotional ploy is to connect the theme park to movies, television, or other interests of young people. The integration of movies, merchandise, and destinations is now an entire segment of the marketing industry.

THEME PARK CENTRAL

The world's most popular vacation site is Orlando, Florida. There are seven major theme parks in Orlando that bring more than 40 million tourists a year to the city. The four Disney parks attract the majority of the visitors, with Universal Studios Escape coming in fifth. In May 1999, Universal opened a second park, Islands of Adventure, a nightlife complex with a water park and hotels. These multibillion-dollar additions put Universal in a strong competitive position with Disney as a travel destination. Disney is a world leader in this industry and is currently considering expanding into China.

Creating an attraction at a theme park requires planning and tailoring ideas to suit potential customers' needs (customizing). New technology has allowed the roller-coaster industry to cater to those who love to hurtle through space at speeds that make the heart pound and the stomach churn. While Universal and Disney have begun adding thrill-seeker rides and young-adult nightlife clubs, theme parks in other countries must have succinct promotional plans to attract visitors. Leisure and Recreation Concepts, Inc. has created a water-mist show at WonderLand, a theme and water park in Dubai, United Arab Emirates. Sunsets, dancing figures, and exotic birds rise out of the water, while colorful flashes explode across a lake. In a desert country such as U.A.E., a water show can quickly become the major attraction.

IT'S NOT ORLANDO

PRODUCT/ SERVICE MANAGEMENT

Between 1993 and 1998, an estimated 2,000 amusement parks opened in China. By 1998, 80 percent of the parks were losing money. Ten percent annual economic growth in China and a huge number of consumers eager for entertainment attracted the glut of parks. The parks have failed because of poor planning and an erroneous presumption of similarities between China and western countries. The theme parks were built an hour or more outside major cities, following the custom in the West. Very few Chinese have cars, and public transportation is generally not available to the theme park locations. The park plans were developed around inadequate or inaccurate marketing information about potential customers.

Attracting first-time visitors and getting repeat business will continue to dominate the marketing plans of theme parks and resorts. Standing out from the great number of choices requires a unique marketing mix.

INTERMISSION

How does a community benefit from a hall of fame, theme park, or resort? Why might a theme park fail? A community benefits from increased restaurant and hotel business. A theme park might fail if planners fail to consider their target market when making style, content, location, and price decisions.

The top three roller coasters in the United States, according to a vote by World of Coasters members, are:

1. The Beast at Paramount's Kings Island, near Cincinnati, Ohio

2. Magnum XL-200 at Cedar Point, near Sandusky, Ohio

3. Apollo's Chariot at Busch Gardens, near Williamsburg, Virginia

UNDERSTAND MARKETING CONCEPTS

Circle the best answer for each of the following questions.

1. **Promotion**   Resorts and theme parks use different marketing strategies because d
   a. theme parks want to draw children and resorts want to draw adults.
   b. theme parks focus on several activities, while resorts usually focus on one.
   c. theme parks are often tied to characters or celebrities but resorts are not.
   d. all of these

2. **Promotion**   Creating a promotional strategy for a theme park includes a
   a. getting children to encourage their parents to take them to the park.
   b. advertising in parenting magazines.
   c. customizing an idea to particular customers' needs.
   d. none of these

THINK CRITICALLY

Answer the following questions as completely as possible. If necessary, use a separate sheet of paper.

3. **Communication**   Write a paragraph explaining ideas for a unique theme park in your town, city, or region. Tie the theme to a special attraction of your area. How will you market this park?

   Answers will vary.

   _____

   _____

   _____

   _____

4. **Geography**   Select a country other than the United States in which to start a resort or theme park. List three pieces of information you would need to have before you construct your plan. List one marketing strategy for each piece of information.

   Answers will vary.

   _____

   _____

   _____

   _____

RECREATION MARKETING CAREERS

CHAPTER 10
LESSON 10.4

OPENING ACT

I n advice to students looking at careers in travel, Megan Epler-Wood once commented, "The more you see your role as an educator, the more travelers will be attracted to what you have to offer, and selling travel will become a much richer experience." Wood is the founder and executive director of The Ecotourism Society, an international, nonprofit organization with 1,500 professional members in 65 countries. The Ecotourism Society was founded to make tourism a tool for conservation of natural resources and sustainable development. Members include travel marketers, entrepreneurs, conservationists, researchers, and tourists.

Work with a group. Discuss what Ms. Epler-Wood meant by "seeing your role as an educator." Present a summary of your discussion to the class.

Describe careers in recreation marketing.

Develop a recreation marketing career plan.

SCHEDULE
Block 90 minutes
Regular 2 class periods

FOCUS
As the population in the U.S. ages, careers in recreation marketing should continue to grow. Ask students why they agree or disagree with the statement.

OPENING ACT
Travel agents can help educate travelers about conservation of natural resources and sustainable development that benefit the local people.

Answers for Opening Act
Cooperative Learning
Discussion should center on providing information to travelers to help them keep from harming the regions in which they travel.

TEACH
Recreation and leisure offers a wide variety of potential employers.

BUILDING A CAREER

M arketing recreation and leisure is a wide-open field for employment. The travel and tourism business is one of the largest employment areas in the world. Recreation and leisure marketing-related positions vary widely. Community recreation programs, campus recreation programs, sports clubs, fitness clubs, resorts, theme parks, airlines, and cruise lines are just a few potential employers.

PLANNING THE TRIP

Recreation marketing has a wide selection of career paths. Before you map the path to your new career, you need to know where you are going. Take some time while in high school to find out about some of the jobs and what they require. This will provide you the opportunity to plan and prepare for your career. When you know where you are going, you will know how to pack educational and work experience opportunities into your life.

WHAT'S OUT THERE?

There are marketing positions in every firm in the recreation business, although in smaller firms the position may include other responsibilities. The Internet has brought about dramatic change in the way jobs are located. Online job hunting sites such as Monster.com and Headhunter.net let you post your resume for hundreds of employers to see. Millions of people are posting their resumes each year and using the Net to search for the perfect job.

MARKETING-INFORMATION MANAGEMENT

The Internet is also a great source for finding out what's available. Employers post job openings as well as other information about their companies on the big job lists, industry association pages, and the companies' own web sites. With a few clicks of the mouse, information is readily available and can help you prepare for a job interview.

Newspapers, school and college career centers, and libraries are other good places to learn about jobs. One of the best sources of such information is people in related jobs. You can begin your career search by talking to people about the kinds of jobs they have and what they did to get ready for them.

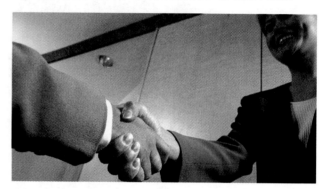

Another good way to research the recreation marketing business is to look at web sites for national agencies, such as Carson Wagonlit. You will also find a wealth of information by clicking on "travel" on the home page of your Internet service provider. Looking at such sites will give you a lesson in the style and flavor of travel marketing language and presentation.

INTERMISSION

Why is recreation marketing a good field of employment? How has the Internet changed the job search process?

It is a good field because there are so many varied positions. Through the Internet, a

job seeker can post a resume for hundreds of companies to read instantly and find

job openings around the world with ease.

GETTING READY

In the section on entertainment marketing careers in Chapter 8, you read about marketing yourself and researching companies with job openings. These same strategies apply to recreation marketing jobs and all jobs in general.

WHAT'S SCHOOL GOT TO DO WITH IT?

The education requirements for recreation marketing careers are as varied as the jobs themselves. Almost all require postsecondary education, and most require a college degree for advancement. Taking advantage of educational opportunities related to marketing while in high school will definitely send you in the right direction. Do not forget to include information on what you learn in your classes when talking with potential employers. In some locations, you may be able to receive college credit for

Businesses related to marketing women's fitness products are growing. Magazines, fitness gear, and fitness clubs are some of the growth area. These firms are looking for the perfect marketing mix to appeal directly to women. People who can develop this and other niche marketing strategies will be in high demand for jobs.

a high school class through a tech prep program. Talk with your teacher and the local community college to determine whether this is an option.

HOW ABOUT THE REAL THING?

Acquiring paid or unpaid work experience is an important stage of your career. Internships offered in the summer and/or during school are opportunities for you to see what companies really do. Working part-time will give you an idea if this area is something of real interest to you.

Sometimes an unpaid internship can be extremely valuable and well worth your time. Even **job shadowing**—spending active work time with someone in a certain job or career—for a few days can give you contacts for the future. Work experience of any kind gives employers a chance to see you in action and lets you meet people in the field. You should assume that everyone you meet is going to have a deciding voice in your next job, and you should behave accordingly.

TEACH
Students need to understand that they are always in competition for the positions that are open. They must learn to market themselves to potential employers.

Students should not forget to mention taking this class if they apply for jobs that are related to sports and entertainment.

This is a great time to bring up Tech Prep and articulation agreements for college credit with local colleges, if available.

Teachers should consider making connections with local businesses that might offer paid or unpaid internships for students.

Letting people in the industry know of your interest is an excellent way to start making contacts for the future.

Getting along with people is one of the single most critical skills. More people are fired for not getting along with others than for any other reason.

Travel-related jobs are a growing field of employment.

PEOPLE SKILLS ARE CRITICAL

Especially in marketing careers, managing your behavior is critical to success. Learning to appreciate your own worth and valuing the worth of others can lead you to tremendous success. Finding someone who motivates people and adopting some of his or her behavior will also help you thrive in your career. Adopting their behavior as your own will provide you with a tool for success.

TRAVEL MARKETING OUTLOOK

According to the *Occupational Outlook Handbook* published by the Bureau of Labor Statistics, employment of travel agents is expected to grow faster than average at least through the year 2006. Top reasons for industry growth are rising household incomes, smaller families, and an increasing number of older people who are likely to travel. However, the travel industry is constantly changing. The agents and agencies that will survive are those that can adapt to the new developments and technology in travel and tourism.

Most travel agents will not get rich. Expect a starting salary of around $20,000 plus commissions in the vacation-travel area to $30,000 and higher without commissions in the corporate-travel area. As with most jobs, earnings change based on effort and creativity. A perk for agents who like to travel is discounted fares and accommodations on their own trips.

INTERMISSION

Why would future employers care about work experience you had in high school? Why should you be concerned about professional behavior? High school work experience demonstrates

a person's interest in a field from an early age. Workers should be concerned with

professional behavior because employees are always being evaluated on the basis of

their behavior.

TAKE A BOW

JESSICA HARVEY

Jessica Harvey markets a naturally splendid part of the world. She is the reservations manager for Maho Bay Camps, Inc., which consists of four resorts on St. John, U.S. Virgin Islands and Florida. Maho Bay, an acclaimed ecotourism site, is the masterpiece of Stanley Selengut, one of the world's experts on ecotourism.

Ms. Harvey was attracted to Maho Bay by her love of St. John. Her college majors were marine biology and resource management for the resorts. According to Ms. Harvey, "Marketing an eco-resort and eco-development company is done a lot by word of mouth with lots of repeat guests. When you have a good thing going, people tend to seek you out."

According to Ms. Harvey, students interested in marketing an eco-resort may find that "it is not as lucrative as many other aspects of marketing." She encourages students to become thoroughly familiar with local and national regulations that may affect a property to be promoted as an ecotourism resort. Additionally, flexibility is a requirement for success on the job. The duties in a small office are many and include preparing press releases, scheduling group reservations, managing guest relations, and developing new programs. Jessica Harvey has the opportunity to be in touch with a beautiful environment while she is selling it to others in a responsible way.

THINK CRITICALLY
1. Why do you think ecotourism marketing is not as lucrative as other types of marketing?
2. How might ecotourism be marketed to travelers in age groups 12-24, 25-34, 35-49, and 50-plus?

UNDERSTAND MARKETING CONCEPTS

Circle the best answer for each of the following questions.

1. **Marketing-Information Management** Good ways to find out about careers in recreation marketing are d
   a. Internet hunting
   b. newspapers and libraries
   c. high school and college career centers
   d. all of these

2. One of the best ways to find out whether you like a career is to
   a. thoroughly research the career c
   b. learn people skills
   c. acquire paid or unpaid work experience in the field
   d. none of these

THINK CRITICALLY

Answer the following questions as completely as possible. If necessary, use a separate sheet of paper.

3. How could you build a career in recreation marketing in your town or neighborhood? What kinds of recreational travel would you promote to your friends and neighbors or to attract tourists to your area?

   Answers will vary.

4. **Communication** Think of someone you know that does not like to travel. In one written page, do your best to sell that person a trip to Hawaii.

   Answers will vary.

CHAPTER 10 REVIEW

REVIEW MARKETING CONCEPTS

Write the letter of the term that matches each definition. Some terms will not be used.

_f_ **1.** a career position expected to grow until the year 2006

_c_ **2.** recreation destinations catering mostly to adults

_b_ **3.** a major source of profit for the travel industry

_d_ **4.** travel reservations bought through the Internet

_a_ **5.** popular indoor winter recreational facilities

a. snowdomes
b. business travelers
c. resorts
d. e-tickets
e. theme parks
f. travel agent

Circle the best answer.

6. Eighty percent of all airline tickets are sold
    a. through airline web pages
 b **b.** by travel agents
    c. by airline reservation specialists
    d. none of these

7. A major annual destination for 15 percent of U.S. adults is
    a. a resort
 c **b.** a theme park with their children
    c. a family reunion
    d. none of these

8. The recreation business is driven by
    a. desire for fitness and good appearance
 d **b.** leisure time and discretionary income
    c. the high price of pay-per-view professional sports
    d. all of these

9. The attempt to minimize the negative impact of visiting sensitive environments is
    a. travel when another country's economy is down
 c **b.** self-indulgence travel
    c. ecotourism
    d. none of these

THINK CRITICALLY

10. Think of five people you know who are over 50 years old. What do they do for recreation? To what destinations do they travel? Ask them what influences their decisions about recreation and travel.

Answers will vary.

11. The Internet and airline caps on commissions have caused concern in the travel marketing industry. Explain the opposing view—that this is a good time to be a travel agent.

Answers will vary. Possible points include: there are a multitude of travel destinations and

options and there are many people travelling.

12. Explain the importance of customizing a recreational area to a particular audience.

Answers will vary.

CHAPTER 10 REVIEW

MAKE CONNECTIONS

13. Mathematics   You have been offered two different travel marketing positions. One pays a starting salary of $20,000 a year, but you have the opportunity to make more through a commission of 8 percent on every trip you sell. The other position is in the travel-planning department of an international corporation. It starts at $28,000 and has no commissions. If you take the first job, how much will you have to earn in commissions in one year in order not to regret not having taken the second position? How many dollars' worth of sales must you make in order to make that commission goal? How many $3,500 trips to Disney World will you need to sell to meet your commission goal? Show your work.

$28,000 − 20,000 = $8,000 needed in commissions to make up the salary difference.

$8,000 ÷ 0.08 = $100,000 in sales needed

$100,000 ÷ 3,500 = 28.57

You will need to sell 29 Disney World trips.

The *Sports and Entertainment Marketing* Teacher's Resource CD includes a spreadsheet

template to help students complete this activity.

Look for the file p242 Make Connections-Mathematics.xls in the Office Templates folder,

or the file p242 Conx.txt in the Text Templates folder.

14. Communications   Using magazines and newspapers, find a local or regional recreational event that has recently occurred or that will occur within the year. Make a copy of at least one advertisement for the event and write a paragraph about the ad. Describe the audience for which the ad is intended. Write a second paragraph about the companies that sponsor the event. Explain why those companies might have selected this event to sponsor.

Answers will vary.

15. History Use the Internet or print items in the library to research the history of amusement parks in the U.S. Search for marketing and advertising strategies. Find out the names of sponsors and vendors. Who patronized the parks? From how far away did travelers come? How did they get there? Incorporate your findings into a three-page report.

Answers will vary.

PROJECT ⚾⚾⚾⚾⚾⚾⚾ EXTRA INNINGS

Ed Boen is the owner and general manager of a small theme park, Thrillville, in southern Florida. Although Thrillville has been successful at attracting visitors—2.5 million a year—and is profitable, Mr. Boen knows he needs to add new rides or attractions. He has hired your team to develop a plan for improving Thrillville. Your plan will be presented in an oral report with visual aids. Assume the following costs:

- Purchase of equipment for a new attraction—$3 million
- Purchase of new equipment can be financed for 3 years with the $3 million in principal plus $600,000 in interest paid in 3 equal payments
- Additional insurance for the new attraction—$25,000 per year
- Additional employees for operation and maintenance of new equipment—$120,000 per year
- Operating costs for all existing personnel, maintenance, marketing and equipment—$87,000,000
- Ticket prices for admission to the park—$35 per person per day
- Thrillville is open 300 days per year

Work with a group and complete the following activities.

1. Brainstorm what the new attraction or ride will be.

2. Decide how you will collect marketing information to determine if the attraction will bring more visitors.

3. Develop a plan for assuring safety of visitors on the new ride or attraction.

4. Determine what percentage increase in attendance will be needed to pay for the new equipment in three years of equal installments. Show your work.

5. Develop a plan for promotion of the new attraction. Include an advertising plan, publicity plan, personal selling plan, and public relations plan.

6. Determine the budget for the promotion plan. Does this cost require additional attendance to cover the costs?

7. Present your new ride or attraction plan to the class using presentation software.

PROJECT
Extra Innings
Suggest students look for ideas in the information found in Make Connections #15 in the Chapter 10 Review.

For Part 4, calculate the increase as follows:

Ticket prices for admission to the park - $ 35.00 per person per day TIMES 2,500,000 visitors =

$87,500,000 current income.

1/3 equipment	$1,000,000
1/3 interest	$200,000
Insurance	$25,000
Employees	$120,000
Costs	$87,000,000
Total needed	$88,345,000
Minus income	$87,500,000
Amount needed	$845,000
Divided by admission	$35

Additional attendance 24,143 (Round up from 24,142.857) Divided by # visitors 2.5 million

Answer % increase = **.965 %**

The *Sports and Entertainment Marketing* Teacher's Resource CD includes a spreadsheet template to help students complete this activity.

Look for the file p243 Extra Innings.xls in the Office Templates folder, or the file p243 XInn.txt in the Text Templates folder.

The *Sports and Entertainment Marketing* Teacher's Resource CD also includes a presentation template to help students complete this activity.

Look for the file p243 Extra Innings.ppt in the Office Templates folder, or the file p243 XInn.rtf in the Text Templates folder.

CHAPTER 11

MARKETING PLANS

LESSONS

WINNING STRATEGIES

ONLINE WITH ADFORCE

Internet advertising is a relatively recent addition to advertising media, and AdForce is one of the dynamic forces in the business. With many sports and entertainment-related clients, AdForce provides services to advertisers, ad agencies, and online publishers of ads. The publishers are the companies that actually sell the advertising space. The advertisers include the firms whose products will be advertised, and the ad agency is generally the creative developer of the actual ad campaign.

AdForce assists advertisers and their agencies in selecting where to advertise, planning and scheduling ads, and gathering and reporting data collected from the ad campaign. AdForce assists web publishers in everything from setting up new clients to billing the clients.

AdForce was founded in 1994, and in 1999 had second quarter revenues of $4.2 million. The revenues represented a 433 percent increase over the same quarter in 1998. AdForce delivers over one billion ads per month and enables advertisers to run their ads on hundreds of Web sites while dealing with just one source. The service minimizes overhead costs for publishers and advertisers while maximizing the ease of setting up and managing an online advertising campaign. Finally, AdForce provides ad performance tracking and information through flexible reports. AdForce has managed to find an advertising service niche with unlimited potential.

THINK CRITICALLY
1. What are the differences in advertising on the Internet and advertising on TV?
2. What would be the major expenses for AdForce?
3. Why would a traditional advertising agency want to work with AdForce?

11-1 CHAPTER
LESSON 11.1

PROMOTION

Explain the purpose of advertising.

Understand the elements of promotion.

OPENING ACT

Network television has been a primary medium for advertising for the past 50 years, but it is no longer the major medium. The Internet and cable networks have taken a sizeable share of advertising revenue due to their capability of targeting specific consumers. For example, cable viewers include high-income/high-education viewers who watch the Arts and Entertainment or Discovery channels, while medium-income/average-education viewers watch USA or TNT. And BET Holding, operator of four cable channels and magazines focusing on African-Americans, has started an online service.

Work with a group. Identify three sports or entertainment advertising campaigns that are focused on a targeted audience. How could the ads be revised to target a different audience?

PROMOTING YOUR PRODUCTS

PROMOTION

Promotion is the most visible of the marketing functions. **Promotion** is communicating with a customer through advertising, publicity, sales promotion, or personal selling. Promotion is directly linked to a company's **image,** which is how a company wants the public to perceive it. Sports and entertainment are used to promote all types of clothing and shoes through the endorsement of an athlete or entertainer.

FOCUS THE ADS

MARKETING-INFORMATION MANAGEMENT

Before developing a promotional plan for a sports team or entertainment event, you must decide who will be the targeted customer group. Marketing research provides information about preferences of the customer group. The demographics of customer groups provide data that will help you make decisions about the content of your ads as well as the appropriate media to use. Demographic groups can be based on many factors, such as the age group of the customers or where they live.

People born after 1979 form a demographic group referred to as the "Millennials." **Millennials** are so named because they will come of age early in the twenty-first century. There are 70.2 million Millennials, more than the Baby Boomers at their peak. This group will attract as much attention as their parents due to the size of the potential market. It is also a much more multicultural and ethnically diverse group than the Boomers.

The Millennials will be the focus of marketing throughout their lifetime, and their opinions and choices of sports and entertainment will be heavily studied. They will challenge marketing decisions with their diversity.

WHICH MEDIA TO USE

After targeting your audience, the next steps in advertising are to design your message and determine the media for delivery to your targeted customer. Data are available that indicate the media to use based on the demographics of the potential customers. The most commonly used media are print (newspapers, magazines, and billboards), broadcast (television and radio), and the Internet. Advertising firms that can create Internet sites that attract customers are in great demand. Internet sites have the potential to become a new source of profit for the advertising firm. By late 1998, the Internet had claimed more than 1 percent of the overall ad budgets in the United States and was forecast to grow significantly.

THE RATINGS

When a company contracts with a TV channel or network to advertise during a specific sports or entertainment event, the ratings drive the

price. If a show is anticipated to have a minimum rating, but the actual rating is lower, the channel will "make good." The channel will provide additional advertising time during other time slots.

The National Hockey League signed a long-term TV contract with the Disney Corporation in 1998. The five-year, $600 million deal allows Disney to dominate national coverage of the NHL on Disney-owned outlets, including ABC, ESPN, and ESPN2. Disney was willing to sign with the NHL despite very low ratings because of the demographics of the viewers. The NHL is reported to draw the highest concentration of young, upscale viewers of any televised sport. Disney hopes these viewers will attract advertisers who will pay for the long-term commitment of air time.

INTERMISSION

How do you decide which medium to use? How is the cost of television advertising figured?

The choice is based on the demographics of the target market. TV advertising cost is

based on program ratings and the demographics of a program's viewers.

THE REST OF PROMOTION

Although advertising plays a major role in promotion, three other categories of marketing are needed to finish the job: publicity, sales promotion, and personal selling. All four categories team together into a promotional mix tailored to the sport or entertainment being promoted.

PUBLICITY COUNTS

PROMOTION

Sponsoring events and getting a company's name in front of customers are methods of promotion called **publicity.** As the primary sponsor of the 1998 Texaco Grand Prix of Houston, Texaco spent over $1 million to place its logo at 60 spots along the racecourse. Sponsoring auto racing is a logical choice for the advertising dollars of gasoline, auto parts, and motor oil companies. Fans are likely to believe that products that are good for race cars will also be good for normal street cars.

The sponsor of an event such as racing counts on getting positive publicity from the event in addition to revenue from fans who buy the sponsor's products. The distinction between publicity and advertisement is the price: publicity is free. Sponsors expect to see newspaper articles written about the event that include the sponsor's name as part of the event title. Since the media control publicity, the publicity can also be negative and discuss, for example, the noise pollution caused by the race.

The amount of publicity received by the hit movie *The Blair Witch Project* was beyond imagination. The low-budget movie, produced for $35,000, received a huge amount of publicity after setting new box office records. The movie became the feature item on TV and radio and in

newspapers, and was featured on the cover of *Time* and *Newsweek* magazines. Publicity of this magnitude is most often only dreamed about by marketing directors.

SALES PROMOTION

Sales promotion is any action or communication that encourages a consumer to buy a product. An example of sales promotion is when a baseball team gives away a baseball cap to each child who attends the game with an adult. The giveaway is a direct incentive for the adult fan to purchase at least two tickets to the game. Teams have sold out games when they gave away certain popular promotional items.

Sales promotion items are often referred to as specialty advertising items. They frequently include the logo of the team or sponsors. Discounts, coupons, and contests are other examples of sales promotions.

PERSONAL SELLING

Personal selling is an in-person, face-to-face communication between a seller and a customer. Large corporations are major clients for sports events, frequently buying huge blocks of tickets or permanently leasing special luxury seating. The director of marketing for a team may be the person who calls on the corporation to make the personal sale.

The Direct Marketing Association (DMA), a trade organization for bulk mailers, announced a deal in 1998 to acquire the Association of Interactive Media (AIM) as a subsidiary. AIM was a nonprofit association of firms on the Internet. The DMA hoped the merger would provide its members with effective use of the Internet. Privacy advocates feared the DMA would bury the Internet in unsolicited e-mail, known as spam.

Jason Catlett, president of Junkbusters Corporation, a promoter of privacy on the Web, believes that in cyberspace, the consumer finds the seller—not the other way around—and that Internet users must be respected by advertisers, not overwhelmed.

THINK CRITICALLY
Discuss as a class whether unsolicited junk e-mail is an ethical way to advertise. How do you feel about athletes and celebrities who appear to be involved in spam campaigns?

INTERMISSION

What are the three types of promotion besides advertising? Provide an example of each one.

The three types of promotion are publicity, sales promotion, and personal selling.

Examples will vary.

A corporation leasing a luxury box at Madison Square Garden in New York City receives 16 tickets to every event held at the arena. Boxes include 16 plush seats, a personal lounge area, and a private restroom. The cost of a luxury box is $1,000,000 per year.

UNDERSTAND MARKETING CONCEPTS

Circle the best answer for each of the following questions.

1. **Marketing-Information Management** The outstanding characteristic of the important new demographic group, the Millennials, is b
   a. its lack of cultural and ethnic diversity
   b. its size
   c. its range of ages
   d. none of these

2. **Promotion** Publicity differs from advertising in that publicity is
   a. more expensive than most advertising b
   b. free
   c. always true
   d. all of these

THINK CRITICALLY

Answer the following questions as completely as possible. If necessary, use a separate sheet of paper.

3. **Promotion** Which promotional medium is most effective for the following age groups: 12–16, 17–28, 29–45, 46–65. Explain your answer for each age group.

   Answers will vary.

   _____

   _____

   _____

   _____

   _____

4. **Promotion** Describe two instances of sales promotion that you have experienced. Did the promotion influence you to later buy the product promoted? Why or why not?

   Answers will vary.

   _____

   _____

   _____

   _____

   _____

MARKETING RESEARCH

OPENING ACT

The oil that keeps sports and entertainment marketing running smoothly is the fans. Fans provide funding by participating as viewers, ticket purchasers, and collectors of memorabilia. To continue to exist, sports and entertainment must make a profit for investors, owners, and sponsors. Sports leagues, entertainment giants, concert promoters, the media, sponsors, and advertisers all are dependent on the goodwill of the fans.

Catering to fans is what marketing is about. To do so requires knowledge of the fans. What are their likes and dislikes, how much disposable income do they have, what is their medium of choice for sports and entertainment, and how will their interests change in the future? These are questions that have to be answered in order to efficiently provide entertainment that will make a profit. Marketing research is used to answer these questions.

Work with a group. Discuss examples of entertainment companies catering to fans. Make a list of what the company has done to attract fans. Make a separate list of actions that have alienated fans. Discuss both lists with the class.

GOALS

Define the purposes of marketing research.

Understand the human element in marketing research.

SCHEDULE
Block 90 minutes
Regular 2 class periods

FOCUS
Ask students what kinds of entertainment they think people over 60 see/hear most? What types of entertainment do people age 20 spend their money on? How do you know?

OPENING ACT
Marketing research answers questions about people who may purchase the products you are selling.

Answers for Opening Act Cooperative Learning
Examples of sports teams catering to fans are the creation of luxury boxes to sell to corporations for entertaining customers.

To attract fans, teams provide giveaways and players sign autographs before games.

Strikes and negative stories about players' illegal activities have alienated fans.

RESEARCHING THE MARKET

In the 1940s, companies learned to use a new marketing medium—television. Firms developed strategies for using TV to market to broad categories of people who were called the **mass market.** At the beginning of the twenty-first century, a new medium, the Internet, is helping marketing strategies become more focused. The focused strategies require companies to obtain and use detailed marketing information in order to build and nurture customer relationships. Finding answers to key questions is the connection between developing the product and actually selling it to customers. Researching the market and managing the research information allow firms to structure their products and messages to customers.

MARKETING INFORMATION

For businesses seeking to thrive in competitive environments, like sports and entertainment marketing, finding marketing information about potential customers is essential. Few customers are undecided about where to spend their money. Thus, to increase market share, firms must take customers away from competitors. To be successful, companies must know what target group of customers they are after and what customers want.

For a company to continue to grow once customers are buying, it must maintain the customer relationship. Developing customer loyalty takes an even deeper understanding of customers.

Marketing research is the process of determining what customers want. Once you know what customers want, you can use that information to improve your product. The process involves collecting data, organizing and managing the data, and looking for patterns in the data. The process must be ongoing, repeated frequently, and revised often. The scientific method of marketing research has five steps:

Step 1 Define the problem.
Step 2 Analyze the situation.
Step 3 Develop the process for collecting data.
Step 4 Collect, organize, and analyze the data.
Step 5 Determine a solution to the problem.

DATA MINING

Digging up data needed to make decisions—or **data mining**—is part of marketing research. Many methods are used to conduct marketing research, but most are based on the scientific method of problem solving. Marketing research is a tool that enables businesses to understand customers. Helping customers state their thoughts and feelings is one method of beginning to understand their needs.

One important marketing firm is Nielsen Media Research. Nielsen's research is based on actions rather than opinions. A newspaper or magazine can count the number of copies sold, but there is no easy method for knowing exactly how many people are watching a TV show. Nielsen Media Research estimates the number of people by selecting a **sample** and then counting the people in the sample. Nielsen uses 5,000 households as the sample of almost 100 million households with TVs in the United States. Each member of the population has the same chance of being chosen for a sample. A top-rated show is one that is watched by the most people during that time slot.

The Nielsen Sports Marketing Service provides complete information for leagues, teams, marketers, stations, networks, and production companies. The information provided allows companies to follow sports teams during the season, for home and away games, during winning and losing streaks, and for long-standing rivalries. This information enables marketers to adjust advertising to fit the sports viewing audience.

INTERMISSION

Why do TV stations need to know their viewers' likes and dislikes? What is meant by a sample in marketing research?

So they will know which programs to air and who to approach about advertising. A sample is a small part of the market that can be monitored closely. A sample is supposed to be representative of the entire market.

WHO IS ASKING?

Some marketing research firms specialize in providing marketing research information for sports, entertainment, and travel industries. Plog Research, Inc. provides studies such as "American Traveler Survey," a comprehensive annual study. The study is based on 6,000 questionnaires from a sample of U.S. travelers and provides information for marketing decisions to companies or services in the travel industry.

ArtsWatch Online is an electronic research service. ArtsWatch tracks changing demographic, cultural, political, and economic forces affecting arts participation and consumption patterns across the United States and the world. Potential sponsors of arts events can track the patterns of ticket buyers and compare them to a national sample. Sponsors want to know their dollars are being spent where their potential customers will see them. Sponsoring fine arts events is viewed as being a socially responsible activity, but it also needs to have a profitable return for the corporations involved.

WHAT'S IN IT FOR ME?

MARKETING-INFORMATION MANAGEMENT

While people are often reluctant to answer personal questions for market researchers, they frequently supply the information in return for something that they want. For example, sometimes moviegoers receive a card that provides discounts in return for filling in information on a sign-up form. The movie theater gains demographic information about where the attendees live, how often they attend movies, and which movies they see. Where someone lives can provide a lead to that person's income and education level.

WORLDWIDE DATA

As the global market for sports, entertainment, and recreation continues to grow at a rapid pace, marketers must expand their knowledge of the culture of potential new customers. In the 1990s, the improving economy in Brazil changed the economic demographics. A black middle class emerged, bringing with it a new profile in the media. As advertisers researched the needs and wants of these potential new customers, more corporate sponsors sought the attention of African-Brazilian consumers. For example, magazines began requesting black models from modeling agencies in Rio de Janeiro.

Assuming that other nations share tastes and values with customers in the United States is often a mistake. Potential customers can

Marketing research provides information about consumers. If an advertiser knows that more viewers under the age of 35 are attracted to the X Games than to football, then the advertiser knows where to spend its promotion dollars.

TEACH

Marketing research firms specialize in providing information to a specific industry.

Point out to students that data can be collected in many ways, including at a point of sale, by telephone, or by face-to-face interviews.

Sponsors use marketing research to decide to sponsor an event so that their dollars are well spent.

Market researchers sometimes provide something in return for answering the questions, for example, a sales promotion giveaway. Ask students if they know anyone who uses a card to get discounts at movies, grocery stores, or other retail stores. The card provides demographic data about the customer.

Marketing research can provide information about an emerging economic group.

MARKETING-INFORMATION MANAGEMENT

be lost forever through lack of information about their wants and needs. The United States continues to dominate the export of sports and entertainment programming, while importing virtually nothing. Lack of sensitivity to the culture of developing nations can be viewed as detrimental to them and can lead to opposition to programming within the developing nation. For growth of a company to occur, marketing information must be used to shape its product for new customers.

INTERMISSION

What kinds of information do marketing information managers need from consumers? Why should marketing managers keep track of social and economic changes?

Age, gender, location, income, preferences, frequency of use, wants, and needs.

Social and economic changes affect the number of consumers who want, need, or can afford a product.

TAKE A BOW

CHARLIE COLON

Charlie Colon turned a summer internship into an exciting career in marketing research. Charlie is currently the Director of Start-up Operations for the Gallup Organization, the world-renowned public opinion polling and marketing research company.

Charlie's summer internship fueled his interest in marketing and people. The project dealt with overall employee satisfaction at a large corporation. Charlie's premise was that more money would make employees happy about their jobs. He was surprised to discover that feeling their supervisors cared about them as human beings was and is still the most important consideration for employee satisfaction.

Today Charlie spends about 60 percent of his time on marketing research for Gallup clients such as CNN. He oversees the research from the inception of the idea to the data collection. He spends 30 percent of his time on the information management technology side of the business. Once the data is collected, it must be made available to clients in a manageable format. Finally, he recruits new employees from colleges and universities. Charlie exemplifies the Gallup strategy of focusing on people's strengths. He is a strong ambassador for Gallup and its people-centered philosophies.

THINK CRITICALLY
1. How is research used to prove or disprove assumptions?
2. How can sports and entertainment companies use research from the Gallup Organization?

UNDERSTAND MARKETING CONCEPTS

Circle the best answer for each of the following questions.

1. Finding data needed to make marketing decisions is c
   a. information marketing
   b. mass marketing
   c. data mining
   d. none of these

2. The process of determining what customers want is b
   a. information marketing
   b. marketing research
   c. mass marketing
   d. none of these

THINK CRITICALLY

Answer the following questions as completely as possible. If necessary, use a separate sheet of paper.

3. Your school's DECA Chapter needs to make some money and is thinking of creating and selling tickets for a talent show. Outline a plan for researching your market. Do you have a chance for success?

Answers will vary.

_____

_____

_____

_____

_____

4. How can you create a student-run research firm for your school? What are some topics you would research?

Answers will vary.

_____

_____

_____

_____

_____

CHAPTER 11
LESSON 11.3

DEVELOP A MARKETING PLAN

GOALS

Comprehend the purpose of a marketing plan.

Understand the components of a strategic marketing plan.

OPENING ACT

Equipped with megabytes of data about consumer likes and dislikes, entertainment firms face the daunting task of forming a marketing plan. Successful firms spend a great deal of time planning. Company leaders must communicate a clear direction as well as provide individual employees with the tools they need to plan their own actions as they move in that direction.

A marketing plan is like a map. It is a guide. The plan is used to fulfill each of the key marketing functions. When everyone in the company knows the plan, decisions on each marketing function can be made in a timely and productive manner.

Work with a group. Discuss how companies can use marketing information to develop marketing plans. How might a plan improve the way entertainment is offered to fans? Present the results of your discussion to the class.

KNOW WHERE YOU ARE HEADED

PRODUCT/ SERVICE MANAGEMENT

A **marketing plan** is a written component of the strategic plan that addresses how the company will carry out the key marketing functions. A marketing plan can be simple or very detailed. Of primary importance in a marketing plan is the development of a **mission statement,** or the identification of the nature of the business or the reasons the business exists. A mission statement naming the company's areas of expertise guides marketers and planners as they develop new products and services. Clarifying the mission of a sports or entertainment business is a critical step, since all further strategies are built upon the mission.

A SENSE OF DIRECTION

Once you know the company's mission, you have direction for your plan. Having completed initial marketing research on your customers, you can begin analyzing the data to decide what your customers or potential customers really want and how to deliver it to them. This information is incorporated into your marketing plan. Your plan must also prepare you for the future needs of your customers. Just as your customers change, so must your plan continually improve.

There is no specific outline or format for a marketing plan. The major components of a marketing plan are determined by the specific needs of the firm and the products or services to be marketed. A tight focus on the customers and their current and future needs should direct the planning. When a company moves its focus away from the customer, it loses the customer's business.

FOCUSING ON THE CUSTOMER

In 1997, video-rental company Blockbuster saw its earnings drop 20 percent. Blockbuster's problems were darkening the dynamic dreams of its parent, media giant Viacom. Viacom also owns Paramount Pictures, Nickelodeon, MTV, and CBS. In 1997, it had sales of $13.2 billion. In response to Blockbuster's poor year, Viacom CEO, Sumner Redstone, hired John Antioco, a manager known for revitalizing slumping profits in other companies. Antioco overhauled Blockbuster's business model and marketing strategy plan. Prior to Antioco's changes, one out of five customers left a Blockbuster store without a purchase or rental. Many more customers left with a disappointing third- or fourth-choice video. Customers grew tired of not getting the movies they wanted, so they stopped coming in.

PRODUCT/ SERVICE MANAGEMENT

With Antioco's leadership and planning, Blockbuster now guarantees that hit movies will be in stock or the customer's next movie is free. Antioco's strategy is surprisingly simple. Blockbuster stocks more of the new releases that customers want. Blockbuster changed its marketing plan to reflect an improved way of purchasing videos from major movie studios. The company backed its new plan with a $160-million advertising blitz that resulted in a worldwide rental revenue increase of 13.3 percent in the second quarter of 1998. Its success came from focusing on the customer.

MARKETING MYTHS

It has become a common practice for corporations to purchase naming rights to sports and entertainment events as part of their marketing plans. Some corporations assume that all free media coverage (publicity) of the event will include several uses of their name. In fact, they count on this publicity in their overall promotion plan. Frequently, though, they are mistaken about the use of their name.

The media have a variety of policies regarding treatment of sponsors' names. Some daily newspapers have policies against such use. Others use the name only once during an article. Media policy may cause sponsors to shy away from sponsorship if the publicity does not follow the money invested.

THINK CRITICALLY
Why would news media refuse to use sponsors' names? Is there a right or wrong belief about these policies? Explain.

INTERMISSION

What is the mission statement of a company? Why must a company focus on its customers?

A mission statement identifies the nature of the business. Customer focus is

necessary because it allows companies to identify customer needs and wants.

WHAT'S THE PLAN?

Sporting events and the athletes who participate in them are consumer products. Fans buy the product by purchasing tickets and viewing the game. Sports are a perishable product much like fruit. Game tickets must be sold or they quickly become as worthless as an overripe banana. Because they are perishable, sports and entertainment must be pre-sold. A marketing plan helps the company make the pre-sale.

COMPONENTS OF A STRATEGIC MARKETING PLAN

1. **Mission of the Business**   Why is the company in business? What does it value?

2. **Goals of the Business**   What does the company intend to accomplish by marketing this product? Is the goal growth or profits?

3. **Product Planning**   What event, product, or service will be marketed?

4. **Marketing-Information Management**   Who are the company's direct and indirect competitors? What are they doing right? Who are the potential and current customers? Who makes up the largest group of people who have the funds to buy what the company is offering? What motivates them to buy? What do they want? What will keep them returning? Who is the next most important group? How can the company retain the loyalty of these customers? Who will the future customers be?

5. **Distribution System**   How will the company's product get to the customer?

6. **Pricing**   What is the best price for the product? How much did it cost to provide it to the fans? How much will the fans pay? How many of them will buy at that price? Would a lower price bring in a larger fan base and consequently more revenue?

7. **Promotional Strategies**   How will the company use advertising, publicity, personal selling, and sales promotion to position the product in the minds of customers? What media will the company use? Does the strategy focus on the goals set by the company? How will the company get the message to its customers or potential customers? Are the ways in which the company delivers the message as important as the message?

8. Financing What is the estimated income from the product? What costs are involved in marketing the product? What are the existing or future economic trends?

9. Purchasing How much can a sports team afford to pay its players? How much can a movie producer pay for scenery for a movie? How much will a web site cost?

10. Risk Management What legal liability might the company incur? What are the laws that will affect marketing this product or event?

11. Selling How will the direct sale of tickets and related merchandise be handled?

12. People Who is responsible for each segment of the plan?

13. Internal Communication Systems How will one department communicate with the other departments within the organization? How will the marketing department know the concerns of the other departments?

14. Timelines for Implementing the Plan What is the scheduled date for the action to commence? What has to get done and in what sequence, starting with completion date and working backwards?

15. Intervals of Review and Evaluation What can be done better, faster, and cheaper? What are the mileposts at which the company will stop and measure progress? Is there a contingency plan for fixing the problems?

16. The Future Where is the business going? What are the next steps for staying ahead of the competition?

Planning is a systematic, ongoing process. As with all processes, it must be reviewed frequently, and revisions must be considered. Constantly looking for ways to improve the plan and the process is the only way to stay ahead of the competition. You can be sure the competition will not stand still.

INTERMISSION

Why must the plan include evaluation and intervals of review?

It is unlikely that any plan will be effective unless it is modified in response to changes in the market or company.

ASSESS
Reteach
Discuss the concept of planning as starting with the end in mind. Know where you are going and think through the whole process. Plans can be changed.

Enrich
Interview someone in the school or community who puts on events. Ask them to share their planning strategies with the class.

CLOSE
Do a role play where each student tells the other everything they know about developing marketing plans, followed by asking the partner every imaginable question relating to marketing plans. Write down the questions. Exchange questions with another pair of students and answer the questions in writing.

UNDERSTAND MARKETING CONCEPTS

Circle the best answer for each of the following questions.

1. **Product/Service Management**   When the reasons a business exists are written down, they are called the **b**
   a. goals of the business
   b. mission statement
   c. internal communication system
   d. none of these

2. The most critical element in a marketing plan is **c**
   a. the budget statement
   b. the timeline for sales
   c. keeping the focus on the customer
   d. none of these

THINK CRITICALLY

Answer the following questions as completely as possible. If necessary, use a separate sheet of paper.

3. **Pricing**   How would you determine the price to charge for admission to a sports event, if you were the event manager? List the information you would need to have to make the decision. List how and where you would obtain the information you need.

   Answers will vary but can include venue costs, advertising costs, salaries, costs

   of other types of entertainment, and customer demographics. Obtain this infor-

   mation by contacting the venue manager, city officials, census bureau data, and

   league statisticians.

   _____

4. **Communication**   Your marketing class is presenting a talent show as a fundraiser. Work in groups and develop a written marketing plan, including all of the components in this lesson. Determine whether this will become a yearly event.

   Answers will vary.

   _____

   _____

   _____

   _____

   _____

THE BOTTOM LINE

OPENING ACT

Entertainers are financing their projects in creative new ways. Performing artists earn royalties, or a share of the profits from the sale or performance of their work. To secure financing for new projects, celebrities are now issuing bonds to investors. The bonds are actually a promise of a share of royalties on future projects. The bonds include a specified amount of money plus interest at a rate higher than other bond investments pay. In a sense, the artist is taking out a loan. Rock star David Bowie secured $55 million in 1997 in the first bond deal of its kind. Singer James Brown completed a successful sale in 1999.

Work with a group. Discuss why an entertainer would want to finance a project through bonds. What are the risks on the part of the bond purchaser? Present the findings of your group to the class.

GOALS

Comprehend the profit motive behind sports and entertainment marketing.

Understand types of financing related to sports and entertainment marketing.

SCHEDULE
Block 90 minutes
Regular 2 class periods

FOCUS
Are sports and entertainment events put on because they are fun to do? If not, what is the motive? Making money is the motive.

OPENING ACT
A new idea for entertainers is for them to get their money up front by selling bonds for their future royalties.

Answers for Opening Act Cooperative Learning
The entertainer can have the money now and the bondholder is sharing the risk that the future royalties may not happen.

TEACH
If a business cannot make a profit in a reasonable period of time, then it should not exist. Inventors need return of their investment plus interest to remain interested in the business.

LET'S MAKE MONEY!

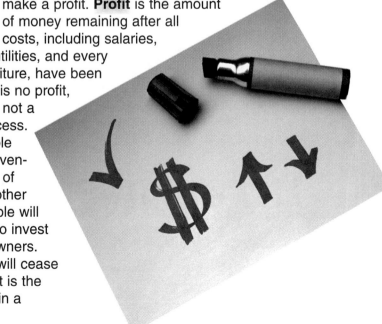

FINANCING

The purpose of all business activity surrounding sports and entertainment marketing is to make a profit. **Profit** is the amount of money remaining after all costs, including salaries, advertising, utilities, and every other expenditure, have been paid. If there is no profit, the activity is not a financial success. An unprofitable venture will eventually run out of money, and other businesspeople will be unwilling to invest or become owners. The venture will cease to exist. Profit is the driving force in a business.

WHO GETS THE MONEY?

Individuals and businesses make profits in the sports and entertainment business at many levels. Since a number of entities generally come together to stage an entertainment or sports event, each entity has the possibility to make or lose money. Money is generated through ticket sales, broadcast sales, licensing, and facility revenues. Facility revenues include venue advertising (signage), parking, luxury boxes, and concessions.

Marketing represents just one activity within each entity. Either the people who are the owners of the event idea must risk their own money to stage and market the event, or they must find others who are willing to invest in or sponsor the event. The owners/originators must market the event to the investors or sponsors with a plan showing the potential for profit. Finally, the event must be marketed to the customers or fans. If no one wants to buy a ticket to an event, then the sponsors have wasted their advertising budget by sponsoring the event.

Companies' demand results from advertising. They want to increase the number of customers and make a profit. Promotion of events through athletes or celebrities can play a major role in earning a profit. Promotion is intended to persuade fans to attend and make a monetary commitment to sports and entertainment.

INTERMISSION

Define profit and discuss its different levels.

Profit is the amount of money left after all expenses have been paid. Ticket sales, broadcast rights, licensing, and facility revenues all generate revenue and contribute to profit.

AND MORE MONEY!

Television networks make a profit by selling commercial time to advertisers and by selling programs to affiliated stations. To clear a profit, they must bring in more revenue than they expend on producing and distributing programs.

Financing a movie can be very expensive. Movies made for teenagers in which young actors star are a money-making asset to filmmakers. They can also cost 50 percent less to advertise than big-budget movies. The salaries paid to young actors, sometimes between $50,000 and $150,000, are certainly more profit-producing for a studio than the $20 million salary of a superstar. By using cable TV channels directed at teens, such as music channels, movie marketers can buy cost-efficient ads and hold down expenses.

CHALLENGES OF PHYSICAL LIMITS

There are physical limits to the number of good seats that can be created for any sport. As a result, the ideal stadium size and seating configuration for each sport does not change. Studies have shown that changes in ticket price or in attendance cause little variance in the amount of revenue from this source. The sources of revenue with potential for growth are concessions, special seating arrangements, and commercial licenses.

Personal Seat Licenses Another form of revenue for sports teams is a **personal seat license** (PSL). A customer pays a fixed fee to obtain the right to buy season tickets. In football and baseball, the PSL fees are sometimes used to pay for part of the costs of a sports stadium. The revenue from the PSL is not shared between home and visiting teams, but ticket revenues are shared. If season ticket prices are lower because of the PSL, the visiting team is paying part of the costs of the stadium. The visiting team does receive a percentage of tickets sold at the gate or on an individual basis.

Concessions and Other Licenses Financing agreements for food concessions and other sports items sold inside and outside the stadium

Internet addresses have a domain name, which is the characters following the dot. There are generic names like "com," "net," and "org," and country domains. There are 236 two-letter country codes.

Tuvalu, an island nation of 10,000, derives most of its revenue from its domain code, "tv." TV Corp., a Toronto firm, charges companies about ten times as much for the use of a URL with domain code "tv" as other firms charge for URLs with "com," "net," and "org." The domain name tv can be a lucrative address, since sites like abc.tv or fox.tv are easy to remember. It will remain with the media firms to create web sites that make a profit.

THINK CRITICALLY
1. How can companies make money from their Internet sites?
2. Why is it important that a company have an Internet address that is easy to remember?

To associate itself with the fans rather than wealthy NBA players or owners during the 1998 lockout, Nike featured nonbasketball celebrities courtside at amateur games. Nike executives wanted their company to be seen as neutral during the lockout.

TEACH
To make a profit, TV stations must sell advertising and programming for more than it costs. Why do young actors make less than superstars? They do not have the fan base to sell tickets at the same level. Why are cable TV channels cheaper to advertise on than broadcast TV? They have fewer viewers.

Ticket price and attendance cause little variance in revenue. Concession, luxury boxes, and licensing are the moneymakers.

Some teams charge an extra fee to obtain the right to buy season tickets. This is called a personal seat license.

Cyber Marketing
TV Corp. is making money for the tiny island of Tuvalu by selling its Internet domain name—tv.

Think Critically
1. Companies can make money from Internet sites by selling space to advertisers and by selling products.

2. An easy-to-remember web site will attract more visitors with less spent on promotion.

are arranged in two different ways. The owners of the rights charge either a fixed fee that is not based on sales, or a royalty that is based on sales. The best way for a team to promote licensed items is to combine up-front fees and royalties. Up-front fees increase the incentive of the licensee to sell licensed products. Likewise, owners have an incentive to field a team that attracts fans.

Sports team owners make money by limiting the amount of the league's revenues going to players. Players make money from their salaries, endorsements from sponsors, and receipt of any part of the team revenue agreed to by a contract.

The 1998–99 basketball lockout was a financial disaster for the hospitality industry in Philadelphia, which was to host the cancelled NBA All-Star Game. The estimated loss was $9 million. The city tax department and retailers incurred other significant losses.

DID WE MAKE MONEY?

As a part of the marketing plan, a forecast must be made. The **forecast** predicts the cost of expenses and expected revenue from the event. Additionally, a budget is developed that details the financial impact of each part of the marketing plan. A **budget** begins the process by providing estimates of expected expenditures and revenues. The budget is in itself a plan for controlling the flow of funds. Experience is the best guide for developing budgets, but everyone has to start somewhere.

Finally, records must be kept of all financial transactions. The records include an income statement and a balance sheet. A **balance sheet** shows the current assets, including cash, property and equipment, and the current liabilities, including debts owed and loans. The balance sheet indicates the current value of the company. The **income statement** is a record of all revenue received and all expenses. The income statement will reveal the profit or loss of the event. If the plan is effective and worth the effort, a profit is made.

INTERMISSION

Explain the different ways owners charge for sports-related licenses and why they are important to a team. Name the major financial records needed for a business.

Owners charge for personal seat licenses and concessions licenses. Crucial financial

statements include balance sheets and income statements.

UNDERSTAND MARKETING CONCEPTS

Circle the best answer for each of the following questions.

1. A business or event is a financial success if it c
   a. is able to pay its bills
   b. continues to exist
   c. makes a profit
   d. none of these

2. Financing   A fixed fee that a customer pays to obtain the right to buy season tickets is a(n) b
   a. up-front fee
   b. personal seat license
   c. distribution fee
   d. none of these

THINK CRITICALLY

Answer the following questions as completely as possible. If necessary, use a separate sheet of paper.

3. If your school cannot increase its seating capacity for basketball games, how can it increase its basketball revenue?

Answers will vary. Possible answers include recruiting more sponsors, increasing

ticket prices, issuing PSLs, playing more games, and increasing concessions

license prices.

4. How are a balance sheet and an income statement important to a business? What would a sports and entertainment company look for on a balance sheet and income statement?

These reports tell lenders and investors how expenses and revenue are

changing and show whether there is profit. Answers will vary.

ASSESS
Reteach
Split the class into several teams. Using a game show format, review the Intermission questions with the teams.

Enrich
Have students prepare a marketing plan for one of their favorite products. Have their plans take advantage of sports or entertainment resources.

CLOSE
Have students review the components of a strategic marketing plan. Ask them if there are any legal or ethical issues they need to consider as marketers develop each of the components.

CHAPTER 11 REVIEW

REVIEW MARKETING CONCEPTS

Write the letter of the term that matches each definition. Some terms will not be used.

<u>b</u> **1.** the figure representing how many people watch a TV show

<u>f</u> **2.** communicating with customers through advertising, publicity, sales promotion, or personal selling

<u>a</u> **3.** the identification of the nature of a business

<u>c</u> **4.** a fixed fee to obtain the right to buy season tickets to a sports event

<u>d</u> **5.** broad categories of consumers

a. mission statement
b. ratings
c. personal seat license
d. mass market
e. up-front fees
f. promotion
g. image

Circle the best answer.

6. A written component of a company's strategic plan that addresses how the company will carry out its key marketing functions is a
    a. customer focus plan
c   **b.** goal strategy
    c. marketing plan
    d. none of these

7. The prediction of expenses and revenue from an event is the
    a. balance sheet.
b   **b.** forecast
    c. income statement
    d. none of these

8. Unsolicited e-mail is known as
    a. mass advertising
b   **b.** spam
    c. mass marketing
    d. none of these

9. Marketing research is
    a. the process of determining what customers want
d   **b.** collecting and organizing data
    c. looking for patterns in data
    d. all of these

THINK CRITICALLY

10. Advertising tobacco products on television is now prohibited. Why would market researchers still want to collect data about sports watched on TV by smokers?

Answers will vary. They might market their products using popular athletes as endorsers

or have sports-related promotions on the Internet.

_____

_____

_____

_____

_____

11. Develop ten questions a firm considering advertising during a college basketball game might want answered about the people who watch the game on TV.

Answers will vary.

_____

_____

_____

_____

_____

_____

12. Consider the Millennials—the group of people born after 1979. Name 15 products or services this group will want and need within the next decade. How will sports and entertainment market researchers learn about these consumers?

Answers will vary.

_____

_____

_____

_____

_____

_____

CHAPTER 11 REVIEW

MAKE CONNECTIONS

13. Mathematics   Based on its market research, your DECA Chapter had 100 T-shirts printed at a reduced cost of $5.50 each. There were 25 shirts of each size (XL, L, M, S). The Club had to pay sales tax of 6 percent on all the shirts it bought. The designer donated time and additional materials, and the school let the club have a sales table at school events. The club priced the shirts at $15.00 each. If the club sold 6 XL, 25 L, 25 M, and 10 S, how much total profit did the Chapter make? How many shirts were left over that couldn't be sold? How much profit could the Club have made if all the shirts had sold? What can the club add to its market research next time?

$5.50 × 100 = $550.00; 6% = 0.06; $550 × 0.06 = $33.00; $550 + 33 = $583.00,

6 + 25 + 25 + 10 = 66 shirts sold; 66 × $15 = $990, $990 − 583 = $407 profit,

100 × $15 = $1500; $1500 − 583 = $917 in potential profit; 100 − 66 = 34 shirts left over.

The club will know next time that large and medium shirts are more popular than small or extra

large. The *Sports and Entertainment Marketing* Teacher's Resource CDincludes a spreadsheet

template to help students complete this activity. Look for the file p268 Make Connections-

Mathematics.xls Office Templates folder, or the file p268 Conx.txt in THe Text Templates folder

14. Communications   Copy three print ads or tape three TV ads for sports or entertainment products or events. Examine the components of the ads and list the items below for each. Then answer the question, "Is this ad targeted at me?" Give a brief explanation of why or why not.

   a. medium used
   b. copy or verbal message
   c. visual image
   d. action ad asks you to take

First Ad   Answers will vary.

_____

_____

Second Ad _____

_____

_____

Third Ad _____

_____

_____

15. Technology Use the Internet for market research on rodeos. Discover all you can about the audience. Suppose that you are in charge of marketing at a small business with an advertising budget of $500. Can your business sponsor anything related to a rodeo? What media would be your best choice for advertising? Who specifically should your ads target?

Answers will vary.

PROJECT ♦♦♦♦♦♦♦♦ EXTRA INNINGS

A new sports-drink company wants your marketing research firm to a) find a sport for the company to sponsor, b) research the market surrounding that sport, and c) prepare a marketing plan. The company prefers a less popular sport rather than, for example, professional football. The company wants consumers to see its product as fresh, exciting, invigorating, young, and daring.

Work with a group and complete the following activities.

1. Use the Internet to find an up-and-coming sport. It can be a team sport or an individual sport. What kind of publicity is the team or individual seeking? Why? What features of this team can be related to the product's characteristics?

2. What are the demographics of the fans of the team or individual athlete? Include age range, gender majority, income, education, and whether the fans participate in any sports. Do many of the fans fall into the "Millennial" group?

3. Prepare a questionnaire to hand out to fans attending an event. What five essential pieces of information do you want? What reward will you offer the fans for filling out the questionnaire?

4. Be able to explain to your client why these fans will be attracted to this particular beverage.

5. Research which media your fan base uses most. Television? The Internet? Mainstream newspapers? Alternative newspapers? What kinds of radio stations?

6. Design a label for your client's drink that will attract the attention of its desired consumer.

7. Plan a promotion program for your client. Include at least two different ideas for publicity (free), advertising (paid), sales promotion, and personal selling.

8. Present the plan to the class as you would a customer, using multimedia presentation software or other visual aids. Include a written outline of the main points.

PROJECT
Extra Innings
Students may take 10 hours or more to complete this project, depending on the ease of access to the Internet. Sports magazines will make good supplemental resources for students.

Set up a group process by requiring a team leader be selected. Set up some interim check points with due dates for the following:

❏ Division of responsibility among the team members

❏ Type of sport to be sponsored

❏ Demographics of fans

❏ Draft questionnaire

❏ Draft label

❏ Promotion plan

❏ Final presentation date and length of presentation

For #1, suggest the students review the definition of publicity before beginning.

For #2, review the definition of demographics and Millennial.

For #3, provide some information on developing questionnaires. Ask the students to practice the questionnaire with other groups before using it outside the class and revise the questions if needed.

For #8, require each team member to have a part in the presentation. The written outline should answer all questions not covered by a visual aid.

The *Sports and Entertainment Marketing* Teacher's Resource CD includes a presentation template to help students complete this activity.

Look for the file p269 Extra Innings.ppt in the Office Templates folder, or the file p269 XInn.rtf in the Text Templates folder.

CHAPTER 12

LEGAL ISSUES FOR SPORTS AND ENTERTAINMENT

LESSONS

WINNING STRATEGIES

SUPERAGENTS

The law firm of Steinberg and Moorad inspired the movie *Jerry McGuire,* and its senior partners were technical advisors for the movie. Leigh Steinberg and Jeff Moorad are best known as the agents for a number of famous pro athletes including Troy Aikman, Steve Young, Drew Bledsoe, and Akili Smith.

At age 25, Leigh Steinberg began his career as an agent by representing his friend Steve Bartkowski. Bartkowski was the number one draft choice of the 1975 NFL draft. Steinberg negotiated with the Atlanta Falcons and secured Bartkowski the largest contract in the NFL at that time. Steinberg and Moorad take pride in the personal relationships they establish with their clients. They negotiate contracts that make their clients some of the highest paid athletes ever, but they also help them become good citizens. The agents believe in treating each athlete as a person who deserves respect on and off the field.

Development as a person, role model, and philanthropist is a requirement of every client signed by the firm. Clients must be willing to give back to the community through charities, foundations, and scholarships. The firm also emphasizes player health. Steinberg has been a leader in initiating research into the prevention of player head injuries. He has worked to improve the design and technology of football helmets to lessen the chance of injury.

THINK CRITICALLY

1. In the complicated world of professional sports contracts, why have Steinberg and Moorad been successful?
2. How might the agents' treatment of athletes as human beings be unusual?
3. Should professional athletes be required to give back to the community? Why or why not?

CHAPTER OVERVIEW
The importance of laws governing sports and entertainment contract negotiations with players and licensing merchandise is covered in this lesson.

Lesson 12.1
Laws and Contracts
This lesson covers risk, copyrights law, and an introduction to contracts.

Lesson 12.2
Unions
Comprehending the impact of strikes and labor laws on sports and entertainment is covered in this lesson.

Lesson 12.3
Licensing
Licensing is presented in this lesson as a critical piece of marketing sports and entertainment.

TEACHING RESOURCES
❑ CNN Video, Chapter 12
❑ CD-ROM Resources, Chapter 12

Winning Strategies
Ask students if they saw the movie *Jerry McGuire.* The movie is about a sports agent who is honest and ethical when others are not.

Think Critically
1. Steinberg and Moorad have been successful at representing players because they are good at negotiating high salaries and providing players that are good citizens as well as good players.

2. Some agents treat players like a piece of property or a cash cow.

3. Yes, pro players should give back to the community as they are role models, make large sums of money, and it is good for their image and the image of the sport.

LAWS AND CONTRACTS

GOALS

Understand risk management in sports and entertainment marketing.

Recognize the importance of copyright law.

Discuss the need for contracts.

SCHEDULE
Block 90 minutes
Regular 2 class periods

FOCUS
Introduce
Sports and entertainment laws require a degree from a law school to completely understand. Why are there so many laws affecting sports and entertainment? The big money involved makes the legal issues very important.

Opening Act
The NFL was exempted from the law forbidding monopolies.

Cooperative Learning
The NFL convinced Congress that they could not exist and make money if they were not a monopoly.

TEACH
Sports and entertainment are perishable products. Tickets to yesterday's game have no value.

OPENING ACT

In 1966, Congress bought what Pete Rozelle, then commissioner of the National Football League, was selling. Mr. Rozelle wanted to merge the NFL with the newly formed American Football League. Additionally, he wanted to form a cartel of the owners of the merged leagues. Both moves required exemption from the Sherman Antitrust Act by Congress and set the stage for football to become big business. This exemption has allowed global domination of the market share of football.

Work with a group. Discuss why professional sports teams need an exemption from the Sherman Antitrust Act to exist.

THE LAW

A glance at the sports section of a newspaper or a quick Internet search confirms that there are an overwhelming number of laws governing sports and entertainment. These laws have a major impact on marketing these products. Sports and entertainment are perishable products. Worse, technology allows easy duplication and transmission of the products. Protecting celebrities, producers, promoters, and investors is the purpose of most of the laws. Laws also increase the safety of the consumers, viewers, and fans.

MANAGING RISK

PRODUCT/
SERVICE
MANAGEMENT

Sports, entertainment, and recreation marketing require an initial examination of the laws and legal issues to ensure compliance and to prevent liability for injury or loss. Being **liable** means you are legally responsible for damages. Becoming familiar with the laws and knowing when to seek legal counsel are prerequisites for business success.

Inviting large groups of people to view an event is asking for potential legal action. Risk management requires an analysis of possible problems and a plan for reducing or preventing the problems. **Risk** is the possibility of financial loss or personal injury.

STEPS TO RISK MANAGEMENT

1. Identify risks

2. Estimate the possibility of each risk

3. Determine how great the consequences are

4. Determine how to control the risk

CONTROL THE RISK

1. Limit the possibility of risk through planning

2. Purchase insurance that transfers the cost of the risk to the insurance company

3. Transfer liability through a contract

4. Cover the risk in the event budget

5. Avoid offering the risky event

One method of transferring the risk to the fans is the inclusion, on the back of most event tickets, of a statement by the promoter that the promoter is not responsible for any harm to the ticket holder. By accepting the ticket, attendees agree to accept liability for their own possible risks. This does not relieve the facility or event management from providing a safe environment. An event sponsor has a legal duty to protect the spectator from unreasonable risk of harm or injury.

INTERMISSION

Why must marketers be concerned with limiting their risks?

Marketers should seek to limit risks in order to maximize the probability of making a

profit. Also, repeated association with profit loss or injury-filled events can make it

more difficult to attract new business.

WHO HAS THE RIGHTS?

Musicians, athletes, and artists make money by selling their product, which happens to be their talent. Laws are necessary to protect the rights of celebrities. When pricing their product, artists and athletes take into consideration that the work is protected by copyright law and is theirs alone to sell. This means that the price of a music CD includes not only the cost of the materials to make the CD, but also an amount to pay the writer of the music to use his or her material on the CD.

Copyright laws protect the unique work of the originator within the geographic boundaries to which the laws apply. Before 1978, works were copyrighted for 28 years and then renewed for 28 more years, for a total of 56 years. Since 1978, though, works may be copyrighted for the lifetime of the artist plus 70 years.

Owners of a copyright have the exclusive right to reproduce, sell, perform, or display the work. For the life of a copyright, the owner must give permission for the copyrighted work to be used in any significant way. Usually, the owner of a copyright is paid for the use of a copyrighted work. This payment is known as a **royalty**. After a copyright expires, the work can be used by anyone without cost or permission.

Many types of works can be copyrighted. The most common items are books, songs, and computer programs. In order for a work to be copyrighted, it must be fixed and original. Fixed means that it must be set down on some permanent medium like writing or printing on paper, or digitally on a computer disk.

For a number of years, the United States has been involved in worldwide negotiation of a trade agreement known as the General Agreement on Trade in Services (GATS). GATS addresses international copyright violation and free access to foreign markets. Both are major problems for audio and video producers. The industry also would like to have foreign markets opened to more liberal trade with U.S. audio and video producers. Other countries struggling with small entertainment industries cite cultural concerns as the reason for keeping the markets closed.

THINK CRITICALLY

1. How can the U.S. entertainment industry encourage other countries to open their markets to more U.S. products?

2. How can the U.S. encourage other countries to obey agreements on copyright?

U.S. LAWS

Laws of the United States are not enforceable in other countries except where the United States is part of an international copyright convention. The United States and China have had verbal battles over piracy of intellectual property, such as music. In the mid-1990s, the United States threatened trade sanctions against China because 90 percent of the compact discs made in China were believed to be illegal copies. The two countries reached an agreement that included closing 15 of 30 factories that produced illegal compact discs. These illegal discs were estimated to have robbed U.S. companies of $2.3 billion in sales in 1995 alone.

The marketability of a celebrity's name, likeness, voice, or image can be a major source of income. A celebrity has the right to give or deny permission to use these attributes for commercial purposes. When a robot resembling Vanna White was used in an ad for Samsung, for example, White sued the company and was awarded $403,000 in damages.

MARKETING MYTHS

Many people are unaware that to legally play music from a radio, TV, CD, or tape as background music at a business requires compliance with copyright laws. Such playing of background music is considered a public performance of the music. A royalty fee should be paid to the copyright owner for the performance by commercial users after obtaining permission for use whether it is live, broadcast, or used as free background music.

THINK CRITICALLY
Why must royalties be paid for public performances of copyrighted works? How should the public be notified of these rules?

TEACH
China does not honor U.S. copyrights.

Celebrities own a right to their name, likeness, voice, music, or image.

The music recording industry is finding it difficult to change and do business with new technology.

Marketing Myths
Public performance of music includes playing a radio as background music during a school's open house.

Think Critically
Public performances must be paid for with royalty fees to comply with copyright laws. This is how the owner of the copyright, the musician, songwriter, or record company makes money and stays in business.

The public is notified by the symbol © or the word "copyright" on the music.
The most affected industries could make an effort to inform people through a promotional campaign or through vigorous enforcement that gained publicity. This could result in a backlash of negative publicity. Disney frequently files charges to enforce copyright laws, but generally settles out of court to hold down the negative publicity of being seen as prosecuting an elementary teacher for using a likeness of Mickey Mouse on his or her bulletin board.

Ongoing Assessment
Use the Intermission as an opportunity to conduct ongoing assessment of student comprehension of the lesson material.

TECH COPIES

DISTRIBUTION

The entertainment industry continues to be worried by new technology that makes it easy for consumers to make quality recordings of audio and video performances. The Recording Industry Association of America tried unsuccessfully to stop Diamond Multimedia Systems Inc. from selling Rio software that allows storage and playback of music transferred from a personal computer. Compact-disc-quality music is available on the Internet in a format known as MP3. The recording industry trade group believes Rio supports illegal copying of music from the Internet. While many artists see Rio as a new means of distribution, the trade group sees it as making illegal copies easier to obtain.

INTERMISSION

Whom do copyright laws protect?

Copyright laws protect the creators of books, songs, films, etc., and companies with

whom they have contracts to produce these works.

TEACH
Have students find examples of how each of these laws affects sports or entertainment.

Congress regulates commerce and some longstanding federal laws affect sports and entertainment. Ask students why a monopoly is a restraint of free trade. Answer – when one large business controls, there is no competition for service or price.

Knowledge of contracts and their impact is critical to doing business.

Technology may make some contracts obsolete.

Ongoing Assessment
Use the Intermission as an opportunity to conduct ongoing assessment of student comprehension of the lesson material.

TEACHING STRATEGIES
Low Achiever
Ask students to form a table labeled "test questions." Divide it into 3 columns – "main idea," "critical information," and "rationale." At the end of the lesson, add potential test questions to the table. Confirm the information with the teacher or other students.

TEACHING STRATEGIES
Auditory Learners
The teacher should provide guided notes with key information omitted. Ask the student to listen and fill in key words. After the lesson, the student should highlight the key words.

FEDERAL LAWS

Federal laws impact sports and entertainment marketing. Article I of the U.S. Constitution gives Congress the power to "regulate commerce." Sports and entertainment are certainly considered commerce. Some long-standing federal acts have major impact on the sports and entertainment industry.

Sherman Antitrust Act (1890)
- declared restraint of trade, as well as price fixing, illegal
- set monopolizing trade as a felony

Clayton Act (1914)
- set up right to sue and receive threefold damages, plus other costs and interest for monopoly and other commercial violations
- gave right to organized labor to confront violations of Sherman Act

National Labor Relations Act (1935)
- gave right of organized labor to collectively bargain and strike
- prohibited companies from coercing employees in union-related matters

CONTRACTS THAT BIND

Contracts are agreements on the transaction of business. Anyone involved in the marketing of sports or entertainment should be familiar with contract law. Although trained legal counsel generally develops contracts, the parties who create the concept of the business need to guide the development of the contract. A contract should be worded so that it is not subject to multiple interpretations. Some examples of the types of contracts involved in sports and entertainment are player or performer contracts, venue concessions, sponsorships, broadcast rights, and facility contracts.

Louis B. Mayer is credited with changing the contract system to enable his MGM film studio to legally bind stars to the company for years. Contracts for movie stars may become a thing of the past during the twenty-first century. For example, The Walt Disney Company is experimenting with animated characters that move their lips and speak words as their scripts are keyed into a computer. In the movie *Titanic*, computer-generated people were shown on the deck. Those "extras" did not require a contract.

INTERMISSION

Is professional baseball legally a game or a business? Who do contracts protect?

Pro baseball is legally a business. Contracts protect businesses, entertainers, and

athletes.

UNDERSTAND MARKETING CONCEPTS

Circle the best answer for each of the following questions.

1. Distribution A controversial issue concerning financial rights of musicians and music publishers revolves around **b**
a. copyright for the artist's lifetime plus 70 years
b. MP3
c. Congress's power to regulate commerce
d. none of these

2. Product/Service Management Event sponsors try to protect themselves from liability by **d**
a. purchasing insurance
b. printing a "not liable" statement on the back of tickets
c. planning well for the event
d. all of these

THINK CRITICALLY

Answer the following questions as completely as possible. If necessary, use a separate sheet of paper.

3. Explain the reasons for copyright laws as they relate to music. List the advantages for the artists involved.

Copyright laws ensure that copyright holders will be compensated for the use of

their works. The laws ensure that creative artists will make money and hopefully

earn a living from their works. Copyright laws require permission from artists

before their works are used or altered, thus giving the artists control over their

works.

4. Discuss why copyright laws should or should not be enforced internationally. Describe who stands to benefit from enforcement and who stands to lose.

Answers will vary. Copyright laws benefit the copyright holders. Foreign

businesses who violate copyright laws stand to lose if these laws are enforced

internationally.

ASSESS
Reteach
Ask students to identify key information in the text and restate it in their own words.

Enrich
Ask students to develop a plan for making money from music that can be freely copied from the Internet.

CLOSE
Ask students to form pairs for a discussion. The topic is whether professional athletes should look out for themselves or if it is the job of the team to protect them from injuries. Discuss as a class. Look for the team's responsibility to provide well-designed equipment and the athlete's responsibility to stay in good condition.

CHAPTER 12
LESSON 12.2

UNIONS

GOALS

Analyze the public relations impact of labor laws on sports.

Assess the financial harm that strikes may cause to a sport.

SCHEDULE
Block 90 minutes
Regular 2 class periods

FOCUS
Are athletes and celebrities members of unions? Answer – yes. What do the students remember about a recent strike in a particular sport?

OPENING ACT
Strikes make fans unhappy.

Answers for Opening Act Cooperative Learning
Fans see both sides as greedy and overpaid.

TEACH
The players are labor and the league is management.

Sponsors face major financial loss during strikes.

The 1998-99 NBA strike hurt people in low-paying, related jobs such as concession sales.

The NBA hoped fans would quickly forget the strike. Ask students if the fans did quickly forget.

OPENING ACT

Fans do not want to choose between the owners and the players during prolonged major league sports strikes. Fans view both groups as selfish and greedy. This was seen during the 1994 baseball season and the 1998-99 basketball season. October 1994 was the first time in 90 years that a World Series was not played in baseball. The baseball players were on strike.

Work with a group. Discuss why fans don't want to side with the players or the owners during a strike.

ORGANIZED LABOR

Athletes in major professional sports have, since the mid-1970s, organized themselves into labor unions, called **players' associations.** Each sport's league has a collective bargaining agreement with the players association. **Collective bargaining** happens when a group of employees join together as a single unit to negotiate with employers. The league is made up of individual teams and includes all non-player employees. The league is the management side. The labor side is made up of players, their agents, and the players' association. Each group has a point of view on how the business should be operated and how the profits should be split.

Sponsors, such as Nike, who depend on NBA stars as promotional outlets, took a major hit in earnings during a 1998 lockout. Nike withheld payment to some NBA players during the strike. The bulk of TV advertising income was not affected, though, because it is generated from the postseason games. The lockout ended before these games.

OWNERS VERSUS PLAYERS

The National Basketball Players Association, formed in the 1950s, was locked out throughout most of the 1998-99 basketball season. The lockout left fans disheartened and disgusted. Other damage included loss of revenue for advertisers, concession sellers, ushers, and maintenance crews.

The image of super-wealthy owners and players refusing to find common ground does not elicit sympathy from most fans. Players and owners hoped that fans had short memories and would quickly return to the games. David Stern, NBA Commissioner, had always taken pride in the good relationship the league had with the union. The NBA had not had the labor problems of other professional sports prior to the six-month lockout.

NBA owners appeared to consider the league in jeopardy of pricing itself out of business with astronomical salaries and debt-ridden clubs. The players blamed the owners for the league's financial problems. The players believed fans would rally to their side and demand games at any cost. Issues in the 1998-99 season standoff included salary caps, rookie contracts, free agency, revenue sources, and NBA authority over the players.

PICKING UP THE PIECES

Sponsorships and advertising are sold about six months prior to games being played. Work stoppages prevent the payment for sponsorships and mean a loss of revenue for all parties. However, if enough support is generated for the third-party victims, such as the maintenance crews mentioned earlier, Congress might take action. Congress can design laws to control the loss of wages by the low-end wage victims.

WINNING BACK FANS

Winning back fans at the end of the six-month lockout in pro basketball required a major promotional effort. Furthering the problems of pro basketball was that it no longer had the charismatic Michael Jordan—the one person who might have been able to soothe angry fans. He had retired at the end of the 1997-98 season, before the strike began. Without him, pleasing fans again was an uphill battle.

Major promotional efforts were instituted at the end of the strike. The league gave away tickets and provided opportunities for sales promotion prizes. But after six months of inactivity, the quality of play was inferior, and fan interest was low. Basketball may have lost its luster.

INTERMISSION

Why would labor conflicts hurt the promotion of a sport?

Unions are intended to protect labor. Owner/player conflicts leave fans and sponsors

standing on the sidelines as two rich groups squabble over money from the pockets

of fans and sponsors.

About 15 percent of Nike's sales come from basketball-related merchandise.

LABOR RELATIONS

As a general rule, people employed in professional sports and entertainment are either in the front office or are members of unions. As interest in sports in the United States broadens from football, basketball, and baseball, new professional leagues are formed. New owners are taking a cue from the experienced leagues in setting up their structures. The new unions of players lack the power of a huge fan base, so they are unable to command huge salaries until the popularity of their league grows.

SOCCER SUCCESS

Soccer is extremely popular in Europe and South America, and it has a great growth potential in the United States as demographics change. It is also an example of one of the newest professional sports leagues.

FINANCING

Major League Soccer is structured as a single-entity league, with the owners as investors in the league itself. The owners are considered business partners rather than competitors, and their power includes selection of player rosters and determination of player salaries. The owners keep 50 percent of the ticket revenues. This structure was designed to keep teams with big audiences from dominating teams from smaller markets. The structure also caps team salaries at $1.6 million.

Soccer team owners believe the structure is necessary to financially support the newly formed league and to prevent major inequality between teams. However, players' union director John Kerr initiated antitrust legal action over the league structure. The union has the players' benefits as its mission even though both owners and players stand to benefit from a strong league. The players' association needs the power to negotiate with owners, but getting that power requires players to be more widely known for their union to have the strength to make the rules.

ENTERTAINMENT LABOR

Nonmanagement employees in the entertainment business are also generally members of organized labor. Celebrities did not always make huge amounts of money for being in the movies. Lew Wasserman was a powerful agent in early Hollywood and is credited with changing the system from employing actors (nonmanagement employees) under long-term, low-paying contracts.

Workers in the entertainment industry have more power now than ever before. As the rate of unemployment reached record lows in the late 1990s, Disney World and other entertainment centers were forced to raise wages to gain and keep employees. About half of the 50,000 employees at Disney World received an hourly raise from $5.95 to $6.25 under a new union contract in December 1998.

GETTING ALONG

Labor and management must cooperate if a business is to succeed. Disputes take energy and funding away from promotion and do not address the other side of the triangle, the fans. Fans like to see action by celebrities on the field or the screen, not by attorneys in conference rooms. Generally, no matter who wins, everyone loses in a game of friction. Squabbles

PRODUCT/
SERVICE
MANAGEMENT

between labor and management may continue to plague sports and entertainment. Winning sports will be those whose efforts are toward finding a balance between the two competing groups. Players and owners need each other, and fans want them to unite and act as a team. Marketing a unified team is much easier and more likely to be successful.

INTERMISSION

How do strikes affect a sports team financially?

Strikes and lockouts reduce the number of games played, revenue, attendance, and sales of licensed products.

TAKE A BOW

OPRAH WINFREY

Oprah Winfrey is one of the most powerful and respected people in entertainment today. She was born in rural Mississippi in 1954 and lived on a farm with her grandmother. When she was six, she moved to Wisconsin to be with her mother. At 13, she ran away from what had turned out to be an abusive home. She eventually moved into her father's home in Nashville, Tennessee, where he demanded that she make something of herself.

Ms. Winfrey got her first job in radio broadcasting in Nashville when she was 19. At 21, she became a television reporter and anchor. Today, her television talk show has 33 million viewers a week from 135 countries. Her influence includes encouraging millions of people to read, supporting Habitat for Humanity in building houses for low-income buyers, working with Congress to build a national database of child abusers, and establishing many college scholarships.

Ms. Winfrey had a brush with the law early in 1998 when she was sued by a group of cattle ranchers in Texas for defamation of the beef industry. A guest on her show had explained how "mad-cow disease" was spread, and Ms. Winfrey commented that she would never eat beef again. Almost immediately, the price of beef dropped. The ranchers sued for more than $11 million under a Texas law against food disparagement, but the jury ruled in Ms. Winfrey's favor. It found that her guest's statements were "informed opinion," and that law protected her own remarks in response.

THINK CRITICALLY

1. Should someone who has the influence of Oprah Winfrey be held to a different standard of free speech than everyone else?
2. Do you think the cattle ranchers were justified in their suit? Why or why not? What does their suit mean for the entertainment industry?

UNDERSTAND MARKETING CONCEPTS
Circle the best answer for each of the following questions.

1. The structure of Major League Soccer is designed to **d**
   a. make owners partners rather than competitors
   b. make soccer a strong competitor to football
   c. keep teams with big audiences from dominating teams from smaller markets
   d. a and c

2. Disney World raised hourly wages in order to keep **b**
   a. pace with other entertainment centers
   b. employees
   c. its happy-go-lucky image
   d. none of these

THINK CRITICALLY
Answer the following questions as completely as possible. If necessary, use a separate sheet of paper.

3. How can disputes between management and labor ever stop without government intervention? Does the government really have a place in mediating sports or entertainment disputes? Explain.

   Answers will vary. Compromise, open dialogue, and the realization that a work

   stoppage reduces revenue for all concerned can result in progress toward an

   end of such a dispute.

   _____

   _____

   _____

4. How are fans partly responsible for the high salaries of owners and players? Can these salaries ever be brought back down? Is there really a ceiling for salaries? Explain your answers.

   Answers will vary. Fans are responsible because they continue to support teams

   and players by purchasing tickets and licensed merchandise and watching

   sports on TV.

   _____

   _____

LICENSING

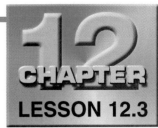

OPENING ACT

NFL Properties has licensing agreements to produce more than 2,500 items bearing the logos of the league, teams, or players. More than 350 manufacturers are involved in making the items. Licensing is a form of marketing used to promote sports teams. Licensing increases the prominence of teams by spreading their names and logos all over the world. More than $60 billion per year is generated through licensing, with about 20 percent of that generated by sports and colleges.

Work with a group. Identify five licensed items from pro sports that are currently very popular and five that are no longer sought after. Discuss with the group why these items fell out of favor.

Explain licensing.

Describe the financial value of licensing sports and entertainment merchandise.

SCHEDULE
Block 90 minutes
Regular 2 class periods

FOCUS
Ask students how many own clothing that has a pro team logo on it. Ask students what other articles, besides clothing, are popular items for sports logos.

OPENING ACT
Licensing of team logos is a huge business.

Answers for Opening Act Cooperative Learning
Look for items to include logos of specific teams that have been winners and losers. Items fall out of favor because people get bored with them and want new items.

TEACH
Items of clothing with logos are an enormously successful type of promotion. Think about an athlete being interviewed wearing a Nike swoosh on his or her shirt. What is the value of that publicity?

WALKING BILLBOARDS

When people wear T-shirts bearing logos, they are proclaiming themselves fans of a team. They are walking billboards. They carry the logos into private homes, schools, and even churches. The licensed merchandise is mobile—it provides publicity no amount of money can buy.

WORLDWIDE DISTRIBUTION

In years past, purchasing T-shirts or other souvenirs with a major team logo on them could take place only at sports facilities. Owning a shirt with a player's name and number on it meant you had met the player. Today, licensed merchandise is sold in malls and shopping centers all over the world. Licensed items are one of the best moneymakers associated with sports events.

The unification of the European market has created new opportunities for international firms to sponsor teams and events through licensing. In

Sports teams all over the country are changing their names, and not just for the overseas market. Many times, the change is out of respect for cultural diversity. Miami University in Oxford, Ohio, for example, in 1997, changed the name of its teams from the Redskins to the Redhawks.

order to open communication for firms doing business across the countries in the European Union, professional teams have begun changing their names. The names selected are more acceptable across a wider region and have appropriate meaning in multiple languages.

Many team logo items are used as sales promotions to promote other products or services. A company may provide the licensed product free with the purchase of an unrelated item. This connects the three key players in sports marketing: the fans, the sponsors, and the sports event.

REACHING AGREEMENT

Licensing is giving permission to copy the logo of a league, athlete, team, entertainer, film, or TV show for a fee paid to the rights holder of the image. A license is issued to another company that will manufacture, market, and sell the products. The purchaser of a license assumes the risk of producing and marketing the product. The league, athlete, or team only approves the product and collects the licensing fees. League management, such as NFL Properties, sells the rights for use of the names of the teams and uniforms. Players' unions, such as the National Basketball Players Association, sell licensing agreements to firms they believe to be viable, since they will also generally receive a percentage of each item sold. This allows the leagues and players' unions to focus on their primary business—which is not merchandising.

INTERMISSION

Who owns the rights to pro team logos? Define licensing.

Pro teams own the rights to their own logos. Licensing is giving permission to copy a

logo for a fee paid to the rights holder of the image.

GETTING LICENSED

The major leagues make it easy to be considered for a license, but actually getting the license is not that simple. Generally, the steps for applying include submitting the following:

1. A complete business plan
2. A sample or drawing of the product
3. The costs of production and distribution
4. A marketing plan
5. The existing distribution channels for the product

EASY TO APPLY, HARD TO OBTAIN

DISTRIBUTION

Obtaining a license for the use of a major league team's logo provides immediate recognition and honor to a product. To maintain this credibility, the leagues in the United States limit the number of licenses granted for a particular category of merchandise. Although the NFL has moved toward globalization of its licensing, many sports teams in other countries have not capitalized on the phenomenon. Finding an item with a licensed logo for Colo Colo, the national soccer team of Chile, requires a search through many stores, even in a city of five million people such as Santiago.

KEEPING CURRENT

As with fashions, uniforms and team logos change, and not without reason. Three major promotional strategies are used to maximize profits of licensed merchandise:

1. Changing the logo, color, or uniform, or reproducing nostalgic items
2. Adding creative new items, licensees, and sales methods
3. Widening the market to the world

MANAGING LICENSING

Major sports and entertainment corporations have divisions whose sole role is managing licensed merchandise related to entertainment or sports events. Their responsibilities include:

- Distribution and collection of license applications
- Review and selection of licensees
- Collection of minimum guarantees or bank guarantees
- Development and dissemination of design handbook and marketing plan
- Determination of how often a new product line will be introduced and how many designs should be allowed
- Development and dissemination of approval process guidelines
- Review of all designs for quality and suitability
- Accounting for all sales and royalties
- Protection against counterfeit merchandise

The web site wallstreetsports.com runs a sports stock market simulation. Visitors get a free account and buy and sell fantasy shares based on athletes. Players win prizes for creating winning portfolios of stocks.

In the NASCAR game, drivers' stock values were based on the real drivers winning races or finishing in the top ten. Also, the buying and selling activities of the game influence the fantasy value of the stocks.

THINK CRITICALLY
1. Why would Wall Street Sports give away prizes?
2. Does Wall Street Sports have a licensing agreement with the teams and athletes in the game? How is it used?

NEW SUCCESS STORY

NASCAR is the sport to watch in the licensing field. Between 1990 and 1998, sales of NASCAR merchandise increased from $80 million to $1.1 billion—or 1,100 percent! Automotive-related businesses are seeing dollars from NASCAR in a new light. For example, the 3M Automotive Aftermarket Division in 1999 signed on as NASCAR's "Officially Licensed Automotive Refinish Supplier." The **aftermarket** is the market for parts and accessories used in the repair or upgrading of a product after the product is sold. 3M believes that NASCAR fans will want to use NASCAR's aftermarket supplies for their own cars.

LEGAL PROTECTION

A logo may be a legally protected property. The placement of an ® next to a logo indicates federal registration as a trademark. An unscrupulous company might put a popular logo on an inferior product without authorization. This sort of misuse carries both civil and criminal penalties for the violators. Development of a protection enforcement plan is needed when an item increases in popularity.

DISTRIBUTION

Although business costs seem to increase without limit, there does seem to be a maximum dollar amount that a fan will pay to experience a sporting event. The money to cover rising business costs must, therefore, come from other sources. The increased funds must come from other sources. Both amateur and professional sports as well as entertainers have derived tremendous financial benefits from the evolution of licensing as a marketing tool. Fans are willing to pay to become walking billboards.

INTERMISSION

Why is the revenue from licensed merchandise so important to sports teams? Why do teams change the designs and colors of their uniforms and logos?

Revenue from licensed merchandise is important because there are a limited number

of seats in a team's stadium, and fans are only willing to pay so much for them.

Teams change their uniforms and logos to increase sales.

UNDERSTAND MARKETING CONCEPTS

Circle the best answer for each of the following questions.

1. When you apply for a license you must submit **d**
   a. a complete business plan
   b. a marketing plan
   c. a sample drawing of the product
   d. all of these

2. **Distribution** Sports leagues limit the number of licenses granted for merchandise in order to **b**
   a. be able to quickly change colors and styles
   b. protect the credibility of the merchandise
   c. keep the prices high
   d. all of these

THINK CRITICALLY

Answer the following questions as completely as possible. If necessary, use a separate sheet of paper.

3. Why do you think U.S.-based sports leagues have had more success with licensing and merchandising than have the leagues of other countries?

Answers will vary. Possible answers:

U.S.-based sporting events are broadcast much more to other countries than

vice-versa. There are more experienced marketers in the U.S. than in any other

country.

4. In sports—as well as in all other areas—is frequently changing styles, colors, logos, etc., a good marketing strategy? Why or why not? Is it ethical? Why or why not?

Answers will vary.

ASSESS
Reteach
Have students review the goals for each lesson. Restate the goals as questions and have students answer them.

Enrich
Have students use the Internet to investigate other laws that apply to sports or entertainment. Have them prepare a presentation for the class summarizing their findings.

CLOSE
Divide students into two teams. Have each team prepare a number of questions about the chapter material to ask the other team. Have the teams ask each other the questions in a game show format.

CHAPTER 12 REVIEW

REVIEW MARKETING CONCEPTS

Write the letter of the term that matches each definition. Some terms will not be used.

_e_ **1.** protect the unique work of an artist

_j_ **2.** professional athletes' labor union

_c_ **3.** addresses international copyright violation and free access to foreign markets

_a_ **4.** copying a logo for a fee paid to the rights holder of the image

_d_ **5.** the possibility of financial loss or personal injury

a. licensing
b. aftermarket
c. GATS
d. risk
e. copyright laws
f. liable
g. royalty
h. collective bargaining
i. contracts
j. players' association

Circle the best answer.

6. People employed in professional sports and entertainment are usually
  a. not contractually obligated to professional organizations
  b. employed in the front office or are members of unions
  c. restricted to the number of hours they can work
  d. none of these

b

7. A major promotional strategy to maximize profits of licensed merchandise is
  a. changing the team logo
  b. increasing prices of merchandise
  c. adding new items
  d. a and c

d

8. Controlling risk can involve
  a. limiting risk through planning
  b. covering the risk in the budget
  c. buying insurance
  d. all of these

d

9. Professional sports teams began changing their names in order to
  a. have appropriate meaning in multiple languages
  b. make the names more acceptable across vast regions
  c. make logo designs simpler
  d. a and b

d

THINK CRITICALLY

10. The settlement of the six-month 1998-99 NBA lockout included the players' union agreeing to reduce its guaranteed licensing revenues from $25 million to $20 million. Why do you think the union would agree to give up this $5 million?

Answers will vary.

_____

_____

_____

_____

_____

11. Should people who voluntarily engage in dangerous activities, such as moshing, be able to sue event promoters, artists, and property owners? Why or why not? Should people who get hurt be able to sue a performing artist if the artist encouraged the behavior? Explain your answer.

Answers will vary.

_____

_____

_____

_____

_____

12. Explain the statement, "Success in business requires a partnership between labor and management."

Answers will vary. Partnership, as opposed to an adversarial situation, is necessary for a

business to maximize its effectiveness. Often, a great deal of energy and time are wasted

through labor/management friction.

_____

_____

_____

CHAPTER 12 REVIEW

MAKE CONNECTIONS

13. Mathematics   A stadium has 8,000 "cheap seats" that sell for $6.00 per game each. The team wants to charge $8.00 each for these seats, but it knows the fans will not pay the increased price. How much money does the team need to make up from some other source? How many additional jerseys will the team need to sell per game if it increases profits from $2.50 to $5.00 per jersey in order to make the money it needs? Suggest three other ways to make this money more quickly.

$8.00 − 6.00 = $2.00 more per seat; 8,000 × $2.00 = $16,000 more per game

$5.00 − 2.50 = $2.50 more profit per shirt; $16,000 ÷ 2.50 = 6,400 additional jerseys

per game. The *Sports and Entertainment Marketing* Teacher's Resource CD includes a

spreadsheet template to help students complete this activity. Look for the file p290 Make

Connections-Mathematics.xls Office Template folder, or the file p290 Conx.txt in the Text

Templates folder.

14. Communication   Write a promotional plan for a sports team to use for the first two weeks after a lengthy strike or lockout in which many games have been missed. Include ideas for advertising, publicity, sales promotion, and personal selling. Your plan has two goals: to bring back angry fans and to increase the number of new fans.

Answers will vary.

15. History   Research the World Series scandal of 1919 and summarize it in one page. Then imagine you are the promoter in charge of making baseball right with the public again. Outline your strategy.

Answers will vary.

16. Technology Use the Internet to research the purpose of contracts. Write a two-page summary about the types of contracts related to sports or entertainment. Be sure to cite your sources.

Answers will vary.

_____

_____

_____

_____

_____

_____

_____

_____

_____

PROJECT EXTRA INNINGS

You are head of the marketing department for a company that wants a new idea for licensed merchandise. Your goal is to produce and market a product that is already desirable, but you want to add a sports league logo that will make the product even more popular.

Work in a group and complete the following activities.

1. Think of items that are not currently merchandised by sports leagues. Discuss new products that could be associated with a sports league licensing agreement.

2. Draw the item or write a very specific description of it.

3. What are the demographics of your potential customers for the product? List the pertinent demographic information about the customers, such as age, gender, or income. Why does your department think these customers will be more interested in this item if it has a sports league logo on it?

4. Develop a complete promotional plan for the product, including advertising, sales promotions, personal selling, and publicity.

5. Discuss why the item selected is not currently a licensed product.

6. Present your product and plans to the class in an oral report.

PROJECT
Extra Innings
Look for original ideas for new merchandise. Students should relate the merchandise to the targeted customer. Suggest students look at the web pages of major league sports teams and consider specialty catalogs for ideas of new products.

Why isn't the item currently licensed? Because nobody thought of it or thinks it will make money.

INDEX

PHOTO CREDITS